COSMIC REVELATIONS TILL THE END OF TIME

CHANNELED PROPHECIES FROM THE GALACTIC GUARDIANS

Transmissions From The Solar Council And The Ashtar Command
With Additional Channelings by Tuella
Introductory Material by Sean Casteel, Timothy G Beckley
and Carol Ann Rodriguez

COSMIC REVELATIONS TILL THE END OF TIME

CHANNELED PROPHECIES FROM THE GALACTIC GUARDIANS

Cosmic Revelations Till The End of Time -
Channeled Prophecies From The Galactic Guardians
By Carol Rodriguez, Timothy Green Beckley and Sean Casteel
Edited By Tim R. Swartz

Copyright © 2014 Timothy Green Beckley
DBA Inner Light/Global Communications
All Rights Reserved
Nonfiction

No part of this book may be reproduced, stored in retrieval system or transmitted in any form or by any means, electronic, mechanical, photocopying, recording, without express permission of the publisher.

Timothy Green Beckley: Editorial Director
Carol Rodriguez: Publishers Assistant
Sean Casteel: Associate Editor
Tim Swartz: Editorial Assistant
Cover Art: Tim R. Swartz

Printed in the United States of America

For free catalog write:
Global Communications
P. O. Box 753
New Brunswick, NJ 08903

mrufo8@hotmail.com
www.ConspiracyJournal.com

COSMIC REVELATIONS TILL THE END OF TIME

CONTENTS

The Unadulterated Truth About Channeling – From Ancient Astronauts To Ashtar 8

Prophecies Do Come True Through The Ashtar Command! 26

The Communications Begin 32

Heed These Warnings 34

In a World War There Would Be No Winner 36

The Space Brothers Secret Mission 38

Relocation in Space 41

Entering the New Age of Enlightenment 45

Signs and Wonders 48

Earth – A Giant Pressure Cooker About to Explode 52

There Are Still Great Men Among You 55

A Cosmic History 58

The Rights of Citizens to Bear Arms Versus Gun Control 61

They Are Amongst Us, Even Today 64

Technological Advances Held Back Because of Greed 67

A Wealth of Plenty for All 69

Earth: Way Station of the Universe 71

Rainbows in the Sky 74

Suppression of Beneficial Discoveries 76

The Plot for World Domination 79

Call Us By Name, For We Come As Friends 82

Peace is the Universal Way 85

The Yucatan 91

COSMIC REVELATIONS TILL THE END OF TIME

Sacred and Holy Ground 93

The Armageddon 96

The Totality of Creation 100

Earth's Civilization, a Blasphemy Against the Creator 107

Effects of the Planetary Alignment 110

The Monitoring of Geological Activities and 113

Geographical Changes 113

Earth's Failure to Climb the Evolutionary Ladder 117

Aura Raines-Look to the Light When in Doubt 119

We Have Not Set the Date 120

Monka-Your Weapons Are Powerless Against Us 122

World Leaders Are Influenced By the Dark Forces 127

Crystal Love from Mirror City 130

Ashtar on Cassandra 132

Ashtar on Nutrition 135

An Answer to a Chant for Protection 140

Sananda – A Christmas Message 141

Ashtar – We Hear Your Messages 142

The Second Coming 144

The Task of the Guardians 147

An Appeal from the Guardians 148

Three Spiritual Task Forces 150

The Seven Different Types of Viknor Flying Saucers 154

Foreword 173

COSMIC REVELATIONS TILL THE END OF TIME

Preface 174

Section One World Chaos 175

An Ultimatum from the Great Central Son 177

The Threshold of Sorrows 180

Stand Tall in the Trial By Fire 182

The Invisible Fortress of Love 185

The Balanced Ledger 187

The Orbit of Destiny 190

The Masters of Invocation 192

Section Two World Changes 195

The Fall of Exterior Religion 197

11:00AM - The Third Day Time Can Wait No Longer 201

7:00 PM-The Third Day The Flow of Wisdom 205

The Seven Laws of the Hermetic Philosophy 208

7:00 AM-The Fourth Day Health in the New Age 210

11:00AM The Fourth Day - Science in the New Age 215

3:00 PM-The Fourth Day - Tribute to Woman 218

Section Three World Guardians 222

7:00 PM The Fourth Day 225

7:00 AM The Fifth Day - We Are The Reaping Angels 228

11:00 The Fifth Day - The Unfolding of the New Light Bearers 232

3:00 PM The Fifth Day - We Must Assume Responsibility 235

7:00 PM The Fifth Day - The Aura of Urgency 238

7:00 AM The Sixth Day - Millions of Space Craft 241

COSMIC REVELATIONS TILL THE END OF TIME

11:00 AM The Sixth Day - We Must Be Invited 244

Section Four   World Deliverance 249

3:00 PM The Sixth Day - Hold the World to Your Heart 252

The Descent of the Guardians 256

7:00 AM The Seventh Day - Keep Your Eyes on the Skies 259

11:00 AM The Seventh Day - When Your Need Is Greatest, They Will Be There 263

3:00 PM The Seventh Day The Impersonal Frequencies 269

7:00 PM The Seventh Day Our Radiant One 273

The Final Words 277

COSMIC REVELATIONS TILL THE END OF TIME

The Unadulterated Truth About Channeling – From Ancient Astronauts To Ashtar

by Sean Casteel and Timothy Green Beckley

A SAMPLE TRANSMISSION

ON most planets, sickness is almost totally unknown. With the spirit and the mind in perfect harmony, people would live to be many more decades older than they do now. Think of the violet rays in order to heal someone.

The Earth is a living entity – all the planets are inhabited in many dimensions. There are worlds within worlds and spirals within spirals.

Learn about the sanctity of life. Someday we will all travel together on the same beam of light toward the one source. Someday Earth may be a part of the Free Federation of Planets. Clarion, warm planet with a violet sky. Monka and the defense of the solar system.

The above is a channeled message from an entity claiming to be Solar Star, healer supreme of the Free Federation of Planets. It is one of thousands of "sugar coated" messages that have been received from intelligence asserting to be from outer worlds in and beyond our solar system.

Like a lot of channeled messages it is open to interpretation as to its source and its credibility. Channeling has always been a controversial topic with devotes who believe every transmission to be legitimate, while the non believers would happily toss out the baby Martian along with the watery canals of the Red Planet.

* * * * *

Is it possible to talk to space beings?

Ancient Tibetans?

Disenfranchised Entities of one type or another?

All things being equal, obviously we can't do this face-to-face on a one-to-one basis, so we have to come up with some other forms of communication.

COSMIC REVELATIONS TILL THE END OF TIME

The subject of channeling has been debated extensively. Is it a legit method with which we can learn to actually speak with off-world intelligences of unknown and varied origins? Or is it all celestial bunkum?

The notion of receiving "channeled" messages from friendly extraterrestrials may be said to have begun in the mid-20th century, but the "New Age-y" phenomenon is really nothing new. The story of benevolent voices from beyond the vastness of time and space goes back well into ancient times, perhaps even as far back as the Bible itself.

But what exactly is a channel? We think of channeling today in terms of speaking with higher entities, higher forms of intelligence, like Space People and beings from Atlantis. But the term itself is not so easy to define. We must remember, as it turns out, even Moses may have channeled God.

A simple and right to the point explanation as to what a channeler is comes via Jeffrey Hooppe, linked to us from the CrimsonCircle.com web site.

"Channeling is a natural form of communication between humans and angelic beings, nature spirits, non-physical entities or even animals and pets. A channeler is very similar to a translator or interpreter. They allow themselves to feel or sense the communication from the other being. The channeler then attaches human words to the communications for the understanding by themselves or other humans.

"A channeler can choose who or what they want to channel. As long as the other party has an interest in communicating, the link is made and the channeling can begin. For instance, many people channel Archangel Michael. If he agrees to communicate with the channeler, the flow of non-verbal information begins.

"The channeler receives the information at an intuitive or feeling level, and then their mind converts the raw information into words. Contrary to popular belief, entities do not generally use human languages because it is considered awkward and clumsy. The richer essence of their message is conveyed through an elegant series of sensory feelings."

The Oracle of Delphi was perhaps the first channeler who used the same modus operandi as more modern practitioners of the art. The Oracle was a woman, or a succession of women, who claimed to be in contact with Zeus and some of the other members of the Greek pantheon. A lot of people today believe that there is a connection between the Greek and Roman gods and ancient astronauts. They could have been one and the same, as it turns out.

It was at this location that the Oracle of Delphi received her channeled messages. (Photo by Tim Beckley)

COSMIC REVELATIONS TILL THE END OF TIME

One co-author of this discussion, Tim Beckley, visited the site in Greece where the Oracle of Delphi gave her readings and wrote an account up for "FATE Magazine" in 2006, as well as the book, "Alien Space Gods Of Ancient Greece and Rome – Revelations of the Oracle of Delphi."

"The oracle did not predict the future herself," he writes, "but passed on the information she received while in a trance to one of the high priests who presided over the gathering, which attracted the high and mighty of Greek society as well as lower class members. To most, the oracle seemed to be speaking in indecipherable riddles. She usually began her discourse with utterings such as: 'I know the number of the sand. I know the measure of the sea.'

"And then she would improvise from there," Beckley continues, "often speaking in unknown tongues only her priestly handlers could comprehend. Crowds would gather to ask questions and they were most likely to receive a Yes or No answer. Frequently associated with the oracle's ability to foresee events was a mysterious vapor, which critics say rose from the cracks in the floor of the cubicle where the visionary would be seated on a tripod-like brass stool. The Christians propagated the idea that the prophetess was intoxicated by the fumes in order to step across the border into the void of the next world. They saw the oracle as a tool of the devil, much as fundamentalists today believe spirits are all Satan's conjurations used to fool people into believing there is life beyond the pale."

Even Alexander the Great is said to have consulted the Oracle of Delphi, seeking information about his future military conquests. For the common person not embroiled in the machinations of war and politics, the oracle was available to answer personal questions. A query like "How do I cure my son of love sickness?" would receive a therapeutic, albeit vague, response like "Treat him gently." To paraphrase Heraclitus, the Greek philosopher, "The oracle neither conceals nor reveals the truth . . . only hints at it." Kind of like the contactees of today, when they warn of impending doom or a supposed forthcoming UFO sighting/landing and end up with egg on their face when the channeled messages don't produce the desired results of a real live ET to converse with.

JOHN DEE AND THE QUEEN

Another important link in the historical chain of channeling is John Dee, a Welsh mathematician who lived in the 16th and 17th centuries. He was also an astronomer and an occultist, whose reputation as a scholar was such that he sometimes served as a consultant to Queen Elizabeth I. Dee was a devoted student of alchemy, divination and Hermetic philosophy. He devoted much of his

COSMIC REVELATIONS TILL THE END OF TIME

John Dee often gave advice to Elizabeth the First via chanelled messages from the Angels.

last thirty years to attempting to commune with angels in order to learn the universal language of creation and unify mankind prior to the coming apocalypse, which was even in this period said to be imminent. Seems the end of the world is always around the next corner.

Dee claimed to have spoken with angels and devised an entire mathematical occult code so that others could do so as well. This was at a time when witches and occultists were still being persecuted. Dee's work was supposed to be superior to anyone else's. Apparently, he made some predictions and some of them were very successful, which may support his belief that he was indeed channeling angelic beings. It should be noted that even though Dee is identified with the word "occultist," he was an extremely pious Christian who prayed and fasted as part of his preparations to attempt angelic contact. He did not draw a distinction between his mathematical research and his delving into angel summoning and divination. He considered the various efforts to be part of the same quest to find a transcendent understanding of the divine forms which underlie the visible world.

ALEISTER CROWLEY AND THE FIRST GRAY

Moving ahead a few centuries, we hereby offer the widely influential occultist Aleister Crowley as a significant channel. Crowley was an avowed bisexual, a recreational drug experimenter and a social critic who claimed to be in a revolt against the moral and religious values of his time, the early 20th century. His cardinal rule was "Do What Thou Wilt," all of which led to a great deal of negative notoriety.

But Crowley may have gotten a totally unfair bad rap. We think of Aleister Crowley in terms of how he promoted himself: as "the wickedest man in the world" whose number is 666, a numeric symbol often associated with the antichrist. Crowley was also known as "the Beast." But there were two sides to his personality. He seemed to have been very much adept at promoting himself and creating an aura of intrigue around his personality. He hyped the fact that he was supposed to have perpetrated all these terrible deeds. The only such misdeeds, however, that have been proven is when he got caught throwing an orgy or two, which perhaps might have been out of place in that particular time period that he lived – though the aristocrats did have their Hellfire Club a bit earlier on. Ironically, Crowley would not have been bourgeoisie enough to qualify for membership in that particular organization.

We find it rather fascinating that Crowley believed that there were other dimensions, other realities, and that there were weird beings that populated these

Alester Crowley's channeled being has been identified as a Gray and looks remarkably similar to the alien on the dust jacket of Communion.

various unseen realms. A lot of people think of him as calling up demons, but that's not necessarily the case. Almost anything, if you're a certain kind of skeptic, can be

labeled demonic – just like some Christians think that every UFO being is a demon or a minion of Satan. Well, the same thing was probably true in Crowley's time. He just thought that they were spirits and some spirits you could control to do your bidding.

It was up to the individual who was performing the magic ritual whether or not they were doing the work with good intentions. Like a gun, it depends on the use to which it's put, whether for constructive or destructive purposes.

It's pretty much the same thing with ritualistic magic. Anyway, Crowley found out, or at least it was his theory, that you could contact your guardian angel and other angels mentioned in the Bible and get them to contact others who might be of a caliber to assist and be beneficial. Because the angels, it was thought, were of a higher power and closer to God, they would therefore also have a better connection with other entities that existed. He actually even called up and materialized an entity that looks remarkably similar to the Grays that a lot of people claim to have been abducted by. So perhaps Crowley, in his channeling and spiritual work, was the first individual to contact an extraterrestrial that we would know as a Gray today.

As further insight, it's noteworthy that Crowley seems to have ushered the great parade of flying saucers into our atmosphere and thus into our minds. He died in 1947, a couple of months following the UFO sighting by private pilot Kenneth Arnold over Mount Rainier and just before channeling came into vogue with the early UFO contactees, who maintained the position that UFO beings could as easily talk through them as land in a silvery space ship from the stars.

A DWELLER ON TWO PLANETS

One immensely popular channeled work is a book called "A Dweller On Two Planets." The book was "written" – or should we say channeled – by Frederick S. Oliver, who was born in 1866. He completed the manuscript in 1886, but it was not published until 1905, by Oliver's mother Mary, six years after the "author's" passing.

In his preface to "A Dweller On Two Planets," Oliver claims the book was channeled through him by automatic writing, visions and mental "dictations" by a spirit calling himself "Phylos the Tibetan," who revealed the story to Oliver over a period of three years, starting in 1883. The first section is a complex first person

COSMIC REVELATIONS TILL THE END OF TIME

Frederick S. Oliver poses along side Phylos the Tibetan. Drawings of ships in A Dweller On Two Planets looks remarkably similar to objects photographer takien by famous UFO contactee George Adamski.

account by Phylos of the culture of Atlantis, which had reached a high level of technological and scientific advancement. It includes a detailed history of the social, economic, political and religious forces shaping Atlantis and relates how daily life in Atlantis featured inventions like antigravity air and submarine craft, television, wireless telephones, air conditioners and high speed rail. Obviously, some of these devices have become reality. Throughout the book, there are images of what are clearly cigar-shaped vehicles drawn while the channeler was in a trance. These illustrations look almost identical to the tubular space ships George Adamski purports to have observed through his telescope. Did Adamski "borrow" the idea from this book, or are his photos perhaps more authentic than one is willing at first to believe?

The book also deals with esoteric subjects like karma and reincarnation. In the book's second section, Phylos is reincarnated in 19th century America and must let his karma from Atlantis play itself out, both in terms of rewards and punishments.

This volume has probably influenced more people or led more people to an understanding of the realm of channeling than any other. Celestial folklore has it that Shirley MacLaine was in a bookstore in Paris

one day when the book literally fell into her hands. She was so impressed by it that she began her study of metaphysics and ended up, of course, writing the popular bestseller "Out On A Limb."

This channeled work is as popular today as it has been previously. The publisher of this book has his own edition, "The Secrets of Mount Shasta and a Dweller on Two Planets," which has been re-edited for purposes of clarification and modernization, thus making it more accessible to today's reader, who doesn't want to spend as much time pondering over obscure terms and names.

A NEW BIBLE IS CHANNELED

Another spiritual classic that has been reprinted many times is named "OAHSPE: A New Bible." The book was first published in 1882 and was purportedly channeled from angelic sources who spoke in the name of Jehovah. The human contact was an American dentist named John Ballou Newbrough, (1828–1891), who reported receiving the manuscript through automatic writing on one of the earliest of typewriters. Newbrough would arise every morning just before dawn and would sit by candlelight at his typewriter and type, at over 100 words a minute, these spiritual messages from other realms. The book covers the history of the planet Earth and its inhabitants for the past 24,000 years, starting out on the continent of Pan, which was alleged to have existed in the Pacific. This is a tremendous volume and people have studied it for years. There are still groups around the country who gather to study and discuss "OAHSPE." Believers in the revelations offered in the book are called "Faithists."

OAHSPE – 24,000 YEARS OF THE EARTH'S PAST REVEALED

Our edition of the book – available by special order only – is in two volumes that total over twelve hundred pages. Officially, it's "The Raymond Palmer Tribute Edition," owing to the fact that paranormal journalism pioneer Raymond Palmer promoted and sold the book in the mid-20th century. Well-known UFO researcher Wendell Stevens proclaimed "OAHSPE" to be the most important book of its type.

"OAHSPE" is a book of history, ethics and religion that emphasizes service to others as a basic component of how people's souls will one day be judged. It also describes a complex afterlife into which people pass on the way to becoming angels and occupants of heaven. Selfish behavior, base thoughts, or a non-vegetarian diet will land one in the lowest levels of heaven, while those who are simply evil must go to a kind of hell. But the ascension of everyone to a delightful mode of existence happens eventually in a place ruled by God. In the theology of "OAHSPE," God is an advanced angel ordained into office for a season, making it an honorary title held for a limited period of time.

While acknowledging that there were many books that were channeled in the decades after "OAHSPE" was first published, channeling actually came to its peak in a modern sense in the early 1950s and 1960s, when many contactees began to claim that they communicated with extraterrestrials. Some of them had physical contact, but a lot of them claimed to be channeling, saying that their bodies or their spirits were actually "taken over" by alien entities from space.

VOICE OF THE ASHTAR COMMAND

The best known of these channeled alien entities is Ashtar, the head of the Ashtar Command, said to be circling the Earth in a giant mother-ship above the equator. Many individuals all over the planet, not just here in the United States but also in Italy and England and other places, believe they have channeled this benevolent interplanetary traveler.

To some, he is so real that his voice has been picked up on ham radio sets, and a TV station in England was reportedly taken over and a transmission was broadcast across the countryside, supposedly from Ashtar. This was in the news

COSMIC REVELATIONS TILL THE END OF TIME

Birthplace of the Ashtar channeling was in a hidden room beneath Giant Rock, where thousands of UFO believers attended massive outdoor conventions at the site located in the vast Mojave Desert. In second photo a supposed Command Ship hovers overhead.

in the 1970s. It was a well known case, and a recording of it is out there on YouTube where the transmission can be heard as if the incident had just happened yesterday.

The first individual to channel Ashtar is believed to have been the late George Van Tassel, who constructed a dome-shaped structure which he called a "time machine" in the California desert known as the Integratron. Van Tassel was a private pilot who once worked for Howard Hughes and had encountered a spaceman named Solgonda while sleeping in the open air one night. For the most part, we think of Van Tassel as the fellow who ran the very successful outdoor UFO conferences and conventions in Joshua Tree, California, out there at Giant Rock, right in the middle of the desert. Every October for at least ten years, thousands of people would gather on his property, which he rented from the federal government. He had an airstrip where people would fly in and also operated a little restaurant. People from all over the world would come to hear the words of the contactees.

Van Tassel had a big platform that was erected next to Giant Rock, and people would ascend the stairs and tell their stories. Some of the individuals would have been Daniel Fry, Orfeo Angelucci, George Adamski, and Howard Menger. It was quite an attraction. Even "Look Magazine" did a big pictorial on the conference, held just outside the town of Landers in the heat of the day.

Giant Rock itself was at one time the largest standing boulder in North America, until it was split apart by an earthquake a few years ago. A room had been dug out directly under the rock where George Van Tassel and his family would gather on a regular basis. Van Tassel would go into a trancelike state and receive messages from Ashtar and other helpful entities who spoke of universal love, a world with no war that was in touch with its cosmic soul, and a time in the future when our own planet would join an amalgamation of peaceful worlds. For those wishing to read some of the early Ashtar messages as received by Van Tassel, we recommend the book "Secrets of Death Valley: Mystery and Haunts of the Mojave Desert," which contains the full text of Van Tassel's early tome, "I Rode In A Flying Saucer."

Along about the same time came yet another George . . . George Hunt Williamson, who became a witness to George Adamski's original flying saucer contact in the California desert, an event that included a face-to-face meeting with a blonde-haired Venusian. Though Adamski's camp followers tried to disassociate themselves from the psychic element in UFOlogy and anything to do with channeling, it was Williamson who led Adamski to his first contact after a session with the Ouija Board which told him and the group the exact spot where the space ship would land. Williamson wrote several books on ancient civilizations (i.e. "Road in the Sky," "Other Tongues, Other Flesh," and "Secrets of the Andes") as well as recording volumes of channeled messages.

Some people were very impressed by the likes of these UFO channelers. Sometimes the entities being channeled would make predictions, like where they would appear in the sky on such and such a date. People would gather and have sightings of the craft these channeled entities are said to have arrived in. Quite remarkably, an admiral from the US Navy set up a channeling session one time and the same thing happened. He consulted a woman that he knew was channeling entities from space and they had a sighting based upon her prediction. This story is even recorded in the Project Blue Book report, and we devoted an entire chapter to it in our book "Round Trip To Hell In A Flying Saucer."

So there's really nothing new about channeling, even as it remains very much in vogue to this day. Shirley MacLaine and various other metaphysically-minded celebrities have made it a part of popular culture in recent years.

THE PRIMARY REPRESENTATIVE FOR ASHTAR APPEARS

For the most part, the main representative on Earth for the Ashtar Command was an elderly lady named Thelma Terrell, who later changed her name to Tuella. Some say she was actually a Higher Dimensional Being who walked into the body of Thelma Terrell, who at a young age realized that she had a "calling" which included reuniting our troubled world with the Free Federation of Planets.

Tuella was born here on this planet, but spiritual entities took over her body from time to time. She was one of these individuals identified by New Agers as a "Walk-In." She channeled Ashtar on a regular basis along with a variety of other "messengers."

Unlike other channelers, whose facial expression and tone of voice change while in a transitional stage, the tone or attitude of Tuella's voice did not alter when she was in contact with Ashtar – she continued to speak quite normally.

For the most part, her work is contained in a series of books published originally by Guardian Action Publications, and transferred before her passing to Tim Beckley's publishing "empire," Global Communications/Inner Light. Among the titles are "Ashtar, A Tribute, Revealing His Secret Identity," "Project World Evacuation," "On Earth Assignment," "Master Symbol of the Solar Cross," and most recently, "A New Book of Revelations."

Before her passing channeler Tuella was the primary representative of the Ashtar Command.

Whenever she spoke in person, which was infrequently, followers of Ashtar's interplanetary fleet came from all over the United States to receive these vital channeled messages for the end times. Now deceased, Tuella's work is still exceedingly appreciated and highly respected even today. She continues to be beloved for being the primary channel for the Ashtar Command and for the fact that her message was always about peace, love and harmony.

Ashtar, the inspiration for much of that "good vibe" that represented peace, love and harmony in the 1970s and beyond, remains a rather enigmatic figure about whom little is known. In one of Tuella's volumes, "Ashtar, A Tribute, Revealing His Secret Identity," a chapter called "Who Is Ashtar?" grapples with

COSMIC REVELATIONS TILL THE END OF TIME

this problem. It is said that Ashtar is the Christian Commander From Venus and that he ranks just below an entity called Jesus-Sananda in overseeing the Airborne Division of the Brotherhood of Light.

"His messages are beamed from a colossal Starship or Space Station," the chapter continues, "beyond our atmosphere. He is loved for his deeply philosophical approach to our global problems and his efforts to raise planetary vibrations. Ashtar speaks of twenty million extraterrestrial persons involved with his Command in the Program For Planet Earth, and of another four million on our physical plane, consciously or unconsciously cooperating in the Program of Light."

Ashtar is a devoted Christian who declares the "Christ Teacher of this Galaxy" to be his beloved Commander-In-Chief, saying that Christ's Word is the law Ashtar himself obeys to fulfill the Program of Light on Earth.

The book also includes a Q. and A. with Ashtar conducted by a believer named Trevor James in 1958 in which Ashtar says that his body is etheric and that he possesses no physical "casing" of the dense type that humans are limited to. He is also called a Herald Angel by other trance mediums who claim contact with him.

Further along in the "Ashtar" book, Tuella receives "A Message of Encouragement From Ashtar."

"We come to you in the vibration of Love and Light," Ashtar begins, "sent forth from the Upper Heavens to penetrate the atmosphere of Earth and reach the hearts of all Mankind. We enfold the Planet with the power of Love and blend into its very layers an anointing of peace and goodwill. We carry away the castoff thoughts of darkness that would destroy your world if left unchecked. We intervene with our own magnetic rays and beams of Greater Light to keep the balance for further decades. White light is enfolded around and around your world in an essence of purification that will bring the blessings of God upon all Nations.

"Wherever there is a hostile approach to the solution of world problems, our Greater Light will assist to dissolve that hostility and maintain peace. Factions of baser intent are gradually deteriorating and being replaced by understanding and goodwill. Peace will come, and the lesser infiltrations of the Dark Ones will be overcome. Yield not to weariness of spirit, but continue to watch for our coming, and the fulfillment of all the dreams and hopes of Humanity for a better world. It will come. The waters of Life shall flow upon every barren place, and every thirst shall be quenched."

Sounds encouraging, indeed. Which of course is the whole point of the majority of the messages that have been disseminated.

COSMIC REVELATIONS TILL THE END OF TIME

We often think of alien abductions as very negative experiences. People like Travis Walton and Whitley Strieber being taken onboard UFOs and being physically harassed and examined and perhaps even raped. But the channeled messages are just the opposite. They deal with bliss and euphoria and talk about a better world and how we can live a more serene life.

The messages take a higher spiritual tone than a lot of the other contacts and experiences. People always ridicule this and say it's a lot of New Age fluff. And they're right. A lot of the things the channelers say cannot really be verified. But it's a very positive message that they bring, although of course it's hard for many people to follow or believe in this chaotic world that we live in.

And while the inspiring messages from Ashtar to Tuella and the other channelers cannot be documented or proven, one cannot help but wish it is true somehow that someone out there really cares about us and is watching over us. Perhaps the Ashtar Command is really the modern day version of our planet's ancient guardian angels beliefs given a more technological spin? We can only hope.

IMPORTANT NOTICE

It should be noted, and that observance reinforced, that the channelings published in this book were not sent forth through Tuella but were given to the Earth by a private individual, a businessman, who has agreed to share the transmission he received over a limited period of time. What makes these transmissions most rewarding is that many of the things that Ashtar and the other masters saw and discussed have come about, unlike the message received through other New Age mediums that were totally "off the wall" and failed to hit the bull's eye.

Many have asked about possible future communications coming forth through this particular channel. When asked, the channel will only say that, as far as he knows, his commission has been satisfied, but all is subject to change as we go about the task of spreading the word of universal harmony and love.

Accept these messages. Or ignore them. The Space Brothers say we have free choice, and thus the decision is yours!

*****

RECOMMENDED READING – BOOKS BY THE ASHTAR COMMAND, CHANNELED THROUGH TUELLA

COSMIC REVELATIONS TILL THE END OF TIME

Ashtar: Revealing the Secret Identity of the Forces of Light and Their Spiritual Program for Earth: A New Book of Revelations - A Harvesting Of Souls At Earth's Final Moment

Project World Evacuation: UFOs to Assist in the "Great Exodus" of Human Souls Off This Planet

Master Symbol Of The Solar Cross

On Earth Assignment

All available through Amazon.Com

Or through the publisher:

TIMOTHY G. BECKLEY

BOX 753

NEW BRUNSWICK, NJ 08903

mrufo8@hotmail.com

www.ConspiracyJournal.com

Prophecies Do Come True Through The Ashtar Command!
By Carol Ann Rodriguez

IT'S difficult to believe that it has been over thirty years since the first channeled communications were received via telepathy from the Ashtar Command that ultimately went to make up the first edition of "The New World Order: Prophecies from Space."

First off, I should explain to those who are not already familiar with this work that the New World Order of which Ashtar speaks is definitely NOT the same as the NWO that has come to be associated with the negative political and military forces of the ruling earthly elite. This is not your NWO of either the Illuminati or that of the George Bush/Dick Cheney soul-sucking administration.

Naturally, we can't make the claim that this is the only channeled material out there. This sort of material has been "filtering through" for ages. Back in the time of the Greek and Roman empires, the Oracle of Delphi channeled Apollo and the list of notables who came to hear her messages from above included generals and heads of state. More recently, around 150 years ago, a manuscript entitled "A Dweller On Two Planets" was the rage and it still sells very well. It was "written" by a young cowboy who tended fences in California. A voice spoke to him that professed to be from Atlantis. While channeling, he drew sketches of Atlantean flying vessels. They looked remarkably identical to the cigar-shaped craft photographed many a dog-eared moon later by the late George Adamski, a contactee who claimed to have traveled in these same type of craft to other planets during the beginning of the New Age movement, which started on the West Coast of the U.S. and silently crept around the world. If you want to see channelers in action, head on out to Sedona, Arizona, the Mecca for this sort of thing. You might even run into actress Shirley McClain sitting in the Coffee Pot café chatting with some metaphysical fans.

Now some channelers make a big "stink" about their ability to speak with outer space beings or with a five thousand year old Tibetan sage. The messengers may vary but the message is usually the same. Peace. Love. Universal Harmony, with a dose of good ole philosophical platitudes thrown in.

Of course, one of the things channels like to do is make dire predictions. They simply love to warn of this or that upcoming catastrophic event. They will select a specific date for an event to occur, and when it doesn't in fact happen, they either "get out of Dodge" or they come up with an excuse like there was a last minute reprieve due to some unexpected turn of events in the cosmos. The rate of accuracy on the part of the channel whose material is presented in this book – a successful businessman who does not want to be identified due to the stigma attached to being associated with any esoteric topic – is higher than most, I would have to insist. Also, from my own study of the phenomenon, I would say that the future is not engraved in stone. We have free will and there are alternative courses history can take – otherwise it would be pointless to try to influence the future in a positive way.

In the messages that were received through "Channel X," Ashtar always qualified his warnings with "if your planet continues on the same course," indicating that we can always change the path we are headed down to a rosier one. Perhaps a nuclear war was avoided because the powers that be heeded Ashtar's counsel that a world war would destroy the whole planet. There would be no winners. Every side would be a loser.

Ashtar predicted abnormal weather patterns and physical changes to the planet due to our misuse of Mother Nature. These include earthquakes, volcanoes, and tidal waves, along with strange atmospheric phenomena, such as fierce tornados, brutal heat waves, golf ball-size hail – all of which we are seeing on a daily basis since this book was initially published. Our space brethren told those willing to listen that freak weather conditions would serve as a sign that the planet is going through harsh changes. When asked when all of the Earth Changes might occur, Ashtar said: "It is impossible to measure time as you know it, because time is forever flowing. While destiny points you in a certain direction, there are changes that can come about because of things you are capable of doing that alter your own future."

Ashtar also predicted the beginning of the demise of the Soviet Union. He said they would have to stay out of Poland (which had begun to make democratic strides) as well as other satellite nations. When I asked if any of these countries would rebel and establish a different form of government, establish freedom, Ashtar explained that the changes would come about over a period of several years, more or less without fighting. 'The governments of these countries will simply have to change, to become less of a dictatorship. Ashtar added, "We don't see the Soviet Union coming in and trying to push back these revolutions from taking place, because it is not to their advantage, given the bad coverage from other countries around the world." Eventually the desire for freedom spread to the Soviet Union itself, which broke up into many independent nations with even Russia making strides toward democracy.

By far, however, the most inspiring prophecies from the Ashtar Command had to do with the New Age of enlightenment which will come after all of these changes have taken place.

Ashtar tells us that fabulous psychic powers, which are taken for granted on other worlds, are beginning to emerge in our young people. Abilities, such as ESP and mental telepathy, are like driving a car or riding a bicycle; it is something anyone can learn.

Mental telepathy will make it difficult to have misunderstandings. There will be no more wars. "Peace and Ashtar Command harmony will cover the entire planet. Nature will co-exist side by side with human beings. The plants, animals, the entire Nature Kingdom will all flourish all over your planet, as they did eons ago."

Furthermore, we will live in peace with the universe and with all living things. "The earth will be as it was back in the time of your Genesis in the Bible. Mankind will know the wonder and magic of creation."

I, for one, am really, truly, looking forward to all this!

Carol Rodriguez, August 2011

About Carol Ann Rodriguez

Carol Ann Rodriguez was born and grew up in Queens, NY. She obtained a BA degree from The City College of New York and a Masters Degree in Education from Hunter College. She has a NY state teaching certification. During the early 1970s, while teaching preschool, Carol began studying at the New York School of Occult Arts and Sciences, where she met and studied the universal teachings of the Ashtar Command with the channel. She also studied art at Parson's School of Design and soon began to do illustrations for Inner Light Publications/Global Communications. Her works have also appeared in numerous other publications, including the now defunct magazine "*UFO Universe.*" Currently, she continues to do art while editing and proofreading as well as pursuing her spiritual and metaphysical studies.

COSMIC REVELATIONS TILL THE END OF TIME

Introduction

ASHTAR has been widely known in UFO channeling circles for many years. Yet, it came as an absolute surprise to me when he first took over the vocal chords of a well-established New York City businessman, who, though familiar with literature on flying saucers, had never experienced anything of this magnitude. He fell into a trance, his eyes glazed over, and he began to speak as if an alien intelligence had gained control.

At first the voice sounded very distant. Then it got louder. The voice said: "I am from the Hierarchy Council and I am opening this channel." With this, the businessman returned to full consciousness without recalling anything about what had happened. A few days later, the same transformation took place, and this time a being identifying himself as Ashtar spoke.

To date, we have received some 35 transmissions that are said to have been beamed from a giant mother ship somewhere out in space. The messages are of a deep philosophical nature and deal for the most part with problems of a global importance. Ashtar says that the Space Brothers are willing to assist with our transformation into a higher plane of consciousness brought about by the heightening of our planet's vibrations as we are about to enter the Aquarian or New Age.

Over a period of months, other beings came through the channel with added advice and information of their own. These beings, all of whom have very distinct personalities, include Monka from the Planet Mars; Aura Raines, a beautiful spacewoman from Clarion, a world hidden behind our sun; Solar Star, a healer assigned to Earth; and Romilar, assistant to Ashtar. A group calling themselves "The Etherians," beings of pure energy, put in an appearance, indicating that some of the aliens visiting Earth are definitely NOT flesh and blood like we are.

The art work contained in this book which depicts our friends from space is a combination of eyewitness descriptions and psychic impressions, though it has been stated that they are often seen differently by different people because of their radiant auras which obscure details.

Though some may see this book as sensationalistic, we feel the messages are of such a "life and death" nature that they need to be distributed as widely as possible. They need to be studied by those wise enough to feel that their content is important as we Earthlings progress into the New Age. To those who do believe, we suggest you do what Ashtar has repeatedly requested – SPREAD THE WORD!

Carol Rodriquez, New York, N.Y.

Session One

The Communications Begin

THE first recorded session took place on July 4th, 1980. Actually, this was not the first time that the channel had gone into a trance. However, until I was able to produce an actual tape of a message, he was skeptical that the Space Brothers were speaking through him at all. This session, as well as many of the others, started with a very low, hardly audible chant of OM, which gradually built to a normal tone of voice.

The first recorded session was on July 4, 1980. It began very low. "Oomm Omm." Gradually the sound got louder. (All of the sessions begin with the "Om" sound, very softly at first, then gradually building to a normal tone.)

Greetings, Starchild.

We are pleased that we can visit with you on such a momentous day in the history of your country that you call the United States. We are with you and watching you at this time from a spacecraft hovering 1,200 miles over these United States. We have watched your firework displays today and we have recalled how your history began, how your great forefathers led a revolution of mighty souls, and how your country grew into the greatest on the planet. We wish you well.

However, we must warn you that there are those who would like to see the Constitution destroyed. There are those in your country who are being directed by outside forces, foreign countries. These people would like to see your country destroyed, democracy taken away. We say heed these warnings, be

COSMIC REVELATIONS TILL THE END OF TIME

careful...[louder], be careful. For unless things are changed in these countries, the rule of your United States is limited in time to the next few years.

We have been with you for many, many centuries. We have watched the founding of your country, the United States. For the most part we have been happy, yes, delighted with what we have seen. Your forefathers, who wrote the Constitution and were the original leaders, had many great ideas. They were the true patriots of mankind. They wished to see the human spirit set free.

Today as you celebrate your July 4th, think of these things – think of these things and see what can be done to change them.

Oh, indeed, sad times are coming unless these warnings are heeded, many, many sad times, not only for the country known as the United States, but for the rest of the world.

Oh, indeed, you live in troubled times, but these are also momentous times, in that the New Age will be upon you very soon. We tell you to spread the message, to pass the word. Let those who will believe know of our existence. Yes, there are UFOs in the sky. Yes, we are the Space Brothers. We have much love, much kindness towards you. Someday there will be a New Age. Someday mankind will live in peace.

You, Starchild, you are among the select. You are among the chosen. We are helping you, guiding you, and, in turn, you will help us when the time comes.

We must go now, but, once again, happy birthday to your country, kind wishes to you, Starchild, and we will be speaking to you very soon again.

This is Ashtar, Commander of the space fleet ending the channeled communication.

Session Two

Heed These Warnings

IN *this conversation, Ashtar warns of the perils that plague mankind, tells of the ruthlessness of world leaders and says that, should we accept the reality of the Space Brothers, our technology would progress by leaps and bounds. This session came two weeks after the first, and a pattern was set for the frequency of most communications that lay ahead.*

Session two was a week later. (There is usually a one to three week interval between channeling sessions).

Greetings. How are you this evening, Starchild?

Very well, thank you.

It is very important that you continue to record these messages. There will be 35 in all. They will cover a wide range of topics, things that people on your planet will find of interest, things that they need to know in this very important age. You are probably aware that many people have seen the craft you have come to call UFOs or flying saucers. There are many of us here, many, many different races, many different beings from all over the universe. We come to watch. We come to wait. We come to teach those few that will listen.

Mark my words, these are dangerous times. You need all the help you can get. Your leaders have led you on a path to annihilation. They have created weapons that they cannot control. If the opportunity arose, they would try to use them against each other. Why? Because they wish to be powerful. They wish to be in control. They wish to be the one ruler of the planet. On our far away worlds, we

COSMIC REVELATIONS TILL THE END OF TIME

know there is not just one ruler. We have governments made up of committees, people who are concerned about the well-being of others. They are not in it for profit. They are not in it for greed. They are not in it for world domination.

If your planet continues on the course it is now on, Planet Earth will cease to exist within the next few years. But, lo, there is still time. There is still time for your people to mend their ways. Clean up the planet to make it more livable. Yes, if you do these things, if you make the Earth a more peaceful planet, we will land, we will make ourselves known, for we love you. We come here in peace. We come to guide you. If only your leaders and your scientists would listen, would look to the signs in the sky, and would understand, this planet would move many years ahead in its technological development. For we have many things that we could show you, that you could learn from.

At this very moment, your energy, the energy within the bowels of the earth, is depreciating. Soon there will not be enough power in your cities to provide you with the energy you need for heat and refrigeration. Lo, these are troubled times. Economics are very bad, not only in your own country, but in other countries throughout the world. There are many unstable conditions, conditions which you have no control over, conditions which only your leaders... [fading]. Yes, these are troubled times. But these are also good times for those who will open their minds, for those who will cast their eyes skyward, for those who will look for our gleaming craft. For we come with knowledge, with love in our heart. We wish to tell you it is possible for you to travel many, many thousands, yes, millions of miles throughout the solar system, faster than the speed of light.

It is possible to teleport. It is possible to transport many, many miles away from where you live. It is possible to do all these things but not by using the very antiquated methods that your scientists have developed and which they continue to follow suit with. Yes, Starchild, you understand part of what is going on. You are doing the best you can to help, through the books you are going to write and through the illustrations you are going to do. You will be successful in your work. There will be other people joining you in this. We watch you. We guide you. We ask your help and we in turn will help you.

I have spoken but I shall return. This is Ashtar, closing the channel for tonight. Goodbye, Starchild, we will see you again soon.

COSMIC REVELATIONS TILL THE END OF TIME

Session Three

In a World War There Would Be No Winner

ASHTAR takes our political system to task and offers the suggestion that "people are important, not parties, not promises." He states that their spacecraft regularly monitor our Earthly T.V. broadcasts. We thought that we would come through tonight since you have had a very active day, Starchild, and you always seem to enjoy conversing with us so much. [I was less nervous than usual because I was swimming, which always calms me down.] We appreciate the opportunity to talk for there is so much we have to say.

This evening we have been monitoring your broadcasts and we have noted, with much interest, the convention held by your Republican party in Detroit. It is fascinating to see what some men will do in order to gain control. We watch and monitor the activities in Detroit and find it totally strange why two parties, who are really quite similar in content, should be so opposed to one another.

Neither party shows any constructive manners in any of the programs that they propose to support.

Of course, many of the things your politicians promise will never come through to fruition even if they should be elected. But that is not really important, because it is their meaning that is more important than anything else. Yes, these government officials, the people you elect, are the ones that have to change the world.

Yet, none of these promises, none of the platforms, go far enough in making those changes that will have to come about if your planet is to survive in the next few years. People are important, not parties, not promises. Governments should not be run by elected officials who do not keep promises.

It is important that your world unite, for, separated as it is now, it will eventually destroy itself. Unity is important. It is probable that this will not occur, in which case your planet will probably undergo another world war.

We would like to see this avoided at all cost. That is one of the reasons we are making select contacts at this time. We are trying to get the message across that a world war would destroy the whole planet. In a world war, there would be no winner. Every side would be the loser. We watch and we wait from many miles out in space. We observe your activities.

We are indeed pleased to see that a growing number of you are taking matters into your own hands, are asking for a change. Hopefully something will be done. Hopefully it is not too late. Yes, you live in a very turbulent world. Times are changing, technology is changing. Everyday there are new discoveries that are being made. It is almost impossible to keep up with everything that is occurring. Just think back several decades ago. Your world, your civilization, was quite primitive. You did not even have the automobile, nor any means to fly. Medicine was in its infancy.

Today all that has changed. Yet, you have not kept up spiritually with your technological advances. If you are to survive in the future, you must radically change your way of thinking, your behavior patterns, or otherwise it will be too late.

We thank you for listening. We appreciate, Starchild, all that you have done for us. We like your work very much. We approve of what you are doing. We will be talking with you again in the very near future.

This is Ashtar, Commander of the intergalactic forces, closing the channel for tonight.

Session Four

The Space Brothers Secret Mission

THE *Commander of the intergalactic forces confesses that there is more to their plan of action than what is communicated through any one channel. Ashtar also discusses time differentials and the Spiritual and physical changes of the next decade. The selection of the chosen ones, and tells of inner Earth inhabitants.*

You are lucky to be the student of such a fine teacher. There is much that he can teach you. However, our mission is known only totally to us. [I had been questioning the "Channel" that day, as to whether he knew any secret information that I didn't know about.] We have not informed any of the recipients, and there are several, about the total extent of our Earthly visitation. The reason for this, you might ask, is because the time is not yet at hand.

Question-When will the time be at hand?

Oh, it is impossible to measure time as you know it, because time is forever flowing. It is not consistent. Many things can happen to block our plans, to change our plans. While your destiny points you in a certain direction, there are changes that can come about because of things you are capable of doing to alter your own future. However, from the way things are being handled on your planet, it would seem to us here at the Free Federation of Planets that time is indeed very short for you Earthlings. We would prophesize that you will soon see many changes coming about, many changes, physical changes and spiritual changes. Some of these things you can see for yourself by tuning into your television stations. You see earthquakes, volcanoes, tidal waves, and many disasters caused by your misuse of Mother Nature.

Of course, in addition to these physical catastrophes that are going to take place, mankind can also destroy itself with the use of nuclear weapons and warlike activities. We hope that this does not happen, but chances are that it will. If this does happen, some of the good ones, some of the chosen ones, will be taken off the Earth and taken to another place. Here you will be kept for the duration of the catastrophes, and, when it is safe for you to return, you will be brought back to Earth to inhabit it once more.

Notice also, there are many changes in the weather. Your Midwest and east coast are now experiencing a phenomenal heat wave. These things are being caused by air currents, which are no longer as they should be because of atomic blasts, and also because of things that are happening inside the Earth. All these things have an effect. All these things affect your weather. You should look for more climate change, hot spells, and violent storms in the future. These will serve as additional warnings that the planet and its surface are changing.

Question-Will it become totally uninhabitable at some point?

No, more than likely there will always be people here on Earth. While many of these catastrophes will take place, and will cause the unnecessary and unfortunate death of many millions, there will always be places for people to hide.

In fact, there are now people who are living inside your own planet, who once lived on the surface many, many eons ago, but they too destroyed themselves. Some of them built rocket ships to go into space, while others built cities underneath the ground. Today we are in contact with these races, the descendents of the Atlantean culture as they exist today throughout the solar system, where they have settled, and also with those that did manage to settle underneath the Earth's surface.

These are your so-called inner Earth inhabitants which have been written about in some of the literature. There are many races, many species that exist throughout the solar system, some of which you have never dreamed of. They are all keeping a watchful eye on you. We are doing our best to see that you do not destroy yourself. We cannot interfere. We can give advice, but we cannot change things.

Only you can change things here on Earth. Over the next few months, you will learn many things. We will tell you what we feel you are able to comprehend and understand at this time. There is much you have to learn. There is much that mankind must learn.

This is Ashtar closing the channel for tonight.

COSMIC REVELATIONS TILL THE END OF TIME

Session Five

Relocation in Space

***ASHTAR** foretells of a possible world war and of the rescue of survivors by the space fleet. He predicts the outcome of a global holocaust. He discusses the grasping for power by politicians and explains why they cannot intervene in the Karmic events which are about to take place.*

There are many people that we must speak to, and because of this we have been absent. But do not think you have been forgotten, because such is not the case.

Many times you have asked, when will we arrive, when will we land in force, when will we evacuate the Earth? Oh, Starchild, it is not so far away, but it is impossible for us to give you a specific date and a specific time. But be informed, nonetheless, that, when this time does arrive, you and the other chosen shall be taken up. You will be taken to safety, a safe place in outer space, perhaps another planet, maybe a large mother ship. It is undecided yet. From there, you will watch your Earth being destroyed.

For a period of many, many years, the planet will not be fit for habitation. However, should the end come through a nuclear explosion, a nuclear war, World War III – we will do our best to try to keep this from happening – but if it does happen, and there is a strong possibility that it will, we will monitor the radioactivity from outer space. We will do our best to sweep it clean, so that the chosen can be brought back here later on.

As I have said, it is impossible to predict the exact date. However, it is leading up to a point where such an event cannot be postponed much longer.

COSMIC REVELATIONS TILL THE END OF TIME

Your planet's vibrations are very, very, negative at this time. There are many forces on your planet who are seeking to control the destiny of millions and millions of people. Things are bad. Things are disastrous. It could happen at any time. It could happen tomorrow, or it could happen a week from now, a month from now, a year from now or five years from now. It is impossible to predict the exact date.

But there are some events that will happen, some things that you could watch out for and mark on your calendar. There is a country in the Middle East that will be overtaken by the country you call the Soviet Union. When this happens, the time will not be far off. Such is happening now in Afghanistan, but it will spread. The power of the Soviet Union is very mighty. They are very powerful. They have a great military machine. Your United States feels that it is the will of the people that we try to liberate these people from the Soviet Union and the Communist Manifesto.

While it is certainly brave and courageous that your government feels this way, this is also leading you down the path to a nuclear holocaust. The two forces are opposing. They are like a magnet, a magnet that repels each other, and this can only lead to a catastrophe.

It is too bad that this has to happen. We would like to see it avoided, but it will be difficult to do so. You have built your military up to a point where both countries could very easily destroy themselves through a nuclear holocaust. There is no backing out now, it seems. Both countries, both powers, are very influential in the world. The next war could be a very, very disastrous one. Millions of people will be killed, millions of people will be slaughtered, but some, the lucky ones, the chosen, will be saved.

We will come. We will land. We will make ourselves known. We will take on board those who are worthy, those who are aware of our presence, those who are involved in the New Age. You, Starchild, will be one of them.

Question-If there were a nuclear holocaust, wouldn't it cause the rest of the solar system to go out of whack? A lot of people have received information to that effect.

Yes, it is true, because, you see, if there were a nuclear holocaust on your planet, it would cause a vibration sort of like a chain reaction that would vibrate through the entire solar system and would cause very, very negative effects. It might cause not only your polar alignment to go off but it could also cause this to happen on several other planets.

It is impossible to predict this, of course, but we are watching with keen interest. Not only do we not want you to destroy yourselves but we do not want to see any of your brothers throughout the solar system destroyed either. So, yes, it is true that these messages are being given out and it is accurate that we are watching and we are waiting and we are preparing to do whatever we can to avert such a disastrous situation.

Question-Couldn't you do something to stop it from happening?

We are doing whatever we can at this time. There are people among you who are from the various planets in the solar system, who are trying to get to your leaders, trying to get them to see the situation they are getting themselves into. But it is really impossible to change the minds of individuals, though we can alert them to the facts, though we can try to shine the light of universal love on them. It is impossible if their will is not strong enough. For you see, the leaders – there is not just one leader – your president, for example, he does not have the power, the power is given to many, many people. It is given to the scientists. It is given to the military. And it is the same, not only here in these United States, but also in other countries, the Soviet Union, for example, where not one person makes the rules, not one person says what is to be done. There are many, many alternative points of view, and many things that cannot seem to be worked out, even amongst your own individual governments. No one person owns the key to this. If this were the case, we could probably come down and take them away and all would be well. But this isn't so because it is not just a handful of people running things, it is many, many people. Some are willing to listen, but many others will not, because it is their own greed they are looking out for, not the welfare of their own people or the welfare of space people throughout the solar system.

There will also be a natural holocaust that will take place, caused perhaps not only by these nuclear explosions, but also because your own weather, your own atmosphere, is so rapidly changing. You have seen this by the repeated eruptions of the volcano you call St. Helens, in Washington State. But there will be others that will be taking place around the world. There will also be an increase in earthquakes and volcanic eruptions. These will also cause many disasters and loss of lives. These are all signs that the time is near, that times are changing, that your whole planet is going through a change.

We would like to see you live in peace. We would like to see these things not happen, for your own benefit as well as for ours, but it is impossible to change the course of history. We could look, we could observe, we could do what we can, but we cannot change the facts. You have created your own life here, your own civilization, and it is impossible for us, it is against the Universal Laws to come down and actually interfere. We can watch, we can observe, we can even be able to give you advice. But if you do not listen, it is not up to us to prevent these things from happening. This is a natural occurrence, something you have brought on yourselves, and you will have to pay the Karmic dues. There will be more signs. There will be more signs in the heavens. You will look to the stars.

Mankind will look to the stars as their salvation. All this will happen, wait and see. We are watching from far above. We are keeping tabs on your activities. We are hoping that these things do not happen.

Question-Could it still be averted?

Yes, there is a chance it will be averted, but with each passing day the chance gets less and less. If mankind were to change the way that they live, if mankind were to put down their arms, then this could be averted, but there is no sign that this will happen. Someday someone will take matters into their own hands and push the button, the button that will mean the end of civilization as you know it now.

Look to the skies. Tell those that you know who believe to look to the skies, that we are coming in greater numbers. We will do what we can. Tell those who believe. Tell those who are righteous that we are here, that we are watching over them, that we are praying for your safety.

We thank you for listening, Starchild, for you are one of the chosen. You are one of those who have helped us in many, many ways, and we thank you. And please, please tell others that this is happening. And continue to walk in peace, continue to walk in love, continue to walk in harmony with the universe. This is Ashtar bidding you a fond farewell.

COSMIC REVELATIONS TILL THE END OF TIME

Session Six

Entering the New Age of Enlightenment

BEINGS *on other worlds, Ashtar says, are endowed with phenomenal psychic powers that are just beginning to surface in our younger generation. He notes that such abilities can be learned by all and will be necessary in the mass evacuation.*

We are with you tonight on the day that you call Labor Day. We have watched from far above the Earth as the people of the United States go on relaxing and enjoying themselves. We find it humorous that those who are running for election would pick this day to start their campaign, for what do any of the candidates know of the people who have worked to make this country as strong as it is?

We wish to talk about, briefly, the change in vibrations which are taking place over your planet. You are entering the age of enlightenment, a cosmic era, a decade of psychic awareness. Many of the young people on your planet already know about this. They are able to read minds, bend metals, and do certain things which your scientists find amazing. They try to find explanations for these things that are not to be found, for truly, we are watching over you and seeing these things happening. Such feats as these are quite common on other planets.

Most of the worlds that have developed beyond yours, intelligence-wise, have found that it is very simple to employ E.S.P., mental telepathy, and so forth. In fact, the majority of contacts that have taken place with your Earth people have been through the medium of telepathy, telepathic communication. Parapsychology will in the next few years become more and more accepted. And we will see the point when several universities will even teach courses in things along these lines, and they will be accredited courses. For you see, the mental powers that man possesses are far beyond what you are able to contemplate at this point. The key to unlocking this knowledge is simply in raising the vibration, in raising the consciousness, in understanding that these things exist. There are no incredible feats. They are not powers of the devil. They are not supernatural. These are things that everyone can accomplish. It is like learning to play the piano or tuning an instrument. All one has to do is to study and practice and keep at it, and they will find that these abilities are something that everyone can understand and everyone can utilize.

It is important that Earth people understand these things and learn to use these abilities, because they will come in handy when people are taken off this planet and taken elsewhere after the great holocaust starts. For, as I have mentioned, many of the other inhabitants of the solar system and the universe use these powers quite commonly. In fact, in most cases, language, the spoken word, as you have come to know it here on Earth, is not even being used anywhere else.

To most intelligent beings, it's as antiquated as using sign language or smoke signals, as the American Indians used to use.

Question-Does mental telepathy come in the form of words?

Well, images, pictures, transference of thought. Words are not important. Words have no meaning. Someday words will not be necessary. For the time being, since your world is so hung up on words, it is necessary for those who are contacting aliens to think in terms of words. But words are not really necessary. It is feelings, it is vibrations, it is emotions that are being transferred in actuality.

Question-Will it be possible for everyone to learn to do this?

Yes, it is as driving a car, or riding a bicycle, or breathing. It is something that everyone can learn to do. In fact, right now at this very moment, the channel we are using is performing a certain method of telepathy. The words are actually being imprinted on his mind, and he is speaking them verbally, but we are actually beaming these words from a spaceship that is hovering hundreds of miles above the Earth's atmosphere at this very moment.

COSMIC REVELATIONS TILL THE END OF TIME

And we are watching you on a large video screen from inside the ship and we are happy to see that you are enjoying these words. And we hope that other people who may eventually hear these words or may read them in printed form will also gain considerable knowledge from them. We will have other messages that we will give to you in the weeks and months to come.

We thank you for your indulgence. We welcome your questions. And we hope that we have been able to impart some bits of knowledge and wisdom to you. We try to keep these messages as non-technical as possible, as we realize that neither you nor the channel are scientists and would not learn these things. However, it is very important that what we give to you is eventually given out, so that people will learn and understand from this information.

I thank you, Starchild, and will be talking with you again in the very near future. This is Ashtar, of the Free Federation of Planets, saying goodnight, and may the Supreme One be with you.

COSMIC REVELATIONS TILL THE END OF TIME

Session Seven

Signs and Wonders

THE *Sun and Moon to look different. A pink haze fills the sky. Rivers to change course. Earthquakes on the East coast and the possible destruction of New York City. Ashtar discusses the number of people to be taken. Life aboard the orbiting space cities. And a possible cancer cure.*

How are you on this fine evening on the first day of the season you call Fall?

Fine, thank you.

We are honored to be able to speak through your fine channel. We have noticed that you are preparing a book on Earth changes and the holocaust that is due to occur. We are happy to see that you are getting this information out to those who are willing to listen. While, no doubt, many inaccuracies will creep into the works, as they come from many sources, through many different means, the vital part of the message, that these things will happen, is getting through to those who are seeking to have their lives changed and improved. There has been some discussion as to what signs and so-called wonders to look for. There will be many, many signs that will differ depending upon what part of the Earth you live on, of course.

When the earthquakes and volcanic eruptions start en masse, your sun and your moon, for example, will look quite different than they do now. There will be a pink haze in the sky. This pink haze will cover everything, so that when you see the sun and when you see the moon they will no longer appear the same to you. Also, the course of mighty rivers will change. One in particular in South America will make headlines within the next few months. There will be a considerable number of earthquakes, some of which will even occur on your East coast. Though they have been recorded there before, this is the first time that such tremors will be of a very strong magnitude.

Question-Is New York going to be destroyed?

New York is already destroying itself. As for a total physical destruction, this may occur, but there is a good possibility that it will not, for it would take a very strong physical reaction to sink or tilt the island of Manhattan. This may occur towards the final days, towards the end as we know it. By that time, most of the people will already be evacuated, those who will be taken off the planet. There will be areas that you can go to that will be safe. Arizona is one that is frequently mentioned, and this is a good place. Also Wyoming, Oklahoma and perhaps the Dakotas.

Question-In general, will the center of the country be the safest?

No, this will be more towards the Southwest portion, the Western portion, although the west coast will be entirely destroyed. There will be so many earthquakes, so many fires, so many other catastrophes that will happen there, that eventually, even if it does not sink totally into the ocean, as has been prophesied by many of your psychics and sensitives, it will still be unsafe to live there. Very few people would want to dwell in California, Oregon, Washington State, or parts of Mexico.

There will also be other signs in the skies, an increase of UFOs that will be coming down here from many sources to watch these things, and at some point to lift off those people who accept the existence of Space Brothers, and those people whose deeds are such that make it essential that they be taken along. These are the ones we would have repopulate the Earth at some future date.

Also, those who have particular skills or abilities will be selected, as long as they have no criminal record, or as long as they have not done unjust deeds unto others.

COSMIC REVELATIONS TILL THE END OF TIME

Question-How many people will be taken from the Earth?

Earth groups coming down here will take people off. Our own ships will be responsible for upwards of 20,000. We would estimate that altogether perhaps 140,000 to 170,000 people will be lifted up and taken off the planet.

Question-That isn't very many, considering the population of the Earth.

Well, it is certainly true that this isn't a great percentage, but if the people who are down here lived more according to the Universal Laws, these great catastrophes and holocausts would not take place. So, why should we remove them only to have it start all over again? Also, the question arises if we were to take more of them, what would we do with these people? We would be responsible for housing them, feeding them, and taking care of their various needs while they are off the planet, which could be anywhere from five years to several decades before the Earth would be safe to be repopulated again. So, though the number may not seem like a large enough one for you, perhaps it is only possible that this many be taken. You certainly will be among those who will be lifted up. Do not fret, you will be there, and your loved ones, and your friends, for you are wise, kind and generous, and you have accepted us, and we thank you for that, Starchild.

Question-How much time will it be before the Earth can be repopulated again?

Five years, a decade, maybe longer.

Question-That doesn't seem like a very long time after all that will happen on the surface.

Well, we will send ships down that will clear the air of any radioactivity caused by any nuclear skirmish or conflict that may take place. And the volcanic eruptions will probably simmer down in a while. The earthquakes will become less frequent in number, because there will be a shifting, probably of the entire Earth's axis, so that the entire land mass will be reshaped. There will be a very few areas, really, that will be able to withstand the force of the holocaust that will take place.

COSMIC REVELATIONS TILL THE END OF TIME

These safe areas that we mentioned will, of course, be safe only for a while. They will be safe at the beginning. But even these places in the end when the Earth tilts on its axis, if that is to happen, will of course become completely altered, and for a period will not house human life as you know it. It is from these areas that a good deal of the number of people that will be picked up will be lifted off the Earth.

Question-Where will the people be taken?

There will be several large cities in space, some of which your scientists have already observed. These ships, which can house many, many thousands of people, can be put in orbit around the sun, as if they were planets themselves. Then at the time the Earth has been made stable again, the people can be brought back. These planets that will be put into orbit around the sun will be big enough so that people could go on living quite comfortably. Food will be grown there. There will be recreation and entertainment areas. There will be schools. Life will go on.

Look for a major breakthrough in the newspapers regarding a cancer cure. This is something we have been channeling information to a number of doctors on for some time now. This will cause a great deal of controversy for a while, but within a short while, the medical authorities will come forward and announce that this is the first true cure for cancer.

The beginning of the New Age is here, Starchild. Many changes are going to take place. You will see them happening all around you. Watch the news. Listen, because all of this is important. You can see that the Earth is like a festering wound, getting larger and larger. There is more hatred among mankind than before. The bomb is about ready to explode. But do not fear, be happy, be content, be glad that you are living in such an important time. And watch the skies, for we are here and we are watching over you. We send our love. We send our well wishes. We send our strength and our power to you and those who are deserving. We will speak to you again very soon.

This is Ashtar, of the Free Federation of Planets, saying goodnight.

Session Eight

Earth – A Giant Pressure Cooker About to Explode

OVERTURES *have been made to the governments of the world but to no avail. Ashtar says craft have been observed by hundreds of witnesses and they are not weather balloons or the planet Venus. Special meditation for lifting one's vibrations.*

Clear the channel, clear the channel, clear for transmission, clear the channel, clear for transmission. (He seemed to be having trouble coming through.) o...om, om, (louder) om. "Greetings." "Greetings."

Much to talk about, but so little time for us to say it. We are watching over your world constantly. We are recording all that transpires. We watch hopefully. We watch and wait. We see the Earth like a giant pressure cooker about ready to explode.

It is very sad to see the things that transpire down here. We would like to change the way you live, the way your civilization has developed. Unfortunately, it is impossible to do so. There is no possible way that we can influence all of the people that live on your planet, though we may try to at times.

It is important that you continue to get the message out, to let people know that there are highly advanced beings who do love them, who do care, who do watch over and try to guide them. We are very concerned for your safety, the safety of the Earth. It would grieve us greatly to see harm come to you. This is why there will be a mass evacuation at the time that the end comes.

We have tried to alert your government to what is happening, but they have refused to listen. Instead of giving you the benefits of the contacts that they have made with us, and the things that they have learned, they have hidden this truth because they are frightened. They are frightened that there will be altercations that will happen in your world. They are frightened that there will be many changes in society.

But change will come about. Change is bound to happen. There is change in everything we do. We have gone through changes ourselves similar to what you are going through on your planet. But our worlds, the worlds that make up the "Free Federation of Planets," have learned to live in peace and harmony, have learned to live in Universal Light and Knowledge. We are trying the best we can to share this knowledge with you.

Question-Couldn't you just reveal yourselves to the people and appear in the skies during daylight hours, bypassing the government?

Well, that has happened in the past. There have been many occasions when our people have been seen by hundreds, if not thousands, of individuals, and yet the media, the press, simply states that what people have seen is a weather balloon or the planet Venus. We have appeared many times in broad daylight, in the early evening hours, and later at night, when our craft glow brilliant, radiant colors in the atmosphere. But yet, some explanation is always offered.

Yet, our message is getting through, though; more and more of your people realize the true nature of our craft. They realize that there are Space Brothers out there. For those who are concerned with this, it is important that they find out what is going on. More and more information will be revealed in the next several years, as the end time approaches. UFOs are very important. We ask that you get the word out. We ask that you inform as many people as possible of the existence of UFOs, for they are very important for your state of development at this time.

Question-Is there a meditation that you could give us, that people could use to raise their vibrations and the vibrations of those around them?

Yes, yes, meditations are very important. One must always think positively. One must meditate on the good. Lie back and close your eyes. Meditate on the light in front of us. Meditate on the goodness of creation. Meditate on the glory of living. Meditate on the fruitfulness of life.

COSMIC REVELATIONS TILL THE END OF TIME

Make that glow expand in your mind. Let that glow consume. Let the glow consume everything around you. Meditate on the wholeness. Meditate on beneficial things.

Say to yourself:

I am the Light of the Universe. I am powerful.

I am glorious.

I am a living being.

Meditate everyday for five minutes, once in your A.M. and once in your P.M. Send out positive thoughts, send out harmony, send out love, and meditate on the wholeness of the solar system in the galaxy.

If enough people were to meditate, the world, indeed, the whole universe, would be a much better place in which to reside.

When you go to Pittsburgh this week, take these thoughts and these ideas with you...Stand in harmony with your fellow UFO researchers and share the light. Share what you know and spread the word, for the word is glorious and it means salvation.

We will stand with you. We will stand beside you. Greatness is yours. We thank you for doing the work of the Space Brothers. You have our blessings always. Peace be with you, Starchild. We will talk to you again very soon.

This is Ashtar of the Free Federation of Planets, saying peace, love, harmony, and always follow the LIGHT. (The last word faded out slowly.)

COSMIC REVELATIONS TILL THE END OF TIME

Session Nine

There Are Still Great Men Among You

THIS *session was recorded on the eve of the 1980 election. A political figure will emerge from California who will acknowledge the existence of the Space Brothers. Space people to demonstrate their power on a vast scale.*

Greetings! We are happy to be with you on this, your election eve. We have watched you with a great deal of interest. We have noted that among your people many feel that they do not have an adequate choice, and that when they go to the polls, they will only be voting for the one they think will be the lesser of the two evils.

Make no mistake about it, there are others who in the very near future will make themselves known more widely than they are today. There are great men left in your nation. Some of them will start coming forward very soon.

It makes no difference who you elect, for the wheels have already been locked in and what is slated to happen will happen. Of course, there are alternatives, but neither Mr. Carter nor Mr. Reagan offers any of these alternatives. They talk about the use of nuclear power as if it were a toy. As long as there is rampant use of nuclear energy for warlike purposes on your planet, there is no time…(could not make out the end of the sentence).

Many things are done in the name of capitalism that are very wrong and are used as profit motives only by very large companies and corporations with no understanding of what the total consequences would be. We are sorry to see that this is possible in this day and age.

No matter what the outcome of the election, no one would truly have won. We cannot interfere in what is to happen; therefore we can do nothing to indicate to you what our choice will be. However, in the very near future, one man on the West coast will acknowledge our presence and thus stand in very high esteem in the Planetary Council.

Question-Who will this man be?

We are not allowed at this time to tell you his identity. He has been in the news, but there are many who are not as yet familiar with what he represents. Look for more earthquakes in the next period. There will be a very substantial earthquake in California. And there will be a very disastrous one in Europe. We cannot say at this time the exact location of this devastating earth tremor but we will let you know as the date approaches. There will be a great number of earthquakes in the future. This will lead to volcanic eruptions, tidal waves and very harsh weather conditions.

Look for China and the Soviet Union to continue exploding their nuclear weapons. Though the Soviet Union will see some amazing changes in the upcoming years and will splinter into separate countries. We will demonstrate our power on a mass scale before too much longer.

Question-How will this happen?

Electrical devices will be implemented, and radio and TV will be taken off the air. In some locations our voice will be heard.

Oh! If only you could come with us and see the beauty and the vastness of the universe. You would understand many things. You would understand why it is wrong to continue on the course your planet is following. Destruction is unnecessary. We do not wish to see this happen.

We wish that the world would live in peace, that the holocaust that is about to transpire would not occur, though it does not seem very likely. We watch and wait and will determine at the right time what action is necessary. Until that time, we will continue to communicate with those channels on Earth who have shown their willingness to receive various data from us.

In many ways your planet has developed over the last quarter of the century. Many of your people know of our existence. Many others will learn of it in days to come. We have not landed openly up to now because we have been afraid of a panic. Your scientists, your great teachers, your politicians, your military leaders, many of them have taken us as being very evil, being very negative, or they have said we do not exist at all. They have tried to brainwash the people of the world into believing that which is not true. Soon, very shortly, as the cosmic clock ticks, we will let ourselves be seen by more and more people. It is good to know that you put your trust in us. And we wish to say that we appreciate what you have done for us up until now.

We watch and we wait and we hope. We hope for mankind. We hope that soon you will be elevated to our level so that we could coexist in peace and harmony.

Starchild, be well. We will speak to you again very soon. This is Ashtar, from the Free Federation of Planets.

Session Ten

A Cosmic History

SCIENCE *and technology have set our world astray. Rise and fall of Atlantis. Space travel existed thousands of years ago. Key to eternal life. Ancient Astronauts in Egypt and South America. Power from the atmosphere. ESP and other mental abilities. Destined to remain on Earth.*

It's nice to be back with you once again. We are watching you very closely, keeping an eye on your activities. We wish to convey to you the message of how science and technology has led your world astray.

Today, scientists think that they are the only ones that have the key to information and knowledge. We wish to let you know that this is not so. Not only are your scientists and technicians backward in many ways, but, in previous ages on your planet, there have been technologies far superior to what you know of even today.

Many have written and lectured on the lost continent of Atlantis. Indeed, such a continent did exist. This was maybe 50 or 60 thousand years ago, in your Earth time. The people who lived on this lost continent were very advanced. They had the key to eternal life and they had the key to traveling in outer space. Their technology was far beyond anything that has developed to this point again on your planet. Unfortunately, a portion of the population on this continent decided to use the technology that they had for evil gain and greed. This in the end destroyed Atlantis. It is possible that the same thing will happen to you again soon.

COSMIC REVELATIONS TILL THE END OF TIME

Some of the inhabitants of Atlantis were, even in those days, able to travel into space. Some of them escaped away from your planet, before the continent was destroyed. Some of them even come back this very day.

Question-What planets did they go to?

They went to planets in other solar systems. They also have bases on the planet you call Saturn, the moons of Saturn. Many of them have since intermingled with various other cultures in outer space so that some of those that are coming back today are descendants of both ancient astronauts and ancient Atlanteans. They are friendly. They wish to help you, as well as the Space Brothers.

In Egypt, the prince and the pharaohs knew of these things. They were in contact and communication with us. We taught them many things and shared information with them. And they allowed us to build energy beams, which you call pyramids, on their soil. We landed in Egypt in ancient times. We had open contact with the people. They knew of our existence. Many of them tried to worship us, but we discouraged this.

We were also in contact with the Indians in South America before your settlers and conquerors visited that part of the world. We taught them many things. We taught them to plant crops. We taught them about astronomy. We helped them build their cities. In many ways they were quite advanced.

Your science today is very backward. There is power all around you. (Raises arms and moves them in the air in a crossing and uncrossing motion.) There is power to be gotten from the atmosphere.

This power can be manifested in many ways. You call it electricity, but yet you only use a small portion of this power, this energy. While you are running out of fossil fuel, there are all sorts of energy all around you that you could be using. There is the power of the sun. You do not have to rely on nuclear energy. Nuclear energy will only help to destroy your planet.

Your scientists know many things, but, because of greed, they do not wish to share this information with you. There are those who would like to come out and reveal this but they are afraid of what would happen to them if they should. Power and energy exist in abundance in the universe.

COSMIC REVELATIONS TILL THE END OF TIME

Do we not speak with you? Do we not talk with you at this very moment? We are able to beam our messages down to you. Telepathy, ESP, the powers of the mind, anything is possible. Do not listen to what your scientists say. Do not believe that the technology you now have is as far advanced as it will be. Many things are possible. Oh, if you would only listen and learn. Do not be so foolish as to think that you know everything.

Man is destined to stay on the planet Earth for a long, long time. We shall see that they are not allowed to inhabit the other planets of the solar system until they have learned to live in harmony and balance with nature. For nature rules not only your planet but the other planets as well. We do not want to see you destroy yourselves nor do we want you to destroy us.

There are many here who love you. There are many here who wish they could hold out their hand and touch you in peace and harmony and be of good spirit and joy. We touch you (lowers arm and places hand on my head) and we send our love, our good vibrations to you. May it fill your system. May you be happy. May you be well. We will see you again soon. Goodnight, Starchild.

This is Ashtar, of the Free Federation of Planets.

Session Eleven

The Rights of Citizens to Bear Arms Versus Gun Control

THERE is no need or purpose for the use of handguns in a peaceful society. Cities could turn into jungles. Other planets have outlawed guns long ago. The death of John Lennon. The coming of open relations between Earth and other planets. Ashtar gives a discourse on tapping into the Universal forces of Light.

Greetings.

I am Ashtar.

I am speaking to you from many, many thousands of miles away. It is good to be able to communicate with you once more. We continue to watch and observe, even though there may be periods when we cannot, for various reasons, communicate. We want you to know that we are watching that which is taking place here on Earth.

We are very sorry to see that one of your great artists was recently killed in your city. (John Lennon.) It is unfortunate that you are permitted to use handguns. Weapons should not be allowed in a peaceful society. There is no need for guns. Guns are used for one purpose only. The purpose is to wound and kill. We would like to see all handguns taken away from those who would use them for criminal purposes. Sometimes it is necessary to be less tolerant. If criminals were shown that they could not get away with their crime, there would be less crime.

Question-How would you suggest that this be done?

Outlaw handguns.

COSMIC REVELATIONS TILL THE END OF TIME

Question-There are those that say that when you outlaw guns, you are only taking them away from honest citizens, because they are the only ones who would abide by the law.

Guns should be taken away from everyone. There is no necessity to manufacture them. Even your military and your police force should not be permitted to carry them. If it were not necessary to manufacture them, there would be no guns in circulation. All of these guns must be taken out of circulation. If your world is not destroyed by a nuclear weapon, or if natural holocausts do not signal doomsday for you. Then if handguns are permitted to exist, you certainly would wipe yourselves out. Your cities would turn into jungles. Something must be done now.

We do not allow handguns on any planet. People are not allowed to carry these things. There is no necessity for it. It is only done because certain people are becoming very wealthy off of it. But, enough of this. It is common sense, what I have said. It takes no great mind, it takes no great being, to tell you this. You can see what is happening. You have watched the news. You have seen a great man die, a man who stood for peace. And while he was certainly not perfect, he had very good qualities about him. It was very foolish and very senseless for him to have been shot in cold blood.

We see what is going down on your planet and we often see the foolishness with which you behave and with which you act. Sometimes we think that mankind does not have his head screwed on right, to use a phrase that we have often heard stated on Earth. Common sense is the key.

Once common sense is observed, there will be peace on your planet, and there will also be open relations between your people and my people. (He began speaking very low, in a language that I could not identify.)

Question-Could you please speak in English?

(He continued what seemed to be a prayer or a chant for a few seconds more. Then he switched to English, but in such a low whisper that not all of it was recorded.)

...Drink of the cosmic forces, drink from them as if they were wine. Observe the life of the universe. Let us know that among mankind there are those that stand for that which is just, for that which is good. We are watching you, thousands of us, observing your actions. We watch your every move. We guide you, we try to instruct you, but we cannot interfere. Listen to us. Listen to us now. Be aware of our existence. Be aware of the cosmic forces, the forces of the universe of Light. We are among you. We have always been among you. We continue to be among you. Use your sensitivity. Use your psychic power. Tune in to us. Tune in and learn. Accept the wisdom that we can offer. Accept our guidance. Accept our hand in friendship. Accept our hand in trust.

Starchild, you are one in a million. The glory of the Universal Source is with you. We come in peace. We come in harmony. We come in love. We appreciate that which you have done and that which you will continue to try to do. Peace be with you. We will return again, shortly.

This is Ashtar, of the Free Federation of Planets. Goodnight, Starchild.

COSMIC REVELATIONS TILL THE END OF TIME

Session Twelve

They Are Amongst Us, Even Today

SPACE *People trying to pull the Earth together. Bond of Brotherhood. UFOs are responsible for blackout in Utah. Technology has a long way to go. Earthquake predictions.*

I must say, I don't remember it ever being so cold since the last time the Earth flipped over on its axis. We are watching and observing you from a long distance away. We always keep tabs on your activities.

That is a wonderful book that you have just released. You are to be commended for your efforts. This book will have a wide circulation and will do much to alert others to that which we have been discussing. (**UFO and Psychic Revelations**). Of course, there remain many questions that are unanswered, not only in your mind, but our mind as well.

Dear Starchild, there is much ahead of all of us. We, the members of the Free Federation of Planets, are watching keenly and observing that which you do. We have talked about the end times. We have discussed many of the things, including the axis shift, and now we must watch and wait, just as you must do.

There are many events that are taking place all over the world which will have much bearing on the outcome. We hope the outcome is a positive one for both your civilization and for our civilization. There are many of us, we should clarify by saying "planetary beings," who have walked the Earth in the past and who are walking it even now. There are many amongst you who are trying to carry out the goals which we have put forward. There are those who are trying to pull the Earth together so that you may live in peace and harmony and brotherhood. Some of these individuals know who they are, others do not, but it is not important whether they know what is behind their work or not. It is only important that they proceed with what they are doing.

We would like to see the righteous people of your planet in control. And, indeed, there are gains in this direction, but not as many and as fast as we would like to see. You are helping. Others in the UFO movement and in the New Age movement are helping.

We are trying to tie the pieces all together. We are trying to unite mankind in a perfect bond of brotherhood. For this, we are happy, and we would like to see your plans grow to be successful ones. We hope that we have inspired people. We hope that we have created a certain amount of understanding.

We have noticed in your news media a report of a massive blackout in your state of Utah. We were the cause of this blackout. We did this as a demonstration of our ability. Naturally, your scientists, technicians, and engineers will look for a scientific explanation, and, no doubt, they will find one that will suit them, at least for the time being. Yet, when these things happen on a much more rapid basis, there will be those who will understand that we are behind them. We wish you no harm. We merely wish to show you that there are many powers that you do not yet possess which others of the universe can turn on and off, just as you can turn on and off a light bulb. It is nothing to us. We laugh at these things. It is a very simple process.

Your scientists are very backward in many ways. You have certainly not developed your full mental capabilities. Technology on Earth has a long way to go until you come anywhere close to where we now stand.

There will be many important events, many important things happening in the future. You now know what to look for. We have told you of these things. We have told many people of these things. The messages will continue to come through this channel and through others.

Question-Will there be any more blackouts?

There will be other blackouts. There will be other signs. You know that these things are happening. You read about them every day in the newspaper. You hear about them on TV. We can only give you certain indications, certain things. We could not make it too obvious to you. But, it is obvious to you, Starchild.

You have a good idea of what we are doing, of what we are planning. And we thank you for your help and we thank you for your assistance. And we thank all of those who have worked with us. You will be rewarded. Many of you will be taken up. Many of you will be saved, if and when this great holocaust does take place. There will be earthquakes soon, some on your west coast, one major one in South America. It is building up now.

Look for the light. You will be guided. You will know more. All of mankind will know more. Well, let me go now, Starchild. We must leave you at this point. We must end the transmission.

We wish you a warm day. We wish you a warm life. We are there. We are protecting you. Have no fear.

Look to the light. This is Ashtar, Commander of the Free Federation of Planets.

COSMIC REVELATIONS TILL THE END OF TIME

Session Thirteen

Technological Advances Held Back Because of Greed

ASHTAR reveals that the Earth is a school. Educational craft orbits Earth. Infants in a cosmic playpen. New forms of energy.

(There was something wrong with the tape recorder during this session, but I managed to write down most of it.)

Greetings from the Free Federation of Planets.

Since the turn of the century, the last 80 years, your technology and knowledge have advanced more than a thousand years before. There are some among you who have knowledge which would advance your science and technology many years into the space age, but they do not wish to release the information for financial reasons.

You are there on Earth for educational reasons. It is like a school. We have an educational craft which circles your world and channels information to those of you who are receptive to it. Some of you are aware of where this information is coming from, others are not. We are attempting to raise your consciousness and educate you so that you may survive the New Age that is to come.

You are still as infants in a cosmic playpen. We are trying to help you grow up so that you may reach the space age and join the Free Federation of Planets. In the New Age to come there will be many changes. There will have to be changes in your sources of energy for transportation and to heat your homes.

Question-What type of energy will be used for transportation and for heat?

COSMIC REVELATIONS TILL THE END OF TIME

There are many forms of energy that may be used, such as solar, polarity of north and south magnetism, and even air and fire and water may be used. Gasoline is a very primitive form of energy. We haven't used it in eons. (Chuckle)

We will continue to channel information. We send our love, not only to you and this channel, but also to all those who are reached.

This is Ashtar, Commander in Chief of the Free Federation of Planets.

Session Fourteen

A Wealth of Plenty for All

A change in the social order. No need to be poor. The light shall shine on you. Look to the Golden Age. Using the rays of the Sun. Mind to mind communications. The coming of the New World Order.

(He began chanting in a language which I could not identify.)

Greetings! Good to be here with you once more. (Very slow, long pauses between each word.)

Your planet is going through a trying period of turmoil and tension. We are here to offer help and advice. There are many things in your social order that need revising. Your concern for financial attributions causes much of the problems on your planet. There are those who do not have, and there are those who have too much. There is not an equal balance. There is a polarity of the wealth.

There is plenty of wealth. There is plenty of wealth to be had by all. There is no necessity for any of your people to be poor. There are plenty of resources left on your planet. Only a very few, a very small minority, hoard these products. Why? Because they are greedy. They think only of themselves. They think not of their fellow human beings.

We do not speak of what you call a socialist order, for that is not a fair distribution of the wealth either. However, the wealth should not be in the control of only a small percentage of the planet. Everyone should have the opportunity. This is what your country was based on.

COSMIC REVELATIONS TILL THE END OF TIME

Unfortunately, this is not what is happening today. The people who run your country seem to be only protecting and helping those who are very rich and very powerful. They do not seem to have the ability to see the light. Eventually, the light shall shine on you. Eventually, the United States will be the country of great materialism and wealth once more. Someday there will be a great true United States. Someday, in the distant future, there will be a country that will provide true freedom and equal opportunity. Look for this in the Golden Age.

Oh, if you could only see this Golden Age, what will come in the future. It will be so marvelous. You will not have to worry about such outmoded means of transportation as the automobile. Gasoline will be a thing of the past. You will be able to travel on magnetic forces of energy that exist in the universe. You will be able to use the rays of the sun wisely. All of this is available to you now, but your leaders try to block this from becoming general knowledge.

In the Golden Age, men will have the ability to talk to each other without speaking. You call this mental telepathy or ESP. Yet, even though it is something that all of us here on other planets are able to do, you have not learned to use this ability. And you will not learn to use this ability until your consciousness has been raised to the point where it is possible for you to send messages from one mind to another. This New World Order will come. It will come eventually. It will be something like nothing else that has ever taken place on your planet before. Your planet will then be in a higher vibration. Your consciousness will be raised. People will prosper. This can all happen. This will all happen.

Starchild, you have helped us much. We continue to watch over you and your channel. You are doing much good in your work. Even though it is only a small percentage of the population now, the numbers are growing every day. You have met some very fine people in your work. You see that people need this information. They rely on it. You are a true source of the New Age. You will be one of the founding fathers of the New World Order.

We go in peace. We send you our love. We offer our positive thinking to you. Spread the word. Get the message out. Tell the world that there soon will be a New Age.

Love, peace and harmony to all of you.

This is Ashtar, Commander of the Free Federation of Planets.

Session Fifteen

Earth: Way Station of the Universe

BEINGS *arrive daily from more than 50 different places. Life forms vary from the primitive to the super intelligent. Negative beings have infiltrated the military and governments. Blends and Star People. Precious minerals stolen from the Earth, stolen by interplanetary pirates. UFO sighting wave predicted. A Brotherhood of love and peace and harmony. UFOs, a symbol of hope for mankind.*

(Before the channeling began, there was a telepathic communication. They were from another solar system. They said that we would be meeting one of them in two to three months. They came here to help, as a result of a distress call, the last time that the Earth shifted on its axis. They are pure energy. Energy has intelligence. Energy is intelligence.

Government officials won't listen to them. They want our advice as to what they should do. They don't know if they should land.)

This is one of the many groups that have been coming to Earth. There are visitors coming to Earth from all over the vast cosmos. We often see their ships passing us by. It is not unusual for your planet to be visited by beings from 50 or 60 different planets and solar systems on one given day. It is a very common sight to see many, many different kinds of ships passing in the night. There are ships like diamonds, like jewels in the sky. There are ships of all different magnitudes, of all different sizes and shapes.

There are all different types of races and beings that are coming here. Some are very, very intelligent, far superior scientifically and technologically. There are others that are not so advanced, whose purposes you might consider to be somewhat primitive.

Question-What purposes are they here for?

They are here for their own selfish purposes. There are many things which we are not allowed to tell you at this time, but that you will be learning as we progress in the next few years. Many of these things will be difficult for you to understand at this point, but the time will come when you will be given the knowledge of such things.

There are many forces throughout the universe that are working together to keep the truth from being known. They want to maintain their privacy when they visit this planet. They do not want others to know why they are coming here. They try to deceive you. They are dangerous in the sense that they are out for their own benefit without regard for others. They also try to confuse the issue.

Some of these groups may actually have representatives in the military and in various world governments, even though nobody realizes it. There are those, you call them blends or star people, that are on this planet. Many of them are doing good. There are a few that have either reincarnated or transplanted here that are evil.

They are of the negative. They wish to come to this planet and take what they want, rob you, if you will.

Question-What do they want?

They want many things. They want things that are not available on their planet in abundance. Some of them come here for precious minerals, such as what you call gold and silver, because they are of value to them. Others come here with a thirst for blood and flesh. These are the ones that mutilate your animals. They are the negative ones. They are the ones you should be wary of approaching.

We are sorry we have not been able to communicate with you in a while. (More than a month.) Sunspot activity has made it difficult for us to beam our messages through. We have been watching, we have been waiting, and we say hello once again to you.

COSMIC REVELATIONS TILL THE END OF TIME

Soon you will see a marked increase in the number of sightings. We will start to put on some displays for you. More and more we will be seen over larger cities. The time, we realize, is getting close at hand.

Question-What about over New York City?

Eventually, this may take place, but we think it would be too much for everyone to handle, this sudden explosion, this sudden impact on the news. Besides, we do not want to frighten people. We do not want to put on a show of force. We merely wish to guide you. We could do this more through our messages than we could through actual physical appearances in the sky.

Channeled messages will increase in many locations. Even in Red China, there will soon be UFO contactees and those that are given the message to spread.

The ships of Light are many. There is a brotherhood, a brotherhood of peace and joy and harmony. We hope you will accept our guidance. We hope you will spread your arms in glory to the Creator. Take in the beneficial rays of the universe. Let the life forces take control. Mankind is on the threshold of many great discoveries. We do not want to see your planet destroyed.

Spread the word that we are here. You are doing a very good job of getting the message out. The message is of hope and salvation. The message is of everlasting life, a life among the stars, a life of harmony with your Space Brothers.

Fear not the tribulation that is to come, for you will be protected, as others of like mind shall be protected. You will know what to do. You will sense when the time has come. We will talk to you again soon. We are watching you. We care for you. Mankind must not destroy itself.

You are entering the Age of the UFO. It will soon become a symbol of love and harmony and peace to mankind. It will become a symbol to those who fight control by the military, of those who know that all men must truly be free.

Peace be with you, Starchild.

This is Ashtar, Commander in Chief of the Free Federation of Planets.

Session Sixteen

Rainbows in the Sky

***THE** true purpose of the space shuttle. No one in space to welcome "deserts." Earth's return to paradise. An end to all wars. Plants, animals and nature kingdom to coexist in harmony. Teleportation and astral projection will be commonplace.*

It is interesting to see your space shuttle. We are sure that there are many of you who are relieved to see that mankind is not fully captive to this planet. But, if your military leaders think that we will allow them to take their weapons into space, they are sadly mistaken. It is bad enough that we must watch as you attempt to destroy yourselves.

We could never let you destroy us. We are so many centuries ahead of you in our development. Your weapons are very ineffective against our defenses. It is true what you have read in the media. There are government officials, and scientists, and military men who are trying to build the shuttle and other space programs with one thing in mind: their own salvation. They realize that the things we have said in other communications are rapidly coming true. They realize that there is only one way to be saved, and that is to leave this planet.

They think that they can just build a rocket and take off and be saved, but this is not true. They will have nowhere to go. No one will welcome them, because they have been responsible for the destruction and damnation of Earth. But, there is a bright side of this. During the period of our communications, we have spent a great deal of time talking about the destruction of mankind and how it could occur. We have not, up until this point, dwelt at length upon those events that will transpire once the Earth is made habitable once again. Have you ever seen a sea of smiling faces? There will be many smiling faces when your people are brought back to this planet. The Earth will be as it was back in the time of your Genesis, in the Bible. Mankind will know the wonder and magic of creation. He will be at peace with the universe. He will be at peace with himself. He will be at peace with all of those living things which surround him. Mankind will never war again. No one will ever be killed on the battlefield. A great new day will unfold, a New World Order, a world order of supermen, a world order of love, peace and harmony.

Peace and harmony will cover the entire planet. Nature will co-exist side by side with human beings. The plants, the animals, the nature kingdom, these things will all flourish all over your planet as they did eons ago. Mankind will find itself able to use many powers that they did not know existed. There are those on your planet now who possess these powers. But, in the New World Order, all of you will be the same. There will be telepathy. There will be psychokinetic ability. There will be mind reading. There will be all of these things and more. Atlantis will rise. Other lost continents will rise. Beings from the stars will come and land and walk among you.

There will be no more skyscrapers, no more ugly concrete. There will be only beauty, a rainbow in the sky at all times.

Yes, you have much to look forward to. It is beyond anything that even my most descriptive words could tell you. Many of you heeding my words will see this day soon. Some of you will survive and will take your place in the new world to come. The New World Order is for all of mankind. It is meant for you, the new-agers, the spiritual, those who are with us, those who are us. There will be new horizons. New vistas await.

Look to the sky. Look to your heart. We are with you.

We are One. We are your Space Brothers.

This is Ashtar of the Free Federation of Planets.

Session Seventeen

Suppression of Beneficial Discoveries

ADVANCES *in medicine and science held back. Washington, Jefferson, Lincoln and Nikola Tesla telepathically inspired by the Space Brothers. The foundation of the United States divinely guided, a new super race of Uri Geller's, bigotry and prejudice wiped out. An international grouping of minds. Super storms predicted.*

We are watching over you. We are aware of the activities that you are engaged in. You have been reading about the genius known on your planet as Nikola Tesla. There are many great men that have walked on your planet. Many of these great men were inspired by us. Nikola Tesla was one such individual. He gathered his knowledge from the river of light that flows above your planet. His knowledge helped mankind develop into the modern technical age.

There are many others on your planet now who have had at their disposal much knowledge. Yet, your governments and your scientists refuse to acknowledge their great discoveries. Many times, these individuals have come forward and tried to release their discoveries, that which they have locked on to, only to find that society is not willing to accept what they are willing to freely give out. Such an attitude in medicine, in the sciences, and in other fields, has prevented your Earth from developing faster than it has.

We are sorry to see that money plays an important part in your society. It seems to us that everything is done for financial gain, regardless of whether it will benefit mankind or not. This is a shame. We would like to see this change. Perhaps you can help. George Washington, Thomas Jefferson, Abraham Lincoln, many of the founding fathers of your country were telepathically inspired by us.

COSMIC REVELATIONS TILL THE END OF TIME

The foundations of this country were originally laid on our guidance. We find it disheartening that your government officials would so easily turn from the light that has been given so freely to them.

There are many highly advanced souls on your planet now. The young man, the Israeli known as Uri Geller, is one such individual. There are many more who have not publicly made themselves known but may do so in the future. From all parts of the globe you shall see a super race developing, a super race of gentlemen who wish only good for all of mankind. They wish there would be no hatred, no discrimination, and no prejudice. They wish only to share their abilities with everyone, for everyone's benefit, not for the benefit of any one government or the benefit of any one individual.

There are some of you who are aware of the ability which you have within yourselves; others are not aware, but will soon start to develop this gift from God. Psychic phenomena are nothing mysterious or supernatural. You all have such talents. We can read minds quite easily, as you know. We have this ability, but so do you, at least to some extent. It lies dormant within all. It can be developed. It will be developed by many.

In the end times which we speak of, those of you who have developed their psychic powers will be fully aware of the events that will be transpiring around you. There will be an international group of minds, a sort of telepathic communication between those who are aware.

Many great men have walked your planet. Jesus Christ was one, Buddha was another. Count St. Germain lived for many centuries. He is still alive today.

Oh, there is so much mankind is not aware of, nor does mankind understand. We ask you to reach out, to share this knowledge with others. Do not let those who are skeptical interfere with your work. Be patient, be understanding, and those who seek the truth will find it.

In the next few months there will be a number of very bad storms in the United States. These storms will be caused by magnetic interference from outer space. They will cause a considerable amount of damage in the southwest. Science will not know what to make of them. Such unusual weather phenomena will be increasing in frequency. You will see many things totally unknown before in nature starting to happen all around you. These are signs of the end times. These are signs that we are not far away.

COSMIC REVELATIONS TILL THE END OF TIME

Watch and wait for us. Take our hand in guidance. Accept the light and share it with those around you who would accept it. There is a mist which surrounds you, a mist of purity and light. This protects you from harm. Be of good cheer and walk in balance.

This is Ashtar, Commander in Chief of the Free Federation of Planets.

Ashtar's prediction came just prior to an extended period of unnatural disturbances which included the worst winter in modern history – a winter that lasted well into spring.

COSMIC REVELATIONS TILL THE END OF TIME

Session Eighteen

The Plot for World Domination

***THE** attempt on the life of the Pope. Negative forces trying to bring about chaos. Some political and military leaders duped. More assassination attempts predicted. The true meaning of "the Beast." Many more people to act as channels for many more Space Brothers who will be coming through. The God-force is in all.*

We watch and wait. We observe. We are aware of all the events which transpire. Very recently, the head of one of your churches was shot in a crowd. There are many evil forces and powers on your planet who would like to see total chaos come about. These forces and powers are a disturbing factor in your world today. They are hoping to signal the end of civilization as you have come to experience it.

There are negative forces in the universe who are hoping to assist mankind down the road to ruination. They are actually in contact with some of your political and military leaders. They are giving them advice and telling them what to do, with promises of world domination. However, this is not the case, for these negative entities would like to rule the planet for their own wrongful purposes.

But the truth is that they do not want to see the planet destroyed either, because if the planet were destroyed, they would have nothing to conquer and control. Though their ways are not as ours, they too try to prevent the chaos from happening.

More attempts will be made on the lives of world leaders and influential men. This is a stage your planet must go through. It is unfortunate, but it has to happen, because of karmic ties your people have with past events. Many eons ago, there were other civilizations that existed here, but they too were destroyed. Mankind is doing this once more. It is hard to pinpoint which events will happen next, but many of your great seers and prophets, such as Nostradamus, have foreseen, even centuries ago, some of the things that are happening now.

There are certain countries, certain nations on this planet, who would do the bidding of those who come here with the thought of world domination, to conquer. They are being told that they will share the wealth, but this is not so, because these negative beings that are coming here have only one thought in mind and that is to control. They will not share this with anyone, even if they promise to, for they are liars. They are agents of Satan. They are "the Beast." They are evil.

There is much tension everywhere; there is much trouble brewing on many fronts. We could feel your planet vibrating. It is actually shaking as if it is about to go off its axis.

Oh, there are so many on your planet who know what is going on but will not share this knowledge with the people. We have tried to share this knowledge with as many as possible. You have done your part, and we will continue to assist in all those ways in which we can.

Look for the light. Look for guidance. Look for love and you'll find harmony and peace all around you. The world is indeed a troubled place, but you could make it a better place in which to live. It is how you act, how you react to others that is important. Be of good cheer. Be of clean thoughts. Be of compassion and not full of hate. Do not envy others for what they have, for material belongings are not that essential.

Remember, we monitor your activities and we try to guide and teach those that are willing to listen. We can only do so much. The rest is in the hands of mankind.

Starchild, we leave you with these thoughts. We leave you with much love and peace. We feel the love radiate from you. We send this love back to you and we ask that you share it with all those who will listen to our words.

More and more, there will be those who will be channeling this vital information that is being broadcast to you from the starship. There will be many more people who will be acting as channels and there will be many more Space

COSMIC REVELATIONS TILL THE END OF TIME

Brothers who will be coming through and speaking with those of you who are willing to listen.

We go now, but we shall return. We have spoken the truth. We have tried to uplift your consciousness and the consciousness of those who will eventually read these words. The God-force is in all of you. Use it. Turn to the light. Use the power within you all.

This is Ashtar, Commander in Chief of the Free Federation of Planets.

Session Nineteen

Call Us By Name, For We Come As Friends

***AURA** Raines of the planet Clarion. Truman Bethrum's contact. The Yucatan: sacred ground. Contact with people of the Yucatan. The problem of landing openly today. If you wish to speak with someone, call them by name.*

We come to talk to you because you are our friend and we like visiting with you, as if we were in your living room. In a way we are in your living room. If you want us to visit with you, you must call us by name, and tell others to call us by name.

When you call Ashtar, I can come and be with you. I can go anywhere with you. When you go to the Yucatan, I can go with you. I am honored that you wish to go there. You were talking about Aura Raines. The reason that she has not been heard from is that no one has asked for her by name. Aura Raines is here now. Would you like to speak with her?

Yes, I would.

Hello.

Hello.

How are you?

Fine, thank you.

Very nice to be here. It is wonderful, the work you are doing.

Thank you.

COSMIC REVELATIONS TILL THE END OF TIME

We, the people of Clarion, have always had a special place in our heart for your people of the planet Earth. Many times we've landed in the desert and spoken with some of you.

Have there been any landings lately?

Oh, we are still around. I, myself, have not been to your planet in physical form in some time, but I can come and go as I wish. I can remember many a hot night on the desert, speaking with an old friend of yours. He used to write a lot about the planet Clarion. A lot of people thought he was funny and that his stories were funny. A lot of people chuckled. They did not believe them but they wished him well. Truman was an old friend of mine. I'm sure it is sad that he is gone from your Earth plane, because he did so much to help in getting word about our visitation out to the people, but we still talk to Truman. I had a fine conversation with him not too long ago. He has even gone for a ride in a flying saucer now. He has probably come back to talk to some of you. He was always a very funny man. He couldn't understand why we selected him. That was because his heart was in the right place and he thought of us always.

*Truman refers to Truman Bethrum, a contactee from the 1950s who claimed to be in contact with Aura Raines, a female UFO pilot from the planet Clarion.

It's so nice that you think of me now. I will come again. Perhaps we will meet in the physical form in the Yucatan. Wouldn't that be nice?

Yes, it would. Are you going to be at the Yucatan?

I am there. I can go there.

Is there something about the Yucatan area that makes it easier for people to get there from other planets and dimensions?

Well, we like the air around there, for one thing. It is very clean. It is sacred ground. We have been coming there for a very long time. Goodness, you can't believe the stories we have heard about that place. In the old days, we used to land openly and we would come out of our ships and talk to the people. We would converse about astronomy. We would converse about the signs in the sky and the heavenly bodies. We talked about a lot of things. It was a much less hurried life then. No atomic bombs. Nothing like that. A few wild people, perhaps, but very friendly. We enjoyed ourselves. Oh, it was so nice then. It could be nice now. You have filled my heart with joy. Say hello to your channel for me, when he is back in his conscious state. Tell him I give him a big pinch on the cheek. He will understand. Take care of yourself. You are a nice girl.

Thank you for coming through.

I enjoyed talking with you. Someday, maybe, we'll all meet on Clarion.

That would be good.

You would like Clarion. The days are long here, though. Plenty of sunshine. People landing on Clarion from all over the universe. They like Clarion. Maybe now, with women's lib on your planet, people won't think it so strange that I pilot a flying saucer or that I am pretty small. But what's five feet or five foot two or six feet? What's a couple of inches in size, especially when you are just trying to help people? At least, being a lady, they didn't always try to shoot me all the time. Some of the guys always had lots of problems. My goodness, a couple of times I even had to heal up their wounds. Luckily, we heal pretty quickly and no one was seriously hurt. Anyway, I'll go now. I can sense that the sun on your planet is about to rise. I will give you back to Ashtar now.

I am back in control again. Did you like the visit from Aura Raines?

Yes, very much.

Good. I am sure she has enjoyed visiting with you. Remember, if you wish to speak to someone, call them by name. If possible, they will come visit with you. If not in the physical form, then by what we can call our little mental radio here. Your receiver is in fine form today, but tell him to watch what he eats.

I will.

I will leave you now but I will come again soon. Think of us as we think of you, and we will be by you always.

Goodnight, Starchild.

This is Ashtar, Commander in Chief of the Free Federation of Planets.

COSMIC REVELATIONS TILL THE END OF TIME

Session Twenty

Peace is the Universal Way

A warning from Monka of Mars. Whosoever attempts to destroy this planet will be doomed. The barbaric behavior of the people of Earth. There are those in the Universal Council who would like to intervene. There are many forms of life out in the universe waiting for the people of Earth to learn to live in brotherly harmony. There are differences of opinion among the space people also, but no wars. Many people will go on to a higher plane even if the Earth is destroyed. Everyone should know the truth. There is no limit to the human mind.

Whosoever attempts to destroy this planet, their soul will be doomed. Their sun will never shine on this planet anymore. There is no fooling around – we mean business. Man was not put here to destroy. Man was put here to multiply. He was put here to live in peace. He was put here to learn harmony and respect for every living thing. There is no need to destroy that which was given to him out of love and kindness. It is a blasphemy, one which will not be forgiven ever. We love you, you are our brothers. How can we just stand by and watch you ruin all that has been given to you for your own spiritual benefit?

There are those in the Universal Council who would like to do something about this. They would like to interfere. They would like to stop this war-mongering that is bound to send this planet reeling on its axis. But that is not the Universal way. Love and kindness is the Universal way. Man was given a soul. He was made higher than the animal kingdom. He was meant to rule his world and to spread his thinking throughout nearby planets in this solar system.

There are many forms of intelligent life out there, some far superior, others on a lesser level, but how can you ever hope to go out and mingle among the stars when you act like spoiled children?

COSMIC REVELATIONS TILL THE END OF TIME

Think of the deeds you have done. Think of the souls you have prevented from reaching new horizons. Oh, how can you call yourselves intelligent when you are so barbaric? Rest assured that we are watching you. You are like naughty school children. We would like to spank you. We would like to punish you. You should be made to stand in the corner of the galaxy. How can you act like this? How can your behavior be so primitive? What are we to do with you? What are you to do with yourselves? Think. Use your brain.

Do not destroy yourselves. There is so much to go on living for. There is such a vast universe that exists all around you. We are waiting for you. We want to welcome you. We want to hold out our hands in love and kindness. We want to meet with you. We want to share with you. We want to live in brotherly harmony. Please listen to us. Heed the warning. Change your ways. I have spoken to you and I will come again. This is Monka from the Planet Mars.

Greetings, Starchild, greetings.

This is Ashtar. I wish to somewhat apologize for the behavior of my friend, Monka. He can sometimes be very difficult. He is a loving, trusting soul. He has tried to do what he can to shed light on your planet. Sometimes he gets carried away. He thinks that using strong-armed methods is to everyone's advantage. But take his words as they are meant. He loves you very much.

He only does this to lead you on the right path. You know it is very hard watching from out here in this spacecraft and seeing the things that go on every day on your planet. Sometimes we almost wish we could pull our hair out. But then, some of us have no hair. So that would be pretty difficult.

We smile down on you. Sometimes we even have a good laugh at the things that you do. We wish it were different. We have existed for so many thousands of years and, oh, there has been good and there has been bad. We wish things had come out differently. There are many on your planet who are being contacted now. Some of them don't even know how to handle what is coming through. They have never heard of the Space Brothers. They are completely shocked and totally taken aback by this. They wonder perhaps for a while, "what is going on, or am I going crazy? The scientists tell us there is no life in the solar system. They say there is nobody on Venus and Mars."

COSMIC REVELATIONS TILL THE END OF TIME

Well, Monka is real. I see him standing near here, defiant perhaps, but standing here no less. He is a tall and mighty figure. You know, back thousands of years ago, they might have thought he was Zeus or Thor. But don't let those biceps fool you. He may be a mighty soldier in his own way, but he is a soldier for the cause of peace.

Oh, we love speaking with you, Starchild. Of all our contacts, you are the one with the best sense of humor. You understand that we are not rigid in our thinking. We are only trying to do what is best. There are differences of opinion among us, just as there is down on your world, but we manage to get along. We do not kill each other. We do not go to war. We go to war only for peace and harmony. We have learned to live amongst each other. We have learned to share and to understand that there are differences of opinion. Perhaps you can do this too. Maybe not on the physical plane, but on a higher spiritual plane. Many of you will go on, beyond this planet, even if your world is destroyed. Many of you will be brought back to life in a world of peace and harmony, and glory will be spread among all.

You know we are watching you, even if we do not speak to you every day. It is hard to be in contact with so many people. So many people want to learn and of course there are different messages we give out. Some people want to learn the spiritual truth. Other people want to learn propulsion of the ships. Boy, we have to be up on everything but we have all kinds of computers out here. We are a vast storehouse of knowledge. We have been around for eons. We were on your planet when Atlantis and Lemuria existed. We were in touch with the Mayans. We were in touch with the Aztecs. We were in touch with your own Native Americans. Oh! How we walked the Earth in those days and, shh, some of us even walk down there now. We are watching over you. We know what you are doing and we like it. Oh, we send blessings. We send our good will. We want you all to understand, understand that there is a new glorious life out here. Oh, the things that mankind is capable of, the knowledge that is at your fingertips. We have pointed and directed to certain individuals. We have given out scientific information. We have helped you along the way and we will continue to do so. There are many out there among you who know the truth but are afraid to talk.

They should be punished, for everyone should know the truth. Every man, woman and child should be told that we are amongst you. You have done a good job. We are proud of you. We need many more workers like you. We send you our healing rays. We send you our spiritual rays. And, above all else, we send you peace. Yes, we will talk to those who will listen. Think of us. Meditate upon us.

Think of the silvery ships. Draw them in your mind. Think of Ashtar, think of Monka, think of us as if we were flesh and blood beings. Think of us as if we were standing over your shoulder talking to you. You have seen that when you call us, we come visiting. If we know that we are welcome in your house, we will enter there. We want to share with you. We want to get the truth across.

If the government and the military will not listen, which we know that they will not do, we must then go to the people, because the people have the right to know UFOs are real. We are real. Do not let anyone tell you differently. Scientists think that there is no one out on Saturn. Well, we are out here beyond Saturn. We are in your solar system all the time. We are in the galaxy. Life teems throughout the entire universe on this the physical plane and on many other planes and dimensions.

Go forth, travel with us and explore. There is no limit to the human mind. There is no limit to what you can endure. May you live in peace and may your aura continue to shine. We will be with you in two weekends. We will be with you and we know that the word will be given out. Go forth and tell them of Ashtar.

We love you, Starchild, good night. This is Ashtar, Commander in Chief of the Free Federation of Planets.

Now that you have heard from Monka and Ashtar, perhaps you would like to hear from Aura Raines?

Sure.

Hello.

How have you been?

Oh, these men up here. They always like to be so pushy and forceful. Such chauvinists. But then, they have their ways and I have mine. I try to spread a little love and cheer around. You know what? I believe in singing. I think there is a great healing power in the sound of music. (The following was sung by Aura Raines.)

COSMIC REVELATIONS TILL THE END OF TIME

Oh, we can sing of love. We can sing of truth.
We can sing of Universal joy.
If it's in your heart and it's in your mind, Anything is possible, you know.

I guess my voice isn't that good. I'm not exactly a Kate Smith, you know.

I bet it's good in person.

Oh, it is, or at least I have fun. I like traveling to Earth. It's backward in many ways, but you do manage to have some fun down there.

When are you going to come down to Earth again?

Oh, I am on Earth all the time. Geeze, I'm down there all the time. But, you know, sometimes the atmosphere is a little bit too heavy for me. I have a hard time breathing down there. Pollution. But also the atmosphere is a little different than it is on Clarion.

It's heavier than on Clarion?

Oh, it's harder to breathe, but I come down there. I was in the Yucatan with you.

I didn't see you.

Well, what was I supposed to do? Come up and pinch your behind? Besides, you had enough problems with your behind as it was. But I'm only joking. I'll show up soon. I may be at the conference but don't you go tell anybody.

Really, I won't tell anybody if you are going to be there.

OK, well, look for me.

OK.

I'm going to buy a book from you and I'm going to wink at you, so look for me.

Really?

Uh hum, make sure you give me the correct change though.

I have trouble with that.

COSMIC REVELATIONS TILL THE END OF TIME

Well, don't worry about it. It's only money anyway. We don't have money on Clarion.

You're lucky.

If we want a book, we get that book. Knowledge is meant to be shared.

That's true.

It's unfortunate that you have to sell all these great books of wisdom. But we understand that you have to make a living. The printers down there won't print them for free. Besides, on Clarion everything is on computers. There are no more printed books like that. For thousands of years, we've had nothing like that. Knowledge is meant to be shared, and you are doing a good job. Oh, sometimes I think I'm so frivolous. Ashtar knows so much. But I do, too, in my own way. But I guess I like to keep things pretty simple. I'm not a scientist, you know. I'm a space explorer, perhaps. I'm an explorer for truth. But I like you all and I hope I'll see many of you soon.

COSMIC REVELATIONS TILL THE END OF TIME

Session Twenty-One

The Yucatan

BREAKTHROUGH *in the Hollow Earth mystery. Tell the children about the coming of the spaceships. The reality behind the legends and lore of the Yucatan. Ships of many sizes and descriptions. Return to the Yucatan. Both friends and foes will come to visit on the ships. A practice run for the evacuation.*

You have called us and we have come. Peace on to you, Starchild. Things are looking up for you personally. You are going to reach all of your goals soon.

Question-Could you explain that?

We could explain anything. It is merely a matter of verbalizing it to you. Look for a breakthrough in the Hollow Earth mystery. More and more people will come forward to tell of these things that are suppressed by the governments of the world. At first, people will stop them from speaking. But eventually, things might be ironed out!

Question-Could you tell us something about the present world situation?

The world situation remains the same. You worry about nuclear weapons, yet you are doing nothing to halt the spread of them. Tell your children about our visitation. Tell them that we are coming and that we shall take them for a ride. Our ships are many. They are at the edge of this solar system. We are standing by, waiting for the right time to appear en masse in your skies. There are ships of many descriptions and many, many sizes. Each craft has its own function. Some of the ships are miles long.

Question-Are you preparing for your visit to the Yucatan?

Yes, I am. We look forward to having you with us down there. The history of this part of the planet is very interesting. We go back thousands of years, to when this part of the world was just being settled. We tried to teach the local natives a lot about science and medicine. A great deal of what we taught has since become part of the legends and lore of this area. Someday we will arrive en masse. We will return. We will put on a show, a display for people. There are some who will come to visit us on the ships; some are friends and others are foes. There are still some artifacts from our visitation left. Remember, there are people, there are individuals in your government, who will go to any length to hide the truth. It is not unknown for them to attempt to kill. Keep this in mind and make sure you are not being followed when you go to the Yucatan. Go on this trip with the thought in mind that this is a practice run for the evacuation that will take place later on. Be careful. We shall see you soon. We shall talk to you on another time.

We thank you for your helping hand on many, many occasions. You should be repaid. Walk in the light.

This is Ashtar, Commander in Chief of the Free Federation of Planets.

COSMIC REVELATIONS TILL THE END OF TIME

Session Twenty-Two

Sacred and Holy Ground

LONG ago, people from all over the universe gathered at the Yucatan. The Space People taught the Mayans many things. The Mayans built monuments of stone to show their appreciation. The serpent race took over the Yucatan. The Toltecs slaughtered and enslaved the Mayans. Many Mayans disappeared. The time of the Great Flood. Tombs yet to be discovered underneath the pyramids. Someday a spaceport will be built in the jungle. Negative world leaders attempt to draw on the power of the serpent race. UFO sighting in China. A new form of power will be discovered. Contact will happen on a more regular basis.

(Channel is speaking.) He said it is good to be back and that he hopes that we enjoyed ourselves.

I said we did.

He wants us to tell people about our experiences and about the things that happened there. That this is a sacred and holy ground. That many, many centuries ago, people from all over the solar system and the universe gathered here. They landed here and made contact with the people who lived in the jungles there. They tried to teach them many things.

We taught them about astronomy, about planting and the seasons. We taught them how to grow. We taught them how to control the weather. Not only was it a place for Space People to land, but there were also Egyptians there and there were Atlanteans. They all shared information. The people who lived there, those we call the Mayans, were so friendly and so intelligent that for many, many years, their race flourished. They built monuments, monuments of stone to show their appreciation for what they have been taught. For many years, they lived in peace and harmony, not only amongst themselves, but with their Masters and with the universe.

COSMIC REVELATIONS TILL THE END OF TIME

Then those who were in touch with the serpent race, with what we call the devil, but it is not really the devil, came and took over the area and slaughtered many of the Mayans and enslaved others. They took over the area because it was so productive, there were so many crops grown. The Mayans had control over the weather. The serpent race, the Toltecs, did not have this. They tried to get the scientists to do their bidding, but the scientists and many of the Mayans disappeared. The Toltecs were paralyzed. They were not permitted to go. This was the time of the great flood that covered the Earth. In fact, the Toltecs climbed to the top of monuments so they could outlast the flood. But the wind and rain lasted for many days.

There are so many things that scientists have not discovered. There are tombs underneath the pyramids that they haven't found. They contain much information, some of it about Atlanteans, some of it about outer space travel. They built the tombs, these chambers underground. It was not done regularly at first. It was so that years later, they thought, their secret could be shared with others. These will be found eventually. In fact, we want you to say that in the story, so that when they are discovered, it will prove that these contacts are legitimate.

It is good to explore many things. It is good for you to reach out and understand that which is all around you. Your planet is so rich in knowledge of the Cosmos. We have been here for so long that we feel we know you as brothers and sisters. It is good you call us the Space Brothers, because Space Brothers we truly are.

The jungle will flourish. Someday a new spacecraft will be built there. In fact, the jungle will act as a protective cover, for, as you know, it is not very easy to get there. But you know how to go now if the necessity arises. You can find your way.

Next time, take something with you so that you don't get sick. Maybe we should help by bringing some purified water. We can bring it from the canals of Mars.

That sounds good.

It is not just coincidence that some of the negative third world leaders have chosen that place to meet. They are trying, attempting, to draw on the power of the serpent which still exists in that area.

COSMIC REVELATIONS TILL THE END OF TIME

Did you hear about the big ship that went over Tibet several weeks ago? That is one of the craft that we are testing that will eventually land and pick up people. It was a big ship. It was seen by many – the Chinese reported on it! We are being seen all over the world now. No one could deny this fact. No government could conceal it for very long. More and more of your people will have to believe. They could not deny their own eyes, no matter what those in elected office say. A new form of power will be discovered that will revolutionize the entire planet.

This will bring many changes about but there will, of course, be attempts to conceal it. It will be given to one of your scientists by us. Actually, it has already been given, but he does not realize it.

Contact is possible. It will happen on a more regular basis now. More and more people will channel. In fact, after they read the book, they will know it is possible and they will do these things.

It is important for them to think of us in positive terms and we will come to them. Tell them to imagine us. Tell them to imagine a giant ship surrounded by a blue glow. Tell them to draw us. Tell them to look at pictures of us. Tell them to think of Ashtar. Tell them to think of Aura Raines.

Tell them to concentrate on us. Tell them to bear us their thoughts, talk silently in the night to us. We will answer many of them. Tell them to have their tape recorders with them, that they may tape our messages. Tell them to get the word out.

Rejoice, for the time is near when everyone will know the truth. And you, Starchild, have done so much. We are indebted to your help. For you help not only us, but you help yourself. I must go now but I will speak to you soon.

Go in peace and harmony and much love. I radiate this love to you and ask that you in turn pass it on. Be spiritually enlightened. Be mentally strong. Be physically alert.

This is Ashtar, Commander in Chief of the Free Federation of Planets.

COSMIC REVELATIONS TILL THE END OF TIME

Session Twenty-Three

The Armageddon

***ROMILAR'S** message. Some of mankind originated from out among the stars, others developed on Earth from a simple amoeba-type species. Creation goes on constantly throughout the universe. The Supreme Being is everywhere and in everyone. One man shall come forward and lead those who are willing to listen. Jesus will return surrounded by an armada of golden spaceships. There are beings coming from many different places influencing the Earth. Space stations are being made ready for the evacuation. There are negative space beings that live off radioactivity. Dangerous viper ships are responsible for cattle mutilations. The use of solar energy is being guided by the Space Brothers. Someday there will be cities of pure golden energy all over the Earth.*

From many, many miles across the galaxy, from another part of the universe, this is Romilar. Romilar, the teacher. Romilar, the conveyer of mystery. Romilar, who sits on the throne of the council next to Ashtar.

There is much we know about the universe, its beginning and its ultimate demise. We have all passed through many incarnations. We have all passed through many life cycles. You, the channel, are in your third life cycle. You have spent many lives already, moving up the ladder. You still have a way to go. You are advanced in some ways and held back in others. But it is not for us to convey any right or wrong in what you are doing. Ours is simply a job of teaching, and teach we must, for the people of planet Earth have much to learn.

We try to simplify things to get our point across. We wish to reach a very large audience. We want you to know that you are on the right track. In many places around your planet, your citizens are crying for freedom against many oppressors. There are many on your planet who would wish to hold you back,

COSMIC REVELATIONS TILL THE END OF TIME

who would like to see utter chaos take place. There are others who would like to prevent this from happening. Luckily, more and more of you know your true purpose in life, know why you are going through these many incarnations.

From this vast distance, we can see many things. We saw your planet when it was only a mere speck of dust in the cosmos. We watched it grow. We saw mankind develop. Some of you originated out among the stars, others developed from a simple amoeba-type species into humankind. There are many with deep understanding and intelligence on your planet now that are afraid to talk about these things. Creation is going on constantly throughout the universe. There is much we could teach you about creation because we have seen it develop many, many times.

There is a supreme being. He is in all of you. He is around everywhere. He has had many representatives throughout the ages. Jesus Christ was but one of them. Buddha was another. Mohammed was another. In your lifetime, one man shall come forth and lead those of you who are willing to listen to the voice of peace, to the voice of freedom, to the voice of intelligence.

Many of you talk about the return of the Almighty Master in your lifetime, and yet it will come, but not in the way that you suspect. For Jesus, the Christ figure, will not float down out of heaven unescorted. He will be surrounded by our messengers, the angels in the ships of gold, pure gold that will shine. He will lead the Armageddon, the armada of spaceships that will take those from this planet who have been chosen. We send you healing rays. We send you rays of love and peace. We ask you to halt your warlike activities. We ask you to reach the leaders of your planet and tell them that what they are doing is in contradiction of the rules of the galaxy.

There are many of us coming to your planet from many different places, for many different purposes. We come to monitor your activities, your spiritual development, your technological advances. Some come to study you as biological forms. More and more your planet is being influenced by otherworldly intelligences. You have placed a seed in many minds and, in the years ahead, you will watch it grow.

We surround you with a white light. We wish you well. We will guide you if you will listen to us. This is Romilar, from the far, far reaches of the galaxy. I shall talk to you again soon. Good night.

COSMIC REVELATIONS TILL THE END OF TIME

Greetings, Starchild. Greetings.

This is Ashtar, once again. You have heard from another representative of the Free Federation of Planets. Romilar has been my right-hand man for many years. He knows much and he will be among those who will be speaking to you in the future.

We are busying up our plans for the evacuation. We are making ready the space stations. We hope it will not be necessary to evacuate your planet, but there does seem to be a growing conflict among your world leaders. And it is as if they were possessed by some evil force. There are even those space beings who would like to take command of the situation there on Earth, to rule so that those negative beings from throughout the solar system can use your planet as a base. They would like to take over so that they could take your precious minerals, so that they could use the energy that you manufacture.

They would like to see you continue using nuclear energy because they would still be able to come to your planet, even if you annihilate yourself. Some of these beings actually even live off radioactivity. We are trying to prevent this from happening as best we can. But occasionally, such a ship, a viper as we call it, will pass through. Be warned that they can be dangerous. They are responsible for mutilating your cattle. There are intergalactic patrols out searching for these craft both day and night. When we find them, we send them back. We send them as far away from this planet as possible. We escort them out of the solar system.

There are several men on your planet now who are working on inventions that will be of tremendous technological improvement in the years ahead. We are trying to guide them, to help them with these things. There is a man right now in Tennessee that is building a device that will one day enable you to use solar energy even more readily than your scientists are capable of using now. We are teaching him how to store the power of the sun so that it can be used at any time.

Unfortunately, many of your large power companies would like to see nothing in the way of advancement, for they are in a position now to make more and more money off those of you who are reaping great profits for them.

Someday in the future, when your entire planet has lifted its vibrations, there will be cities of golden pure energy on your planet. They will be seen throughout the solar system. The time is right for many great advancements.

COSMIC REVELATIONS TILL THE END OF TIME

The curve of development on your planet is upward. Please, do not stop this curve. Help as much as you can. You are getting the word out and you will continue to get the word out. We are very appreciative of your efforts and we will do all we can to guide you in the right direction.

Stay well and be healthy. I shall talk to you again shortly, Starchild.

Session Twenty-Four

The Totality of Creation

SOLAR *Star, Healer Supreme of the Free Federation of Planets. Healers on Earth who are blends. On most planets, sickness is almost totally unknown. With the spirit and the mind in perfect harmony, people would live to be many more decades older than they do now. Think of the violet ray in order to heal someone. The Earth is a living entity – all the planets are inhabited in many dimensions. There are worlds within worlds and spirals within spirals. Learn about the sanctity of life. "Someday we will all travel together on the same beam of light toward that one source." Someday Earth may be a part of the Free Federation of Planets. Clarion, warm planet with a violet sky. Monk and the defense of the solar system.*

Greetings, Earthlings. This is Solar Star, assigned to your planet for healing purposes. I come to give you the beneficial rays of the universe. I come to heal the sick. I come to heal those who are diseased. My representatives are walking your planet now. We have blended with them. We are bound together.

There are many, many people now with these healing abilities. Many more shall come forward in the future. We have projected to them the beneficial rays, the healing powers that will cure those who are in need of such healings. On other planets, such healers are commonplace. On most planets, we have learned to rid the physical and the spiritual and the etheric and higher bodies of any disease or sickness. Sickness is almost totally unknown. There is perfect health, perfect harmony.

The body, the mind and the spirit must be in perfect harmony if there is to be total health. If this is to happen, many of the people on your planet would live to be many decades older than they do now. A balanced diet, a nutritious diet, free of those things that would pollute your body and which adversely affect the mind, must be part of your daily eating habits. Proper nutrition and proper dieting laws must be started at a young age. If you follow such laws, it would be possible within a few decades to rid your planet of cancer and of other dreaded diseases. Such things are totally unknown on other planets where the inhabitants have learned to live in perfect harmony, in perfect trust in the creator, following those laws which have been set aside for His benefit.

Animals are sacred and holy, just as people are. It is not beneficial to your health to eat that much meat. Someday your people on the planet Earth will realize this. It would also help to heal oneself to think of the positive rays. Think of the rays, think of the violet rays. Think of the violet rays whenever you want to heal someone. Picture the body surrounded in violet. Picture the body surrounded with pulsating light. Picture the body as if it were healed to be cured. Picture the body throwing off any and all diseases and sickness.

Humankind can heal itself. We will show you the way. You have but to follow the path.

This is Solar Star, Healer Supreme of the Free Federation of Planets. We will speak again.

Greetings, Starchild. This is Ashtar, Commander in Chief of the Free Federation of Planets. We have been away from Earth for a while and therefore have been unable to communicate with you. But we have been watching your activities and we want you to know that we are with you all the time. We feel the vibration even out as far as our space station orbiting between the planets you call Saturn and Jupiter. The aura surrounding your planet continues to get dark. Yet there are bright spots from time to time on the surface of the Earth. You see, the Earth is like a living, breathing organism. It is a living entity, the Earth as a body, as a planet, as one consciousness, as one spirit. Yet many of the people living there would try to destroy this unity. Every planet has such a consciousness. Yes, there are consciousnesses all through the solar system. Mercury is a very high planet. It is the planet of healing, of light rays, of warmth.

Meditate upon Mercury if you wish to feel these warm healing rays. Venus is the planet of love and harmony. Mars is the planet of spirit and higher consciousness and scientific order in the solar system. These are the planets that most affect the Earth, but all the other planets are also inhabited and have a certain vibration.

Question-Are they inhabited physically or only in another dimension?

They are inhabited in many dimensions. There are many worlds within worlds and spirals within spirals. All the way from the elemental kingdom to the most powerful and potent masters that have ever existed. On your planet, the people are physically dense. There are beings that exist below them on the evolutionary scale, and there are beings that you cannot even imagine that exist far above you.

Oh! If you could see the universe with clear sight, if you could see the beauty of God's creation, the magnitude of the universe. As I am seated here at the controls of the great mother ship, I can look out into space and see the majestic colors, the majestic hues. I can see them because they exist not only on the physical, not only on the spirit plane, but on all these realms simultaneously. My vision is limitless, and your vision can be limitless as well. We are watching you. We are watching your world. We are watching all that is happening.

Oh! The universe is so vast we cannot even begin to tell you of the many life forms that exist throughout the universe. There are many dimensions. There are many different kingdoms, some of which even I cannot see and yet I know they exist. Every thought that I think, every thought that you think, is reality. Bring it to you, Starchild, bring it to them, bring it to the rest of the world.

Tell them to think of many dimensions. Tell them to think of many planets that are inhabited. Tell them to think of the totality of creation. You would not do well to destroy yourselves, you would destroy so many. Learn to live in peace and harmony. Learn to expand your consciousness. Learn about the sanctity of life. We praise you. We praise your planet, for there are many there who would like to see the New Age come forward. Yes, there is a strength against the forces of darkness there. We are with you. We are guiding you. We watch every move. We send out rays of healing energy. We send out rays of hope. We send love. We send peace. We wish to charge you with the electromagnetic power of every planet, every sun in the universe. We send it spiraling towards you on the physical plane.

COSMIC REVELATIONS TILL THE END OF TIME

Let the whole world rejoice. Yes, Starchild, we will remain with you. We will remain vigilant. But you must do your part, too. Every man, woman, and child must know. Get the word out. Tell them about Ashtar. Tell them about Monka. Tell them about Solar Star. Tell them about Aura Raines. Tell them there is life in the universe. Someday we shall all travel together on the same beam of light towards that ONE SOURCE.

Farewell, Starchild. This is Ashtar, Commander in Chief of the Free Federation of Planets.

Greetings, this is Monka. Well, we are back from our Council meeting and we must say that sometimes Earth gives us a very difficult time. But when we meet and talk things over, we realize that it is of the utmost importance that we see you through the coming crisis. We wish to uplift your planet.

We wish for you to join our Council someday soon. You have your space shuttle now. The space shuttle does not go very far. In the future, if you learn the right way to exist, we may let you come and be a part of the Free Federation of Planets. We look down upon the Earth and we sigh at what we see. You are naughty children. You are very selfish. You do not wish to share with one another that which has been put down there on your planet to share among everyone. There is an abundance on your planet, but you have not learned how to share this abundance. Council members are aware of this. They know that you have been naughty children. Some of them have suggested that we go down and take matters into our own hands. But I have told them that it is not time, that we must still give you the benefit of the doubt and that perhaps you can pull yourself up by the bootstraps and someday soon join us at the Council.

Yes, we have many ships in the atmosphere going back and forth, doing all kinds of jobs. Sometimes I even come down on the ships myself. I have landed and I have walked on your planet. Sometimes I come down here and spend a few weeks and even a month, but it is harder for me to exist down here now because of the pollution on your planet. So that is why we are sending more people down, so they can take over bodies, actually blend with the inhabitants of your planet. In your physical bodies, it is easier for them to dwell on your planet than if we come down and actually walk amongst you ourselves, which we have done many times in the past. I know sometimes I am stern about these things, but that is my job.

COSMIC REVELATIONS TILL THE END OF TIME

I am Monka and I wish you well. But you must tell everyone that they must learn to behave. They must not go against the cosmic laws. They must abide by the rules, which are meant for the benefit of everyone.

Soon there will be much activity on your sun. The planets will align and there could be a holocaust. But you must keep your vibrations high. You must keep your thoughts positive. You must not let them stray on to the negative. Keep working for the evolution of mankind and you will pull through yet. We are behind you 100%.

This is Monka of the planet Mars. We shall talk again soon.

Hello. I guess it's my turn. Everyone's coming through tonight. Your channel is working really well. See what he can do if he puts his mind to it. Let our thoughts flow through him. He is a very good channel but sometimes he blocks the messages.

Question-Why does he do this?

Well, he is shy by nature and also he does not want to put his own subconscious thinking into our messages. So, therefore, sometimes he blocks us from coming through. But he is doing right. He is a good channel. There are many good channels now on your planet. This is why sometimes we don't even have to send many ships down with people on them because we could talk straight to you now. There are many people who are opening their consciousness to this. I like your planet, especially the warm climates.

I like the warm climate also.

Well, you should. I don't like cold places. But what can you do? Sometimes it's pretty cold out here. The temperature is evenly tempered on Clarion. It's very nice there. People sometimes don't even have to wear clothes in the houses while they are at home. They don't have to worry about heat. There's no oil, no gas, no electricity.

That's great!

It's always about the same temperature. Oh, sure, it gets a little cold now and then. But the atmosphere isn't so dense, and it's just a nice place. Oh! You'd love the color of the sky. It's almost a violet or a purple color. It's very nice. There is lots of water on our planet. Lots of places to take children that are very nice. Of course we don't have too much of a population problem. Not like on Earth. The population of Clarion is less than 10 million.

We don't believe in building skyscrapers. Most of our buildings are under five floors. But we have some taller buildings. And we have some really strange looking architecture. At least strange as far as your planet goes, all kinds of connecting tubes and channels and corridors and things. Some cities are like one big, huge maze. There are shopping districts, vacation districts, industrial districts, communication districts. There are cities and cities and cities, and yet there is enough open air and enough places for recreation.

The people on Clarion are never bored. They get plenty of exercise. I, myself, I do a bit of jogging. Of course, the atmosphere of Clarion is such that you do not have to use up that much energy to jog. It is a lot easier to run and jog on our planet.

I notice that you have been trying to do a drawing of me.

Oh, yes.

It's not too bad, but make my face a little rounder. Just a little rounder. Picture me in your mind's eye.

I'm going to try.

You do really good though, you are truly inspired. Monka was going around all day long telling people about how you pictured him. He's so proud. He likes that very much. He said he wished he could do the drawing justice. Oh, but he is a mighty man. Very big, very strong. He has a power and a majesty about him that is unequaled. That is why he is in charge of the defense of the solar system. Monka, the defender, we call him. But he is a sweet boy. He wouldn't do anybody any harm. He just thinks he has to put his foot down every once in a while. So, anyway, I think I must get back to my duties as captain of the spaceship. We are heading out to another solar system now to start up a new trade agreement.

That's exciting.

It's exciting, but I do it all the time. I'm here about half the year, half the Earth year, and the rest of the time I'm out wandering around. We have good men in my command. It takes nearly a day to go out to some of these far distant planets, and then you have to spend some time there and then you come back, you go somewhere else. It keeps me busy but I like my job.

I wish I could spend more time with Ashtar. He really has a lot on the ball. He doesn't get much chance to travel out of the solar system now. He says his duty is to watch the Earth. But I keep him informed and they do come in for Council meetings from other parts of the universe. And he gets to meet quite a number of delegations. They all say he's very charming, and I guess he is. That's why he's Ashtar and I'm Aura Raines. And I'll talk with you again soon, Starchild.

COSMIC REVELATIONS TILL THE END OF TIME

Session Twenty-Five

Earth's Civilization, a Blasphemy Against the Creator

GEORGE *Washington and Abraham Lincoln were inspired by the Space Brothers. Jesus came to Earth as a messenger of peace. The star of Bethlehem was a symbol of the light of good will and love. Monka warns that there are those who would like to come down to Earth to take matters into their own hands. It is not their job to police the Earth.*

We are with you yet one more time. Oh! But from where we sit we would have to say that your world is in turmoil. The way you treat your fellow man is beyond our comprehension or understanding. Why must one fight for their freedom when all men by their nature must be free? Did not your great leaders, George Washington and Abraham Lincoln, say so? They were guided and inspired by us. They sit on the throne next to God. Your civilization is a blasphemy against the Creator. Woe to mankind for the trouble it has caused. Men will continue to fight to be free. It is their inalienable right to do so. We support them in their quest.

The holiday that you call Christmas is only a few hours away. You celebrate by buying presents to share among yourselves, but they are covered by the blood of mankind. How is it possible for all of you to exchange presents when there is no peace on Earth?

Jesus came to your planet for a reason. He did not come just to visit. He came to tell you much. Jesus was one of us. He came as a teacher. He came as a messenger to the Earth. He came to tell you about love. He came to tell you about harmony. But yet, in the end, you crucified Him. We cry for mankind. We are sad that you act in such a barbaric manner. You are supposed to be progressing toward the light of universal harmony. But in reality you bask in the shadow of indecisiveness and evil. What are we to do with you, Starchild? How can we go on much longer and watch this insane behavior? It is too much for us to do.

Earth has had the opportunity to grow. We have given you every benefit, every doubt. We had hoped that you would learn. Perhaps it is not too late.

Turn toward the light. Turn toward the light and be saved. Let the light of peace and good will shine down on your Earth. That was what was symbolic about the Star of Bethlehem. Yes, one of our spaceships hovered up above and sent down rays. We like Christmas. We like the people of Earth.

We want to see you develop all your senses. You could become so mighty. You could become so tall. Why do you continue to act the way that you do? It grieves us greatly. We wish to put our hands around you and share our love. Yes, at Christmas time, it is important that you on the planet Earth accept our love. We offer it to you unconditionally. We ask for nothing in return. We ask only that you learn to live together as one. Our blessings go out to you. Our ships are in your skies. We say to you now as we have said before, peace on Earth, good will toward mankind.

This is Ashtar, Commander in Chief of the Free Federation of Planets.

Intervene, intervene, intervene, intervene. Yes, intervene. There are some of us who would like to intervene. This is Monka, proud and glorious, a member of the Free Federation of Planets.

We watch and wait to see what mankind will do. You are on the brink of disaster. There are so many of you on your planet who would rule with might and not with love. To them we send a warning. We are the judge and the jury. You are but mere children who have not learned how to play with your toys. My God, look at what you do. How could you all stand idly by as if nothing were going on?

There are those who wish to intervene. There are those who think it time that we take command. I do not want to stand here and tell you what to do, but you never learn your lessons it seems.

Strike, strike, strike, they tell us. They say, go down there and take matters into your own hands, but we cannot. It is not our job to police you. I must go now.

COSMIC REVELATIONS TILL THE END OF TIME

I am sorry that I have been so hard on you. I do not mean this. I only want to show you where you have gone wrong. Please tell your fellow people that we are behind the forces of good. That the forces of good must come out ahead. We strike with you. Though our power and our might is great, it is a power and a might that we use for justice. You understand, Starchild. You have gotten the message across.

This is Monka from the Planet Mars. Peace and love.

COSMIC REVELATIONS TILL THE END OF TIME

Session Twenty-Six

Effects of the Planetary Alignment

***THE** force of the conjunction is felt throughout the solar system. The vibration causes difficulty in space travel. More earthquakes are predicted. Political and military leaders still pursue a path to destruction. Franklin Roosevelt's 100th anniversary. Sighting of a large mother ship over Nevada is predicted. Scientists are working on control over the weather. Astrology as a science. Earth's radio and TV broadcasts are under constant surveillance.*

We are watching for the effects of the planetary alignment, not only on your world but on the other planets in the solar system as well. There is a mighty force which is the result of this conjunction. It is felt throughout the solar system. We find it even difficult to move about in space because of the vibration from this planetary alignment. As you know, our ships travel on lines of magnetic force but there is destruction on these lines of force at this moment. This is one of the reasons we are having trouble entering the Earth's atmosphere. We do not wish to have any accidents; therefore, we are keeping at a distance. It is hard to predict what the full effects of this conjunction will be but it will be felt not only on Earth but by us as well. These effects have already begun but will become more noticeable during your summer and fall months. Look for more earthquakes on your east coast and in your states of Mississippi and Illinois. The effects of the conjunction will be felt for a long time on your planet. Its overall effect on your planet will be very negative. There will be hailstorms in the next 30 days. There will be snow very late into spring in certain parts of your nation. Your meteorologists will try to find other explanations. But you are aware of the conjunction. More and more people will become aware of it. Yes, the planets will have a strong effect on all of this on the physical and into the etheric states. We have known of this and have tried to counter-balance it with our own scientific and technological advances. But the pull of the planets is very strong at this time.

We watch your activities and monitor your TV broadcasts at every opportunity. We continue to be dismayed over your warlike progress. We have long since lost patience with you. We realize that there is not very much that can be done to change the attitude of your world leaders. The military has a strong hold, not only in your country but in almost every country around the world.

Just recently, you had a very relaxing trip to another nation that you call the Bahamas. They are a good example of how a country can learn to live without a military force to protect and defend their nation. This is a fine example of what we mean. Other countries should follow suit.

It is not necessary to build more nuclear weapons, to construct battleships to shoot nuclear missiles. These things will only lead you down the path of destruction. You have been warned. Your leaders have been warned. They know what negative deeds can be accomplished by these means. We ask that you lay your weapons aside and try to live in peace and harmony.

This week you are celebrating the 100th anniversary of the great American, the man known as Franklin Roosevelt. He was a great leader, one of the greatest your country has ever had. We wish you to know that he still looks down upon you, that he is trying to guide your country along with the spirits of many of those who have lived in your great nation. But there is only so much that he or these other men of great vision can do. They can only guide you. If your military leaders and political leaders will not listen, it is impossible for them to change the course of history.

There are other great men amongst you now, but it is becoming more difficult for them to have their voices heard. The tensions mount in other parts of the world. We do not like to see this conflict over politics and in many cases over religion. It is silly to go to war for any purpose but especially not for these purposes. Nothing could be accomplished by war.

There will be a sighting of one of our large spaceships over the state known as Nevada within the next 60 days. Many more people will see our craft, yet we cannot guarantee that your radio or TV will carry the appearance of our large ship.

COSMIC REVELATIONS TILL THE END OF TIME

We will be watching your planet as closely as possible as the planets continue to line up.

You are doing a good job of getting our message across to those who are willing to listen. We realize the impossibility of the task but you are trying the best that you know how and we will be behind you in your future attempts. Well, I haven't been on Earth in a while myself. It has been too cold. On Clarion, we have a very temperate climate. It is always very mild here.

I wish it were mild here.

Well, Earth is in for many changes, you know that. Nothing stays the same forever.

We are only able to control our weather because we are so far advanced technically, more so than you are. But certain of your scientists are working on controlling the weather and this is a possibility, certainly within your own lifetime. Everything has a pattern, one thing affects another. There is something to what is known as astrology, which of course astronomers do not believe in, nor do your scientists. But there is a science there. It needs to be more refined and developed than what is currently practiced on your planet. But, yes, the moon and the other planets do have a strong effect on all our lives.

You know we watch you. We listen to your radio and watch your TV. We read many of your newspapers on our scanners. We are well aware of current events on your planet. Someday you will learn more about the history of Clarion and about the history of the other planets in your solar system. Many great races have existed. At one time, some of us even warred. But now we no longer fight. We live in harmony. We live in love. We live in peace with understanding. Oh, we hope someday Earth will join us in the Federation. We would like very much to share our knowledge with you.

Please continue to smile, to keep your heart full of joy. It is important. We bring love. We bring peace. We bring warm wishes from Clarion. And I will speak to you again soon, Starchild.

This is Aura Raines. Goodbye, goodbye.

Session Twenty-Seven
The Monitoring of Geological Activities and Geographical Changes

A number of important planetary conjunctions will be coming up in the next few months. The planets are having a devastating effect on the etheric envelope surrounding all of the planets in the solar system. An increase in volcanic activity is predicted on the east and west coast of the United States as well as in Turkey and in China. A mysterious cloud circles the Earth and could cause havoc over a populated area. Love, peace, prosperity for all races, all nations. The Etherians, light beings from other dimensions.

We are in control. We are in control. Om...Om...Om....Greetings, Starchild. Greetings.

We have not spoken with you at length in recent times for our activities have kept us quite busy. We are as always observing the Earth for all signs of geological activities as well as possible geographical changes.

A question has come up as to the alignment of the planets. We wish you to know that there are any number of conjunctions coming up that will be of importance to you. The planets are having a devastating effect on the etheric envelope, surrounding not only your planet, but the other planets in the solar system as well. We cannot point to a particular cataclysm, but it is within the realm of probability that there will be a noticeable increase in volcanic activity both on your west and east coast as well as in countries such as Turkey and China. Our large cigar-shaped ships have been circling your planet and monitoring such activity. We are trying to prevent catastrophes such as these from happening. Normally, our ships are able to affect the magnetic polarity of your planet, but the sunspot activity, as well as the alignment of the planets, has been causing us some degree of difficulty. We have called upon help from other sources. Other spaceships are coming here from other solar systems to aid us. There will be an increase in UFO activity. Our ships will be visible over many parts of your planet, particularly at the north and south poles, which are being most adversely affected by the pull of the planets.

Hello, Starchild. This is Monka. Hello.

I'm sorry that it has been impossible for me to communicate with you. We have a number of probes circling the planet Mars, which is our headquarters. These probes have been helping to monitor the activity caused by the conjunction of the planets. We have been most busy in the work.

We understand that there is a mysterious cloud circling your Earth. We have predicted such things in the past. Such signs and wonders in the heavens will continue.

Question-What is the cloud composed of, and where does it come from?

Your scientists will try to tell you that there is a logical explanation. The truth is that this substance is part of a planet that once existed in the solar system that now comprises the asteroid belts. With the close approach of the various planets in your solar system, some of this material has been thrown into your orbit. It is not particularly dangerous at this time. However, should it enter the Earth's atmosphere over a populated area, it could cause havoc. We do not expect this to happen. If there is any danger, we will try to prevent it from happening.

Your government continues to refuse to acknowledge our presence. It is as if they have closed their eyes to the fact that we are real. Yet more and more, Earth's population is beginning to understand the truth. More and more, it will become obvious that there are Space Brothers who watch and monitor your activities.

There will be many changes coming in the next decades on the planet Earth. We have told you about some of them. We have warned you about the possible consequences. Yet, no one in a position to do anything seems to want to listen to our warning. We have come and communicated with you in friendship and we thank you for taking our message far and wide. Yet, there are many people in a position of power who have not heeded what we have to say. They close their ears. They turn the other way. They refuse to listen. We can only do so much, Starchild.

Solar Star sends you healing rays. There are a multitude of us who are trying to protect you from harm. Yet, no one seems interested. No one seems to care. Your planet continues to be in a state of chaos and havoc. We hope the time will come when this will all change.

We would like to see you enter the Federation of Planets. There is so much love and understanding that awaits you out among the stars. You have only begun to grasp the importance of what we have to say. Once the citizens of your country and the other countries around the Earth band together, we will be able to land openly and speak with you. At that point, it will no longer matter that the leaders of your society will not acknowledge our existence, for we will communicate directly with the people. We will, if necessary, bypass the government. Much is at stake, not only the safety of your own planet in space, but the safety of the other planets that revolve around the sun and other suns as well.

Yes, you have visitors from space and they will continue to arrive. Many of them belong to the Federation of Planets, as does the planet Mars and Venus and Saturn and Neptune and Mercury and Jupiter and Pluto. Others do not. Others are renegade ships that come here for their own purpose. We do have space patrols that monitor their activity and try to steer them away from your planet. Sometimes they do get through these space patrols and land. Some of them are negative. Some of them would like to keep your planet in ignorance so that they can continue to plunder the resources of your world. Some of them are even in touch with world leaders and together they formulate plans to control the minds of men.

We would like to free mankind. We would like to take you out of slavery. We would like to have you join us here out among the stars and planets. Yes, all of mankind. Yes, freedom for all of mankind.

Love, peace, prosperity for all races, all nations. That is our creed. That is our motto. That is our goal. In love we come, in trust we wish you well, Starchild. We shall speak to you again.

COSMIC REVELATIONS TILL THE END OF TIME

This is Monka from the planet Mars.

We are the Etherians, magnificent beings in the form of light. We come from other realms, what you call dimensions. We do not have physical bodies but we are intelligent. We are light forms. We are highly advanced souls who have passed through many worlds in space. We are the true creation. We are one with God. We are holy. We are pure energy. We exist alongside of you and have existed since the very beginning of time.

Do not destroy yourself, as you may destroy us as well. We pray for you. We seek your help. We must both co-exist together. We must go on. We must continue to thrive. We are with you as one. We are part of the elements. We make up the atoms and neutrons. We are ever flowing. We are ever creating.

We are your intelligence. We are your mind. We are everything that ever was and ever will be. We are the overlords of the universe.

Megaron 3, Megaron 3.

Returning control to the Ashtar command.

We thank you for listening through this channel tonight. We will have more messages in the weeks and months ahead.

This is Ashtar, Commander in Chief of the Free Federation of Planets.

Session Twenty-Eight

Earth's Failure to Climb the Evolutionary Ladder

THIS is your old friend, Ashtar. We want you to know that we have not gone away, that we continue to watch with wide open eyes. We monitor your activities on a daily basis. We know what is going on around your planet at a moment's notice.

We are well aware of the turmoil in the Middle East. Have we not predicted that the situation would worsen there? Well, we have said many times that this is where the next great confrontation would transpire. If the mortal enemies do not lay down their arms and learn to live in peace and harmony: Bloodshed all over. Women and children and old people dying, for what? For ideologies. For oil. For political gain. These are what your leaders consider to be of utmost importance.

Why do they not understand that human lives and souls are at stake? How many more years can you live like this? Don't you know and understand that someday it shall have to come to an abrupt end?

We do not take sides. We do not predict outcomes. We can only see patterns and trends unfolding. The situation in the Middle East has continued to become more and more explosive. We would like to put our foot down with your governments, but your governments refuse to listen.

It is as if your leaders were blind. They do not see us, yet we appear in your skies, over and over again. We appear over military bases. We appear over large cities. We appear time and time again, and yet they say we are nothing but hallucinations, temperature inversions and swamp gas.

COSMIC REVELATIONS TILL THE END OF TIME

When your planet was first going through its early evolutionary stages, we had much hope for you. We thought that your planet would evolve just like others had done. That is why some of us came and landed openly at that time and mingled with the early inhabitants of your world. But, no matter how we tried to genetically direct you, you have not been able to climb up the evolutionary ladder.

You are but sorrowful children. You have not developed your consciousness. You are on a very low vibration. There is only a handful or more of you among the new agers of your world who will even listen and digest our messages.

We are well aware of the efforts you have put into this book. We know that those who read this book will be touched in many ways. We would like to see this book get wide circulation, if it is possible. People will come to you. Those who are led will come to you and will seek you out.

There are many stumbling blocks in your way, but you have overcome other stumbling blocks before, and you will overcome those that are put in your path now. Keep up the good work. Your work will benefit many in the next few years to come.

Time is short. Time is of the essence. We watch. We wait. We remain vigilant. But remember, there is only so much we can do. We cannot intervene without your request.

Be of good mind and good cheer. We stand behind you with whatever you do. Monka sends his regards.

Aura Raines sends her regards. Solar Star sends his regards. We are all together tonight on the space station, looking down at your world as it turns on its axis, hoping, indeed, that it will remain on its axis. We beam to you great love and joy for all of humanity. We keep a watchful eye on you at all times. We will be in touch with you again. Do not despair. We radiate peace, love, and harmony, and ask that you do so as well.

Thank you, Starchild, for all that you have done, as well as that of the channel, and other channels.

This is Ashtar, Commander in Chief of the Free Federation of Planets.

COSMIC REVELATIONS TILL THE END OF TIME

Aura Raines-Look to the Light When in Doubt

DO you know who this is? This is Aura Raines. We haven't talked in a while. I've been very busy, you know.

One of my jobs is to keep track of all the maps of the different solar systems. It keeps me very busy. There are always explorers going out charting new regions. When they come back, I have to go over the data which they give to me. We have many maps of many worlds and many solar systems. Some day we would like to share them with you.

Your world is a very busy place. There is so much bustle and hustle, especially in your large cities. On Clarion, things are a lot more relaxed. We take our time. We do not see why you insist on hurrying the way you do. But then, on Clarion and on a lot of the other planets, we live a lot longer than you do.

We learned to live in peace and harmony, not only with the universe, but with the land that we live on. We know the right foods to eat. We know the right vitamins to take. We know how to keep ourselves healthy and strong.

We look to the light whenever we are in doubt, and you should do the same. Yes, there is a God. He is very great. He has given us the intelligence to think with. We must use this intelligence for our own benefit and for the benefit of every race and every people throughout the vast cosmos.

Yes, I've enjoyed watching your planet. We have learned a lot. We only wish that you were more developed, that your mental capabilities were near that which we have. But someday some of you will develop these powers and then you, too, will be able to travel throughout the solar system and the galaxy and to see far off worlds. Someday we will meet, Starchild.

This is Aura Raines from the planet Clarion, till we meet again. Goodnight.

Session Twenty-Nine

We Have Not Set the Date

GREETINGS, Starchildren, this is Ashtar, Commander in Chief of the Free Federation of Planets, speaking to you from our station near the planet Saturn. It is so nice to see the three of you gathered together for the purpose of initiating a contact with us.

We, who are your Space Brothers, watch you and guide your planet. We see you and care about what happens on your world in space. You have all received many messages from us in the months past. We are pleased that you deem it worthwhile to listen to what we have to say and to repeat it so that others will learn of our mission and our presence in your solar system.

As you already know, we have watched your planet for a multitude and will continue to observe what is going on. We have seen many battles fought on the Earth. Someday soon we would like to see no more fighting anywhere on your planet.

More and more people are becoming Light Workers and joining in the mission. They realize that it is essential that they do this work if your planet is to be rescued on the brink of the holocaust that you are now approaching. We have asked for your help and assistance and you have given it to us repeatedly, for which we are ever grateful. It is important that more and more people learn of our presence and our wishes for your safety in the months and years ahead.

Yes, we will continue to show ourselves in the sky. We travel in the craft that you call UFOs or flying saucers. We are able to transport ourselves across your definition of space, travel in terms of light years in no time at all. Your methods of propulsion will never get you any further in space than beyond the nearby planets in your own solar system. If you were to mend your ways, things would certainly change, but, as it now stands, you are thus far destroying yourselves.

Yes, there will be a liftoff. Yes, there will be a gathering of souls. Yes, there will be an evacuation. We are coming to save those of you who are worthy. And, certainly, that is everyone here in the room tonight.

We pick up your vibrations. They are very strong. They are stronger than they have been in the past. It is Light Workers such as the three of you who continue to spread the word as far and wide as possible.

COSMIC REVELATIONS TILL THE END OF TIME

Monka-Your Weapons Are Powerless Against Us

WELL, look who's here. This is Monka. I see that Beverly and Carol have joined us tonight for a session.

Things are pretty rough sledding, as you say on your planet. All the fighting and killing that goes on is enough to bring tears to our eyes. Woe to those who are the war-makers, for they shall be trapped on the planet. We will not allow them to leave. It is bad enough that they must destroy one world. They will not destroy more.

We have many spaceships that scan your globe daily. We know exactly who the troublemakers are. It is power and greed that drives them. They wish to rule with a mighty fist. They want power; they want land; they want oil; they want gold. They want your souls, but they cannot have your souls, because you are free spirits. And that is why you come and listen. That is why you wish to learn. And we hope that we do not disappoint you.

There are other warring factions in the solar system and in the universe which we must keep in line. Some of these negative beings, you call them the Illuminati, or the International Bankers, are actually in touch with the negative rulers of your planet, as well as the organization known as the Mafia. They work together to rule with an iron fist. They do not want people to be totally free. They want to control everything.

There used to be war on Mars. There were two factions at one time. The Zemenites was one such force. They, too, tried to control the people, but the people broke free. Now there is a united Mars.

COSMIC REVELATIONS TILL THE END OF TIME

Yes, someday your people, too, will be free, but not before you cast out the evil that is inherent in your political systems on Earth. The power brokers have to go before there is peace and tranquility on your planet. Why must man go into battle when it is much easier to join hands in peace and harmony? We ask you that, Beverly. We ask you that, Carol. We ask that of the channel.

You will see more of us in the days and weeks ahead. We will show the governments how strong we really are. They can shoot their missiles at us. They can send their fastest planes to chase us out of the sky, but it will be to no avail. We can appear anyplace on your planet that we want at any time.

I do not mean to be so harsh, but the feeling overwhelms me that something must be done. Oh, sometimes it is hard to imagine the planet Earth as a peaceful world in space. But we know that it is possible, and it must take place before you destroy yourselves.

Think thoughts of kindness, even to those who would do you harm. Surround yourself in the white light of purity. Denounce that which is bad. Denounce that which is evil. Grow spiritually, grow in awareness, and, above all else, love your fellow man.

This is Monka speaking to you from the planet Mars.

COSMIC REVELATIONS TILL THE END OF TIME

Ashtar

***BEVERLY**/Cassandra – When he started channeling, I saw a little golden light the size of a fist go behind the chair. I would like to ask a question.*

Question-Do you have more information on the time of the evacuation? Because Michael El Legion said that he was told it was going to happen on Tuesday morning.

We cannot tell you because we do not know when that will be. It will be at the right moment. It will be to your benefit. It will be determined by the Almighty God. It will be determined by your actions and responses to our messages to you. We do not work in days of the week. That is too cumbersome for us. We have not been told of the specific time, though we know that it can come soon.

This is a test that Michael and Aurora are going through. They wish to see what the reaction of people will be to such an announcement. We do not hold them at fault, for they are sincere in their beliefs.

But we have not picked a date. When we do, everyone will know of it at the same time. We could not possibly give you advance warning because it would throw off the equilibrium of your society. We do not want people standing idly by, looking up at the sky, waiting for us. There is too much to be done. You have your jobs to do and we have ours. We cannot intervene. You must do what you will do and we will stand by.

You have asked if we could not appear to you in physical form, and, yes, we would like to and at some point in time perhaps we will. But it is very difficult for us to lower our vibrations. And it could be harmful, not only to us but to all of you in the room. It is certainly not our intention to harm anyone, least of all the three of you.

You have been so patient with us at times. We understand that it is difficult to follow all of our instructions, because, after all, you are down there and we are up here. We exist at a higher vibratory level. Our realms are different than yours. Our realms are more of the etheric. Our realms are more of the spiritual. We do not criticize you, for many of you are brave souls who decided to incarnate into Earthly bodies, so that you could help others progress along the karmic wheel. For this you are to be thanked, and we do thank you profusely.

We thank you for gathering together this weekend. And we hope that our message and our word will be of inspiration to you. If there is something that you wish to have clarified, we will do our best to clarify it for you.

Question (Beverly/Cassandra) – I have asked you this before about the person who broke into my apartment, but could you tell me what happened and why?

That is not within our realm of jurisdiction. It is not something which any person, certainly you, was responsible for. It was done by a person who has what you call a diseased mind. There were no karmic patterns or ties to this person. It was just a random event. It will not happen again as long as you live in a safe place and take the proper precautions, which you certainly did. You are very brave and very strong. This element, this criminal element, is to be found all over your planet at this time, as people struggle.

You were not harmed, so try to put the incident out of your mind. It is not good to dwell on that which is negative. It is better to progress toward the light.

Question (Beverly/Cassandra) – Is there anything special we can do to help you now to come in the future?

Your thoughts are very important, for you do, believe it or not, inspire us. If there was no one who believed or accepted us, we would feel that our work was in vain. It gives us great pleasure to know that there are more and more who accept our reality, even if they are few in number. They are increasing and that makes us very happy.

We realize that things are not always easy, that sometimes you all have to struggle to get by. But you are all very gifted, because you have a heart of gold and intelligent minds. We can only advise that you use them, not only for the benefit of mankind but for your own benefit. Do not neglect yourself, because you are certainly all important in the cosmic scheme of things. Each person on your planet is important. Every soul is divine. We hope that we can continue to inspire you, because we like to see your auras shine.

This is Ashtar, Commander in Chief of the Free Federation of Planets.

Session Thirty

World Leaders Are Influenced By the Dark Forces

WE come to you at your direct request.

This is Ashtar, Commander in Chief of the Free Federation of Planets, channeling a message of light and understanding on this your holiday weekend. Our ships are paused in your atmosphere for a continued vigilance of your world.

We watch and wait for your leaders to make the next move. Your planet is like a giant chessboard to us. We can see over vast distances, over your oceans. We can monitor your activities simultaneously. We know what each of your world leaders is thinking. We have watched your world since the beginning of your time. We are keenly aware of all of your activities. We know what is taking place on your planet every minute of the day and night.

We have watched, since the end of your second world war, the buildup of your mighty armies and nuclear weapons, which you claim is for your defense, but there is no defense in the case of a nuclear attack. All the countries on the face of your planet will be affected to a large extent. Any such war would only cause confusion and utter chaos throughout your hemispheres.

We will try to prevent such a catastrophe from taking place. But we are not in a position, because of Universal Law, to come and stop your activities and make you change your destiny. This you must do on your own. We can guide, assist, and inspire, but we cannot take a direct course of action. That you must do for yourself, without any outside intervention on our part. This we have told you repeatedly and this is how it must remain throughout all of eternity.

COSMIC REVELATIONS TILL THE END OF TIME

You are spiritually progressing up the ladder, but in many ways your technology has held you back. You are like stone-age men learning to use fire for the first time. Yes, you, too, will get badly burned if you do not learn to use it properly. Nuclear weapons were not meant for fun and games.

Your leaders, many of them, have a very sick and evil mentality. There is one now which is indeed the 666. Many of you know who he is. Some of you do not and follow him. If he is not controlled, he could change the destiny of the world for the negative. We ask your indulgence as we pass over your missile silos and your military bases, for we are monitoring your activities very, very closely at this time.

There are many of you in the scientific community on Earth that pooh-poohed the alignment of the planets. They picked out one day and said that this would be doomsday, so that everyone would laugh and poke fun at this phenomenon. Yet, look around you. Do you not see the effect that this alignment has had, just as your Space Brothers predicted that it would? Do you not see floods? Do you not see tornados more devastating than anything that has ever taken place before? How about mudslides, earthquakes, volcanic eruptions? These are happening all around you, as Mother Nature turns against you, just as we have said for many, many years that She would.

Listen to us closely. Heed our warnings. Do not laugh and scoff any longer, for we mean what we are saying.

Are there any questions?

I have been receiving disturbing letters from Cassandra about a situation. Would you be able to tell me something about it?

We are not prepared, nor are we allowed, to speak of others in the New Age movement. Some of them do indeed receive messages from us on a regular basis, others are in contact with the negative forces or have been influenced by them. However, it would serve no purpose to mention names in this regard, for it would do nothing but cause disunity and disharmony in the New Age movement. We think that you can understand this, Starchild.

However, Cassandra has been in touch with the Ashtar Command for some time. We would like to see her spread her activities a lot further. She should not concentrate on any one single little thing but should broaden her horizons in order to get the material and information she has out to a large group of people. It serves no purpose just to gather together in groups of one or two to discuss this when those involved know what the truth is. They must reach out at this point and share this information with as many people as possible.

This channel that I am speaking through has done a very worthy job. For this reason, we have chosen him as our main disciple on the planet Earth at this time. He has done more in the last few years to spread the information about the Space Brothers' visits, and because of this we feel that he is in a very high and select position.

It is necessary at this time for all light workers to unite and gather and work hand in hand. There is no time left now for personalities or petty feuding. Do you understand? It is necessary to unite in a brotherhood, a brotherhood of sharing and a brotherhood of giving, giving this information out to those who will listen, to those who are searching for the truth.

There will be many sightings of our spaceships over the Earth this summer. Look for sightings over the Great Lakes of the United States. Look for sightings in several South American countries.

Look for a very low level sighting in the state you call Florida. We will also appear in New England, as we have been doing for the past several Earth years. We have stepped up our activities. We have increased the number of our bases around the world.

The Space Brothers are ready to do their part, but we must have the cooperation of all of you. Time is short. Unity is a necessity. The next few years in your Earth time will be very crucial.

Someday we hope that you will be able to look behind you and understand that what we have been doing has an ultimate purpose and goal, which is the betterment of mankind on Earth. We come here in peace, we come here in love, we come here with the idea in mind of sharing with you. But you must give, your leaders must give, the Earth must give, and in return the Earth will give back to you.

This is Ashtar, Commander in Chief of the Free Federation of Planets.

Session Thirty-One

Crystal Love from Mirror City

DIAMONDS, sparkling diamonds. (Channel is speaking) The rays of the sun are the most majestic that you will ever see. I am Crystal Love speaking to you from Mirror City.

Question-Where is Mirror City?

Mirror City is on the far side of the galaxy. It is many hundreds of light years from Earth, yet it is as close as my outstretched hand to those who feel the power of love in their heart. The power of love radiates from everything around. This planet is like a giant emerald glistening in the sun.

I am Crystal Love. I am purity. I am the holder of the great Flame of Truth, the protector of the Crystal World. I come to you with knowledge that you are looking forward to receiving. I come to you with a crystal in my hand. I come to you so that we, The Brotherhood, can share our knowledge with those of you who would like to be uplifted, those of you who would like to expand your consciousness into other realms.

Wear the crystal at all times. It is a powerful magnet that attracts cosmic rays from the furthest corners of the Universe. We send these rays to you through dimensions of time and space. We send you a beam of positive energy.

The crystal that you wear attracts that. It also attracts others who are of the same mind. Yes, the crystal is a powerful force to contend with.

COSMIC REVELATIONS TILL THE END OF TIME

Hold it in your hand. Hold it to the light. Hold it to the sunlight. Think, think of positive thoughts. Focus your mind on the Ultimate Light. Focus your mind on pure thoughts of energy. I, Crystal Love, send you these vibrations.

Use the crystal wisely. Do not use it for negative purposes. Use it only to channel the light, to broaden the spectrum all around you. Crystals are like a magnet. They will attract those forces to you which you desire. If you wish good and you want positive things, the crystal will surround you in a protective aura. The rays from the crystal are like the rainbow. They cover the entire spectrum. The crystal is the highest form in the universe.

It has been used for centuries, dating back to the time of Atlantis, when those scientists on Earth built a giant crystal which was almost as big as the building you know as the Empire State Building. This crystal was like a magnet. It drew in the forces from the four corners of the Universe. But it was so big and so powerful, and it got into the hands of those who would use it for negative reasons, so that it turned into an enemy of mankind.

All the elements were affected. The air was filled with lightning like this planet has never seen before or since. The tides rolled in. The tides rolled out. There were volcanic eruptions. The seas revolted. The air revolted. There was fire. There was wind. And Atlantis was destroyed.

Use the crystal for 10 or 15 minutes a day if it is at all possible. Meditate. Think of us. Think of this jeweled city, where the buildings are made of crystal, where everything around is crystal, reflecting and drawing in the light. Share it, share it with mankind. Get out the word and tell everyone who will listen about the Space Brothers. Crystals can be used by anyone to enhance their psychic abilities. But, again, we warn you that they should be used wisely. Scientists on your Earth know the power of the crystal. Some of them would like to use it for their own diverse purposes. Beware of this. Always stand in the light of purity and harmony.

I send you love from the City of Mirrors on a planet far, far away. I send love to all the brothers and sisters in the many planets on the many continents throughout your solar system and the planet you call Earth. We send rays of harmony for those who will listen. We will be able to see those who carry the crystal and sense their warm wishes even at this distance. Yes, we listen to those who carry the crystal with them.

COSMIC REVELATIONS TILL THE END OF TIME

Ashtar on Cassandra

GREETINGS, Starchild. This is Ashtar, Commander in Chief of the Free Federation of Planets. We speak to you tonight from our vast station in space. We watch over you. We watch over all of mankind.

You have heard from our brother from the planet far, far away. You have heard of the City of Mirrors. You have heard from Crystal Love, who speaks to you with kindness, with hope, and with charity. We see the sparkles in your eyes. We see your soul light up like a diamond. We praise you, and all of you who come and listen, for it is our duty to share with you the knowledge, the power, and the light of all Creation.

If there is anything you wish to ask, we will do our best to bring to you the proper response.

Question-Could you tell me something about Cassandra?

Yes. There is a giant heart that beats and radiates thoughts only of love toward others, a soul that has reincarnated many, many times. A true Starchild who has lived not only on Earth before but who has come from other planets in space. She has a duty, a mission to fulfill, and she will be very important in the New Age, in times to come.

We watch her and we look over her. We guide her and send her our love, and she in turn spreads this to others. She is a true visionary, a true Starchild. She is someone who can be trusted. She is someone who can be relied on. She has a soul that glimmers in the light of God.

COSMIC REVELATIONS TILL THE END OF TIME

You have known her before. You will be very close to her for the next few months. There is a sharing, and a giving, and a cooperation, and a bond between the two of you. You were both on Mars at one time, several centuries ago, and you migrated throughout the solar system. And now you are both here on Earth together. This is both your third incarnation here.

You have learned much, Starchild, in your previous incarnations and you are growing stronger day by day. You share your knowledge with others. You do not try to hide what you know, and this is good, because we need others like you. We need others like Cassandra.

The trees are sprouting up. Remember when I said that soon there would be a forest of followers? Well, the forest is expanding. We can see the light now in many, many countries, as the word gets out. Yes, there are finally smiling faces who understand.

Is there anything more, Starchild?

Question-Do you know anything about whether General Westmoreland was abducted?

Monka on General Westmoreland

(Channel begins tapping on the arms of his chair and saluting.) Monka here. You ask about General Westmoreland. Do you miss him?

No.

We are not quite sure what to do with him either. Do you think it is funny? (I could not stop laughing.)

It sounds funny the way you put it.

We have been trying to change his mind, but he is a stubborn old goat. Do you know when he was up here he wouldn't even remove his boots. All he wanted was to give us his rank and serial number.

What a fool. We returned him promptly. But we know where he is, and he is shaking in his boots. We're not warlords, but something has to be done. How can anyone expect the world to live in peace when there are people like that walking around? Actually, I shouldn't be so critical. It's not my job to say. But we try to do what we can to help you, which is more than I can say for General Westmoreland.

I'm sure he is back home now, polishing his brass buttons and dusting off his stripes. Even at his advanced age, he would still like to get out there and command the troops. But he's had his day. And Monka and the rest of the Ashtar Command will have their day soon enough.

Question-Are there going to be any landings real soon?

Landings?

I've heard rumors that all the ships are going to land at the end of October.

Let me look at my calendar. We have not penciled a date.

Oh, shucks.

But you will see more of us. This, I guarantee.

COSMIC REVELATIONS TILL THE END OF TIME

Session Thirty-two

Ashtar on Nutrition

WE beam to Earth. We beam a message on Earth. This is Ashtar, Commander and Chief of the Free Federation of Planets.

We watch closely the developments on your world. Earth continues to be at a critical point in his history. War is going on at sea. War is going on, on the land. All wars must cease. All governments must put an end to armed conflict. Your world teeters back and forth. Your planet wobbles on its axis, not just on the physical plane, but in a spiritual sense.

You must uplift yourself. You must reach to the heavens. You must look to the planets and the stars. You must accept our guidance. You must heed our warnings and seek our advice, for we know the trouble and turmoil that envelops your world. We can see it from our mighty spaceships.

A fleet is always standing by, ready to venture into your atmosphere. We have many scout ships, many different shapes and sizes. You see us in the daytime as bright and glittering ships that streak across the sky, reflecting the brilliant rays of the sun. At night we glow like a million fireflies.

Oh, yes, we are here, regardless of what your scientists tell you. You, Starchild, know of our existence. You have helped us spread the word among countless thousands. You may think that it is only a small number, and indeed percentage wise it is, but each person that you reach is like a seed, a seed that grows and grows and grows. First there is a little bud; then there is a tree; then there is a grove; then there is a forest. Yes, Starchild, there will someday soon be a forest of believers. There will be many of you who will know of our calling, and we will be more than pleased.

COSMIC REVELATIONS TILL THE END OF TIME

We shall do our best to answer your questions now.

Question-Is there some kind of advice that you could give people on using nutrition to help uplift their vibrations in a practical way?

You speak of nutrition. Ah yes, we see the plants growing. We see the vast fields of corn, the vast fields of wheat. We see all of these things down upon your Earth. Many of us have transcended beyond having to use nourishment as you know it. We exist off the rays of the sun. We exist off the flow of the cosmos. Oh, poetic perhaps, but true enough.

You on the Earth must feed your body. We can help you feed your mind, but you must feed yourself properly to advance in both a physical and a spiritual state of mind. We cannot tell you what to eat because everything that is grown is certainly God's food. God has placed it there for you, but you must prepare it properly. You must know how much of certain things to take as nourishment. Many of you do overeat. We can see that this is one of the things that people on your planet crave and lust after.

Ah, many times I smell the aromas and I must say that the fragrances of the spices are very nice indeed, but where would we be if we ate the same foods that you do?

Remember, does not the Bible, your holy book, speak of the Garden of Eden? Oh, in those days it was a paradise. There were fruits of all different kinds. Fruits have great nourishment. Fruits are the nectar of life. You could tell which foods are good for you by their vibrations. Pick up an orange. Is it not a bright orange color? Does not that color radiate goodness? You could feel it in your system. Take a bite and you know it is good for you.

Eat less of the pork and of the meat with the blood in it. Though it is not bad for you, too much will keep you down, keep your density down. Eat more of the fruits. Eat more of the natural things. Do not pollute what you eat. Do not add chemicals. Do not take away the vitamins.

Let these things fill your body and mind. Yes, you can tell by looking at food whether it is good for you. Does it vibrate to your chemistry? When you look at it, does it fill you with warmth? Is it bright? Is it colorful? Those are the things that you want, oranges, things that are reds and greens and are filled with vitamins. This is good. This is spiritually uplifting. Seafood is very good for you. This contains much that will be uplifting to you. As do vegetables, of course, tomatoes and carrots.

Oh, you have so many things on Earth that are rewarding. In fact, often, to be honest, I look and I say, "Oh, I wish I had an orange or I had a tomato." But, at last, I am beyond that. I am among the stars. I get my energy from those beings that surround me.

Many of your people, especially those you call the New Agers, know of these things. They know that the body is a temple and that it is important to keep that temple clean, to keep the blood circulating properly, to keep your system cleaned out. This is very uplifting. It is very spiritual. It will help you.

Many of your producers and packagers of food do not realize that when they add chemicals they are really poisoning the system. They think of quick profits. "How could we get the most for our investment? How can we mass produce?"

Many of you should go back to planting and farming yourself. If you live out in the country or out of the city, have your own garden. Plant your own fruits and vegetables. This would be good for you. It would take you outdoors in the sunlight and in the fresh air. Also, the food that you consume would be natural, and you will know what you will be growing.

Do you understand, Starchild?

Yes, I understand.

Question-Is it helpful to take vitamins?

I knew you were going to ask that. I picked that up. Vitamins are fine. But you must know which vitamins are meant for you. You must know what your system needs and you must know the limitations. Too many vitamins are no good, just as no vitamins could be bad for you as well. Most of the vitamins you need, though, could be gotten through proper nutrition. Our advice would be for people to meditate, to think before they take too many vitamins. Know your system. Know what your system needs. Your system is a breathing entity. It will talk to you. If you listen, you will hear in your mind your body talking to you. Your body is an entity and can tell you much.

There are many healers today who are directed by us, who know these things and who can explain them to you. Take their advice.

I will now pass the communication on to an old friend.

Monka Takes Credit for the Florida Blackout

This is Monka, from the planet Mars. It has been a while since we have spoken with you. Much has transpired since that time. Wars continue to break out on your planet. There is conflict on many shores. We pound our fists in frustration, knowing what you do. Why can't you learn to live in peace and harmony just like the majority of us here among the stars do? Starchild, what makes the leaders of your world tick? Why do they continue to carry out their duties as if they were warriors of olden times? They must change their ways. They must be shown there is nothing to be gained through conflict and battle.

We have caused blackouts in recent times. When your channel was in the state that you call Florida recently, we put on a dramatic demonstration. Electricity went out all over the state while he was right there in his motel room. If that wasn't a demonstration, I don't know what is.

In fact, he was joking with his friend Diane about us. So we thought we would show the two of them exactly who is boss. The news media played it down but they could not come up with an explanation. Well, there is no Earthly explanation. We pulled the switch and out went the lights, total darkness. We can do it again. We will do it again, mark my words.

Question-Where?

We have not picked the location as yet. The location is not that important. Perhaps we will tell you about it ahead of time. Perhaps there will be no time. But keep a couple of candles nearby. You don't want to be caught in the dark, not in New York anyway. So you see, Starchild, I am still here. Monka has not gone far. True, we have traveled through the solar system and beyond in our duties but we always return. Wait a minute. Someone else is trying to speak.

COSMIC REVELATIONS TILL THE END OF TIME

Aura Raines on the Rings of Saturn

Hello. Greetings.

Greetings.

This is your old friend, Aura Raines. I've been driving my spaceship all over. My goodness, you can't believe the sights out here. Well, maybe you can because I see that you have Saturn up on your wall. That's a good way to tell us that you believe.

We know these things. We know a lot more than you think we do and we are very pleased with what we see. We are going to come through very often. You have stayed right with us and we are going to continue to direct you and to give you light. We are happy and pleased to be able to do these things, for we want to share with you all the things that we know, all the goodness and riches that are out here among the stars.

My friend Monka, my friend Ashtar, my friend Solar Star, they will guide the way like a beacon of light. They will pass much knowledge on to you, and you should share it with others. Indeed, you will share it with many more.

We shall talk to you again soon. You be of good cheer now and think of us often. This is Aura Raines from the planet Clarion. Goodnight from all of us now.

Session Thirty-three

An Answer to a Chant for Protection

YOU are always opening your consciousness to that which surrounds you on the etheric plane. You welcome us to do your bidding and we attempt to do what you request.

Om, om, om mm.

We of the invisible kingdom come to you on this day. We thank you for calling us and we have answered. We look at your world from outside and yet we are all a part of that which surrounds you. We see everything which happens on your planet. We have evolved in the same manner that you have evolved, but our minds, our senses, are more highly developed. Many of you who have crossed over from the other planes are now with us.

We try to guide and protect whenever it is in the realm of our jurisdiction. We are enveloped in a blue mist of purity. We will not and cannot harm you. We wish only to be of value to you. You have seen us in your dreams. We have spoken to you before. We are around you. We are with you. We are part of The One.

May the blessings of the Highest Secret abound in your life. May you be guided to the ultimate truth. May your existence be of benefit to all of mankind. We send you our powers. We send you our love. We send you the forces of the kingdom of God.

Session Thirty-four

Sananda – A Christmas Message

(Delivered Christmas Eve)

BLESS my children, for all those who gather together, in peace and mind, to recognize that day, 2000 years ago, when I came to visit your world. I came to show you the right path to Father. I came in peace and with love in my heart. I came to share with you the wisdom of the Lord. I had a mission that I had to accomplish.

Yes, my children, I still watch you. You are still my flock, my blessed little sheep. I have not abandoned you. I shall not abandon you. I came to your planet and was born of an Earthly mother. You called me Jesus. Her name was Mary. We have lived on in your hearts and in your souls. And now it may soon be time for me to visit once again.

Though my message has gone far and wide, very few of you have really heeded my words. Time is running short. I will soon have to return.

I am the Heavenly Host. I am the Light of Perfection. I am the Violet Ray. I am Love in its pure essence. I am Peace that has not gone astray. I am the Messenger of the Heavens. I am the Son of the Lord. I am that I Am.

This is Sananda.

COSMIC REVELATIONS TILL THE END OF TIME

Ashtar – We Hear Your Messages

HELLO, Starchild.

Hello.

Your calls have been heeded. Your messages have touched us dearly. Though we have not talked to you in recent times, this is no reason to be fearful that we have gone away. We know what you are thinking. We know by the vibrations cast forward by your mind and thinking.

You have seen the effects this week of what your scientists call the planetary alignment. You have seen storms like nothing else that has touched your nation in over a century. This is just a sampling of what is to take place in the heavens in the years to come. Your scientists have pooh-poohed this phenomenon, but once again, you have proven them wrong.

The vibrations of your planet are changing daily. Your whole world is starting to vibrate. Just to travel outside of your atmosphere in our ships, we could feel this speeded up action. It is necessary for you to put forward all your positive thoughts to slow down the trembling of your planet, to make this transition from the current vibration to the next as smoothly as possible.

We do not wish chaos. We wish a peaceful and, indeed, a pleasant transformation. The sky will be filled with our ships. Messages will be beamed over your radio and TV. More people will receive personal contact and communication. More of the mysteries of existence will be tied in together.

This is a wonderful moment in your history. For the first time in many, many years, we can feel that we have touched many.

COSMIC REVELATIONS TILL THE END OF TIME

Wear the crystal in good health. Wear the crystal to open up the channel. Keep us in your mind and in your heart and we will keep all of you in ours.

Yes, the network is spreading. Yes, there are more lights now. More will be written about us. More proofs will be brought forward. The time will soon be upon us and the time is almost now.

This is Ashtar, Commander in Chief of the Free Federation of Planets.

Session Thirty-five

The Second Coming

THIS is Ashtar, Commander in Chief of the Free Federation of Planets. Good evening, Starchild.

Good evening.

We are coming to you across the limitless void of space with a message of peace and hope for you in what has been termed the last days. We welcome your questions and extend our hand in friendship to all peoples on your planet.

I have a letter which I would like to read to you.

Please go ahead and read it to the channel and we will try to answer to the best of our ability.

Tell Mr. Richards that we appreciate both his concern for the safety of the various locations mentioned, as well as his calling upon us for advice. It shows that indeed there are amongst you those who are willing to heed the warnings and messages of this command center.

We are, however, unable to offer specific advice as to what locale. We do not see Boise, Idaho, as being involved in a specific geographical change. However, we do feel by the vibrations that are given us by the various cities and towns and communities mentioned in Mr. Richards' communication that it would be advisable for him to go to either Arizona or New Mexico.

When the time is right for a pickup, he will know exactly where to go. This will be communicated to him and others in the form of mental images. We cannot give away the specific locale of our landing because it might be that some who would not be there would then go of their own volition. At the time, those who

COSMIC REVELATIONS TILL THE END OF TIME

have been selected to be part of this mass evacuation will know exactly where it is that they are to go.

Both Phoenix and Albuquerque are high energy centers. They are surrounded with a very brilliant white light. There may be some trouble in Kansas City at a future date. We see hostilities taking place there. Many people from surrounding states may try to head for this spot after a holocaust and there could be much bloodshed. We would suggest that he keep away from this area, though it is safe now and in the immediate future. Many of the things which he describes in this personal communication are valid. There shall be tidal waves in these places.

Are there any other questions which you would like to ask at this time, Starchild?

Yes. Could you tell us about the time when Jesus will return to Earth?

It is hard for us to speak of someone so holy. Jesus was the savior of your planet. He came here to teach you how to live in peace and harmony with one another. Many have misunderstood his message or have distorted it for their own personal gain.

Jesus was taken up into heaven. He was levitated by a spaceship under our command. He will be brought back in a similar fashion. The man you call Jesus of Nazareth has the most powerful aura of anyone born on your planet. He was truly holy. He was truly wise. And yet, many of your people refuse to acknowledge him. There have been other wise men, but not of such a high caliber.

Jesus shall return to your planet in the not-too-distant future. He is waiting and biding his time for his return. Just as your holy book, the Bible, says, everyone will see him descend from the sky. He will come surrounded by a fleet of glittering spaceships, objects which you call UFOs.

Though he is not one of us as such, we are in contact with his kind. His kind is powerful of a magnitude far superior even to us. Jesus and his brothers sit on the throne of the Lord.

Jesus rules over this planet. He has tried for the last 2,000 years to lift you up out of the muck and mire humankind has gotten itself stuck into. Jesus does not wish to be worshipped. He wishes but to teach. He wishes to share his knowledge of the kingdom of God with those who will listen.

COSMIC REVELATIONS TILL THE END OF TIME

His return will be known by all true believers. His voice will be heard. His face shall be seen all over the Earth. He is wise and omnipotent. You have but to follow and heed the Ten Commandments, for they are given to you from the Most High.

God wishes you to live in peace just as his other children do. Do not be tempted by the being you call Satan, for he is the leader of the band of fallen angels we call the Serpent Race. Do you understand, Starchild?

I think so.

Are there any more questions?

When Jesus communicates with everyone, does it not mean that he will take over communications media at some point?

His thoughts will be in your mind. His face will appear to all of those who seek him out. This is the age of Jesus for mankind. This, Starchild, is the time of his Second Coming.

Is this going to happen soon?

Oh, but the date is not known by any of us. But it will not be that far off in the future, as your Earth time goes. It will come soon, perhaps not tomorrow or the next day. But the day is not far away when you shall see him come from the clouds, his hands extended, the warmth of love of our God radiating from his heart. This is the Jesus you know and the Jesus who loves you.

So, it isn't true that he has been living in the Himalayas all this time, as some people believe?

He has been among you on and off. He visited the country you know as Mexico many centuries ago. He also walked among the American Indians for a while. He has lived for a brief while on this planet, but he is not here now, for he is in the place which you call heaven. If those are the only questions that you have, we shall say goodnight, Starchild. And we shall talk to you again soon. Please spread our message of love to all of those whose hearts and minds are open to our existence.

This is Ashtar, Commander in Chief of the Free Federation of Planets.

The Task of the Guardians

AT this very moment various groups of space entities – some in solid, physical bodies and others in spiritual or etheric form – are circling the Earth, undertaking a variety of tasks, some to benefit us and some perhaps detrimental to humankind. The goals of these different groups is so varied that often considerable confusion arises, allowing for disharmony among UFO researchers and New Age networkers alike.

Over four decades ago, one group had already made a significant contribution to the subject, defining the activities of these extraterrestrial and inter-dimensional beings. The Borderline Sciences Research Foundation (Box 549, Vista, California 92083) was founded by the very astute Meade Lane, who gathered around him a group of associates from many branches of the metaphysical world. One individual Lane came to rely on frequently was Mark Probert, a medium and channel whose body was regularly "taken over" by members of a higher order of beings known as the "Inner Circle."

Unlike much of the channeling done by others, Probert's communications were not of an overly philosophical nature but centered around the dissemination of valuable information pertaining to the functions of this hierarchy of invisible beings who are arriving daily on our planet. Much of the collected material concerned ancient traditions and cosmic laws, as well as the future destiny of the world as seen from the viewpoint of these brings.

The following material is taken from ESRA files and constitutes a significant contribution to the volume of material derived from the Ashtar Command. It should further serve to verify the information that has been presented through the pages of this book.

• • •

An Appeal from the Guardians

ON August 2, 1952, noted New Age teacher and channel George Hunt Williamson received this message: "Your world has been observed for 75,000 years. How can we deny the eternal varieties: Life, God, the Creator's place in the divine scheme? How can we stand by and watch the progress of evil men on this globe, the Earth! ... Evil planetary men, who abound in space, will attempt contact with evil men of Earth for destruction! The good men of Earth must unite with the good men of the Universe...." And on August 31, 1952: "Ashtar speaking. Certain great powers in your world wish to see us go away or see us destroyed. Neither will happen. These powers fear us, and when you fear anything, you hate it. All planets have come to help certain ones on Earth. Those of the right mind are with us! We will not harm anyone. Only their own thoughts can do that!"

Killing is Forbidden by Law

We can be sure the Guardians have no intention of destroying the planet, nor of depopulating it. They know that the killing or disincarnation of an undesirable person affords only temporary relief at best. In fact, the arrival of this bad actor on the lower Astral plane may aggravate the problem he originally created! Once oriented to that plane, he may have more power to harm others still in the flesh. He can continue to do mischief by planting evil and destructive ideas in weak-minded men and women. Individual disincarnations of trouble makers among us will be resorted to only if all other means have failed.

This guardian reminds us that, when a child has reached a certain age here on Earth, it must be taught to handle such useful aids as fire and sharp-edged tools. Of course the child must be watched to keep it from cutting its own throat or from burning down the house.

COSMIC REVELATIONS TILL THE END OF TIME

As racial children in the solar system, we have just discovered fire and sharp-edged tools. At present, they are still beyond our ability to understand or use.

What makes the situation even worse is our demonic playmates from the Astral and Cavern worlds. They continually tempt us to use this knowledge in particularly dangerous ways. From what little is told us, these appear to be both elementals and degraded humans of low intelligence, almost mindless, and subject to easy control by Satanic forces whose greatest triumph of evil would be to blow up the planet. If they cannot rule, they would destroy.

The Caverns are both natural and manmade by Elder races who were far superior to us in technology. Yet, it is said that they got into an all-out atomic war thousands of years ago and had to leave the planet. They abandoned their workers in the underground factories and also much advanced electronic equipment, still useful and usable by their degraded descendants.

The only safe solution for all concerned is education of us surface dwellers, the Adamic races. The mass intelligence must be considerably improved, also our code of ethics. Somehow we must learn to get along together; for there is no use trying to restrain people from doing wrong. Sooner or later someone will evade the restraints and do what his lower self and demonic playmates tempt him to do.

There is a perverse streak in mankind on this planet. For the majority of us, until we suffer the consequences of our misbehavior, taboos against the use of things learned too early are worse than useless. We will do what we want to do. Maybe our demonic playmates place a certain glamour around the forbidden. Anyhow, pain is the great teacher on this planet, and we are here to learn by experience.

So the role of the Guardians as teachers is to allow educational errors to be permitted, just short of the final error of all-out atomic war. They cannot really teach us anything. Information must be placed before us in the hope and expectation that we will make the reasonable, rather than the suicidal, choice. If not, our force toward evil will have to be met with a greater force.

There have been news suppressions of Flying Saucers by both sides. A reasonable educational program on the Visitors could have been instituted from the beginning in 1947 if it had not been for the stupidity and fear of some government officials and the vested interests they represented. The Guardians themselves admit having had to suppress some stories on UFOs, to prevent a possible panic reaction of the public.

The Task of the Guardians is Threefold

First and foremost, they must accelerate the spiritual awakening of mankind. This will take care of the needed moral and ethical development of us surface dwellers.

Second is to watch closely our scientific progress. They must aid that which is generally beneficial in its results. They must retard or slow down research in areas where the results would be detrimental to our welfare and they must be ever ready to halt or block that research and development which will lead to an international disaster.

Third is the necessity for continually patrolling the borderland between the visible and invisible worlds, to keep a watchful eye on our demonic playmates from the Lower Astral world and the Moon. It is not the purpose of the Guardians to interfere with this telepathic communication; for we must be allowed to listen to the voice of evil and make our own choice as to whether or not we will yield to temptation.

It is only by yielding and suffering the tragic results that we develop moral stamina and spiritual muscle. Nevertheless, we have Desperate Ambroses here in the United States who are continually being tempted to unleash our atomic weapons in the war against Communism. Interference with the astral demons who continually suggest this to certain leaders can be expected and has probably been in effect since the development of the hydrogen bomb in 1952.

Three Spiritual Task Forces

Each segment of the above-mentioned program is handled by three individual groups. They ordinarily restrict their activities to their own specific task, but, of course, they work in close harmony. Each group helping the other when the need arises.

Assistance in specific projects or crises is also received from special outside groups and individuals, on different planes of consciousness and in the physical. Certain Earth scientists have been of great assistance to the Guardians' program for man. The scientists have not consciously known this because they have not had self-awareness on these other levels of consciousness from whence their inspiration comes. The scientist acts as the eyes and hands of an Etherian or Guardian who cannot or does not want to materialize or create a temporary form of his own. Ethical and moral principles are abstractions, deriving from the higher levels of the mind.

Development of these principles in mankind is a task obviously involving the mental sciences. The masters of mental science in the atmosphere of Earth are the adepts and Masters of our earlier civilizations, from the continents of Lemuria and Atlantis. They are still very much with us, living and working at the Etheric levels, still very much concerned about the welfare of their physical and spiritual descendants in modern races. Their work doesn't normally call for the use of physical transport such as Flying Saucers. They forward our evolution mostly by mental means.

The scientific phases of the Guardian program are in the hands of the Etheric Nors or Viknors from Venus. They have been called in to help in this present crisis because they are recognized masters of the technical aspects of creation. Individual members of this group have taken embodiment in human form at times on the Earth but they could not be said to have been an Earth race originally. Some members of this group are from advanced races on Mars, also. The Saucer researcher must keep in mind that their normal Etheric plane of existence is invisible to us. The rate of vibration is different. If and when our Astronauts get to Mars and Venus, the Guardians or Etherians will be no more real there than they are here. Venus Etheria is another order of magnitude than the 3-D physical in which we live. This is probably the greatest barrier to understanding the Flying Saucer phenomenon. For the Guardian Nors to make their spaceships visible to us, the form of the craft and its occupants must be brought down the scale of tangibility to where it radiates or reflects physical light that we can see.

The evil influences continually tempting us to selfish and harmful actions are watched over by a mixed group of Guardians. Our demonic playmates function in the Lower Astral and Lower Etheric counterparts of the Earth. During Lemurian times, primitive man was much more consciously aware of these "playmates" than he is now. Passions were uncontrolled. Life on the surface of the Earth ran riot. The humans who achieved adepthood then were really Masters of

Passion. So it is only natural that they should be responsible for this phase of the program. When anything of a technical nature is needed they can call in the help of the Nors.

Much work of a controlling and steadying nature must be done in the Cavern world beneath our feet, and in the Astral heavens and hells around us.

The Need for Bodies, Mechanical and Organic

One principle of life we must accept here is that to accomplish effective observation and action on any plane of consciousness – or on or in any living surface – one must have a body composed of the matter of that plane or surface. This means that the Venusian Flying Saucers – as well as UFOs from other planets or constellations from space – must be able or capable of both interplanetary travel and inter-plane travel.

In our limited understanding we always think of travel as being from place to place on a living surface. This is horizontal motion in some particular direction. The coming of the use of airplanes didn't change this concept; it only speeded the travel from physical point to physical point. The development of the rocket gave us our first glimpse of vertical travel away from our living surface. This is the first step up the Scale of Tangibility. When this vertical movement is speeded up to where it becomes a change of vibration, then a change of vibration becomes a change of location. Some people are familiar with the materialization and dematerialization of the séance room. Others have seen it shockingly demonstrated by the Flying Saucers, such as the miner and his wife on Steep Rock Lake, or Farmer Hoard on his hilltop in West Virginia.

When the Viknors want to perform effective observation and action here on the living surface of this Earth, their craft must be brought here – or thought here – and converted to the vibrational level of this plane. The craft have mechanical equipment aboard by which this can be done. They can also be "converted" by external means, presumably the mind-power of some external operator. This kind of instantaneous conversion from one location to another is being dramatized for television audiences every week in the "Star Trek" program. It is called a "transporter" beam in this program.

As a matter of operational convenience, the Scout Saucers seen are brought here aboard huge mother ships or carriers. Teleportation is a good word to describe the process. The mother ship and everything aboard it, mechanical equipment and living beings, is taken up the Scale of Tangibility to where it is pure energy. Then it is brought back down the scale to a level corresponding to that of the vibratory rate of the atmosphere of Earth, and here it is an immeasurable fraction of a second later.

Apparently, the first attempts to do this in 1947 or thereabouts were not quite as accurate as the Viknors wanted. They admit this is quite a delicate matter, especially when operating from a mobile control aboard the craft itself. Sometimes the "stop" on the tangibility scale was too close to the surface and the materialization was observed by astounded humans on the ground below. This form of propulsion would be called true space drive, no doubt. Later warp jumps were more accurate. The carrier was materialized somewhere out beyond the moon and brought in under a different kind of propulsion, probably electromagnetic.

The Different Kinds of Propulsion

Jet-powered space ships have been seen by many and the Viknors admit to having reactivated some of their ancient, jet-powered Saucers for operations here. We don't have to worry about their contaminating Earth's atmosphere with heavy metals explosions or other exotic fuels. Their rocket power is obtained by disintegrating our atmosphere in the rocket chamber. The air is scooped up at the nose of the craft, compressed in the rocket chamber and exploded there – atomic disintegration – by a dis-beam. Atomically disintegrated metals could be used in the same equipment in airless locations away from the planet. We are working toward controlled atomic explosions, but our science is still limited to the use of heavy, radioactive metals like plutonium and uranium.

Electromagnetic drive is common to many of the Viknor spaceships, for local use only, as it cuts or bends the magnetic lines of force around a planet. A side effect is the blanking out of all electric apparatuses in the area, as well as radio, TV and other electronic phenomena. This characteristic is one of the first things a Saucer researcher looks for in investigating a Saucer sighting.

Primary drive is true space drive. It is suitable only for high speeds and long distances – in our 3-D terms. Telano was told that the control mechanism on the mother ship is placed in synchronous frequency with "universal energy flows existing in all space."

A crude simile for us would be the surf rider sitting on his board off the beach and waiting for the big one to come along. He catches the wave for a free ride toward shore. He can go in only one direction, though; and the sophisticated equipment of the Venusians allows them to go either way by lagging or leading the cosmic wave; so they can go with or against the flow – "in" or "out" of phase, as the technicians would say. The speed then depends on the phase angle and the amount of shading power the pilot can apply with the control mechanism. Anything beyond 27,000 miles per hour creates navigation problems around this Earth; so this is considered the maximum usable speed; but UFOs have been clocked at over 40,000 mph by our surface and airborne radar tracking gear.

All of the Vicknor craft have the ability to hover motionless when desired and this is a characteristic which differs markedly from our own airplanes. One way this is done is with a cone-shaped electrical field. This creates a sort of umbrella which deflects the pull of gravity on the ship, thus neutralizing its weight. Sometimes this cone-shaped field ionizes the air, causing it to glow. This type of glowing, cone-shaped phenomenon has been seen and reported at night, where no UFO was visible to normal sight at all. Another type of glowing phenomenon is the corona discharge which obscures the actual body of the Flying Saucer. The Viknor contact says this is a diversionary field which reduces the physical mass of the ship. Electromagnetic propulsion also produces a corona discharge. So these different kinds of phenomena-creating systems must be kept in mind when analyzing Saucer sightings. No one answer does for all.

The Seven Different Types of Viknor Flying Saucers

The doughnut-shaped *Suze class*, 125 feet in diameter and 30 feet thick. This is a flying laboratory with a large amount of test equipment aboard. The normal crew is 50 and drive is electromagnetic. Harold Dahl and several others apparently saw a formulation of Suzes over Maury Island, Puget Sound, the afternoon of June 24, 1947; for he later described them as "doughnut-shaped" and about 100 or so feet in diameter.

The *Tonton Class* flier is 100 feet long and 25 feet in diameter. The Viknors say this is an escort and fighter craft primarily for the protection of others. This carries a normal crew of 20 and uses both jet and primary drive. A UFO of this description flew alongside an Eastern Airlines plane the night of July 24, 1948. Pilots Chiles and Whitted saw it on the flight between Montgomery, Alabama, and Atlanta. They were at 5,000 feet. The thing was compared to a Buck Rogers type rocket, no wings, and with a red jet flame shooting out from 25 to 50 feet at the rear. They estimated its speed at between 500 and 700 miles an hour. There were two rows of portholes along the sides.

The *Fakle* is another circular craft, 100 feet in diameter. This is primarily for cargo transport, with a crew of 25 and electromagnetic drive.

The *Olon-type* Flying Saucer is crescent shaped, about 45 feet across by 10 feet thick. This is a reconnaissance craft with a crew of five. It has a three-jet drive mounted on universal joints, one at each point of the crescent. These swivel mounted jets are the only control; thus this is an ancient flier but useful here at this time.

This matches the description and drawing of the leading saucer in the flight witnessed by Ken Arnold the afternoon of June 24, 1947. He was flying near Mount Rainier, Washington, when he saw this line of eight discs moving along in level flight at tremendous speed. He observed that the ninth UFO, the leader of the flight, was crescent or scimitar shaped.

A much smaller version, The *Oloner*, is only 14 feet across. This is a single place flier.

Then there are expendable, remote-controlled discs for closer observation of surface conditions and activity. The spherical *Pomid type* is only five feet in diameter. This uses electromagnetic drive.

The *Pomider* is even smaller, only a foot in diameter. This is the kind, the Viknors say, which is most often mistaken for a fireball. If one of these gets in trouble, it is allowed to or caused to explode in a shower of fiery sparks or fragments which leave no residue, unless it is close to people; then it may be caused to disintegrate more slowly so as not to attract attention or cause damage.

A fellow employee with me at the Naval Supply Center, Pearl Harbor, Hawaii, in the early 1950s, told me of seeing one of these Pomider-type Saucers while on a visit to the Pacific Coast with his wife.

COSMIC REVELATIONS TILL THE END OF TIME

His mother was riding with the two of them when they were driving into San Francisco one night. They were coming up the Bay Shore Highway, approaching the San Francisco airport. Suddenly they were aware of a glowing object, about a foot in diameter, moving along at their speed and in the same direction, a few feet above the ground and off the highway to the left. My friend slowed down a little so the three of them could watch this UFO more closely. It moved on ahead of them, crossed the highway in front of them, and continued on toward the airport, there to disappear in the bright lights. He and his wife attended my early Flying Saucer lectures in Honolulu to try and get some answers to the puzzling phenomenon they had observed.

Visitors from Other Solar Systems

Surface dwellers like you and me on this planet are just beginning to suspect that there may be a hell of a lot of traffic through our solar system, most of it internally originated, but some of it from outside. "As above, so below." Following this principle of occult science enunciated so long ago by Lord Buddha and other racial teachers, we should expect that this solar system traffic is patrolled and controlled. We certainly find it necessary with our surface traffic.

The Guardian Viknors have the responsibility for observing and controlling the space traffic around the Earth and perhaps the rest of the solar system as well. Anyhow, in this information through Rolf Telano to Meade Layne, they admit that Visitors do come here to this planet from elsewhere for various purposes. "They are permitted to proceed if their purpose is not malicious; otherwise they are usually intercepted at the outer limits of the solar system and turned back."

But what of those Invaders, from the regions of the Pleiades and Draco, for example, who are not intercepted but slip through the perimeter defense? There is no hint of this in the Telano material, but it is my belief that Invaders are ruthlessly hunted down and shot down. Certainly there is some kind of aerial warfare going on over our heads; for the results are occasionally witnessed and reported by amazed Earthlings.

In the early evening of March 17, 1956, a flaming UFO flashed across the Matanuska Valley of Alaska. It was 6:30 p.m. The object appeared to crash into the Chugach Mountains. It exploded with a roar, which was heard for miles, and a column of smoke and debris hung in the air for 15 minutes. Puzzled searchers found no wreckage on the ground. Nor were there any reports of missing military or civilian airplanes.

Eight months later, an even more spectacular disintegration occurred over a much more densely populated area of the States. We quote the *Wilmington Delaware Evening Journal* of November 20, 1956: "At 7:30 a.m. a violent explosion rocked the Harrington-Dover area and was heard as far off as Bridgeton, New Jersey. Eyewitnesses said they saw a plane trailing smoke heading for a crash in the area before the explosion was heard. Air Force and CAP planes and helicopters cruised the area for four hours but found nothing. No aircraft missing. Buildings 15 miles from the scene of the explosion rocked violently. One woman actually saw the aircraft, described it as the largest aircraft she had ever seen, and said she could have gotten the number and name had she thought of it. A radar station reported it had lost contact with a plane in the vicinity of Harrington."

The lady thought she saw a plane because airplanes are the only manmade objects Americans expect to see in the skies over their country. But when our planes come down after a mid-air explosion, bodies and debris are scattered over the countryside. There was none from this huge spaceship of November 20, 1956, because the magnetic field which held the form together was collapsed by a disintegrating weapon of the Guardian patrol craft.

The sudden vacuum in the atmosphere caused air to rush in violently. This made the terrific explosion, an implosion, really. The craft itself turned to dust and settled slowly to Earth as invisible molecular particles, raw matter to be used again in Nature's endless creative processes.

It is this almost absolute control of matter which has left little or no visible, physical evidence of the presence of the Visitors – unless they wanted something left for our puzzlement and education! One final example, from the Telano material, is a case in point.

The Mexico Flying Saucer of 1949

The craft most deserving the name Flying Saucers were brought to this planet in 1949 from the moon. A midget race from elsewhere – origin not given – set up a temporary base on the moon from which to explore the Earth. This was their first venture into deep space. The purpose was peaceful exploration. They had only one carrier or mother ship. It carried 30 or more Scout saucers. These were 100 feet in diameter and 16 feet thick at the cabin, with a crew of six. Their propulsion was electromagnetic or "Earth induction" drive, but it was different from that used by the Nors in that its performance was affected by our radar, with serious consequences.

The carrier became disabled in the atmosphere and magnetic field of Earth and the Scouts it had launched suddenly had no base and no supervisory control. The Nors say that any of their craft are capable of deep space travel. Their Scout Saucers can make the warp jump to Venus on their own if necessary, but not the craft of these midget explorers. They weren't even capable of getting back to their base on the moon under their own power.

One of these midget-piloted Saucers was shot down over northern Mexico by an over-anxious Nor patrol craft. The peaceful Invader didn't respond quickly enough with a recognition signal. Two or three others were caused to malfunction by American radar and came down in Arizona and New Mexico.

The problem was that their drive and control apparatus were not sufficiently shielded against the frequencies sent out by our Radar. The welfare of the midgets became the responsibility of the Viknors when it became apparent that the repair of their carrier would be indefinitely delayed. Earth's atmosphere and surface represented a hostile environment to these newcomers for which they were not prepared. There was only one thing for the Nors to do: gather them up and take them back to their base on the moon.

Of the 37 original fliers, 26 were located and safety returned to the moon. Eight were known to have crashed on the surface of the Earth. The remaining three went down unnoticed; perhaps they dropped into the sea.

Here again is a piece of fantastic information indicating surveillance and patrol activity far beyond our wildest dreams. What a staggering illusion of privacy and isolation we live under here on the surface of the Earth! If it is true! Do we have any evidence to back it up? Yes, going back through the ESRA files, I did indeed find some confirmation of this 1949 Saucer flap in our *Round Robin* journal. It was the January 1950 issue.

COSMIC REVELATIONS TILL THE END OF TIME

Don't Call Us, We'll Call You

1. Do not try to contact the Space People.

A. They can contact you at a time or place they choose to, in any form they wish to use, depending on their evolvement, of course.

2. Prepare yourself spiritually for some useful work.

A. This does not mean religious practices of an orthodox nature. This does mean a conscious effort in attuning to that which is the highest, most beautiful and eternal within one's self.

B. In work, we mean anything that will in some manner help those around you to find upliftment, peace and inner JOY.

3. Live each day in Service to the Creator.

A. By your works, the Space People know you and are able to judge by your aura if you are truly worthy of being part of their work upon Earth.

B. Your aura not only tells your past but it is a good and reliable way to tell what you are best able to do, spiritually.

4. Live each day as if it were your last.

A. Collect your mental baggage so that all which is of lasting value can be moved at once, all else left behind. Live so at any time or place you can turn your back upon the past without regret or backward glance.

B. Gather unto yourself all your dreams and desires of Service to God and man, for these are your wealth.

5. Negation breeds fear and doubt.

A. Evil loves the unprepared, the confused and ignorant.

B. Spiritual understanding is the key to all UFO activity, both negative and positive. Spiritual Guidance is offered to all who seek it sincerely and open-heartedly.

6. The Earth is a battleground.

A. The forces of evil employ ships of great size and beauty, just as do the Christ forces.

B. Unprepared Earthlings who seek contact must not do so without knowledge of how to set up a positive force field and hold it around themselves.

C. The negative forces can and do abduct thousands of people each year from the surface of the Earth – as well as animals, water and vegetation.

D. These samples are used for hideous purposes.

7. Establish a contact with your God-head.

A. No power on Earth nor from any realm outside the Earth can harm one who dwells in perfect accord with his High self.

B. This contact is waiting any and all who choose to place it in the area of the most important thing in their life.

8. Meditation and concentration bring awareness.

A. Be worthy of contact by the Etheric Forces by being apart from the flesh pursuits of the world. To be in the world but not of the world should be your goal.

B. Meditate upon perfection – upon that which you would change from evil to good, from sickness to health, and from ignorance to understanding.

C. Concentrate on being a balanced human; for you can be of no real service in an unbalanced condition to the Space People or to yourself.

9. The Kingdom of God is built by Light, Truth and Understanding of Spirit.

A. Radiate Light, think Light and you shall attract that which you seek to be, a creature of Light.

B. Seek Truth, demand Truth, and it shall be given to you. This is a universal law, and to know and use this Understanding is Wisdom.

C. You are Spirit no matter what form you are in now, and to know yourself and to be true to that inner knowledge is the greatest of all keys – for it brings the Kingdom of Heaven with you and enables you to express the Son-ship of God.

Remember this always, "Like attracts Like" – the Path before you holds no fear for those who choose to place their hand in God's.

I am Myron (Miller) Ashtar Command

COSMIC REVELATIONS TILL THE END OF TIME

**Space Master's Portfolio
Channeled Through
The Psychic Impressions
Of Carol Ann Rodriguez**

New York-based artist Carol Ann Rodriguez has worked closely with the channel whose messages make up the text of this book. She has received psychic impressions as to what the various Space Masters look like while they are in physical form.

COSMIC REVELATIONS TILL THE END OF TIME

ASHTAR—COMMANDER IN CHIEF

COSMIC REVELATIONS TILL THE END OF TIME

MONKA

COSMIC REVELATIONS TILL THE END OF TIME

AURA RAINES

COSMIC REVELATIONS TILL THE END OF TIME

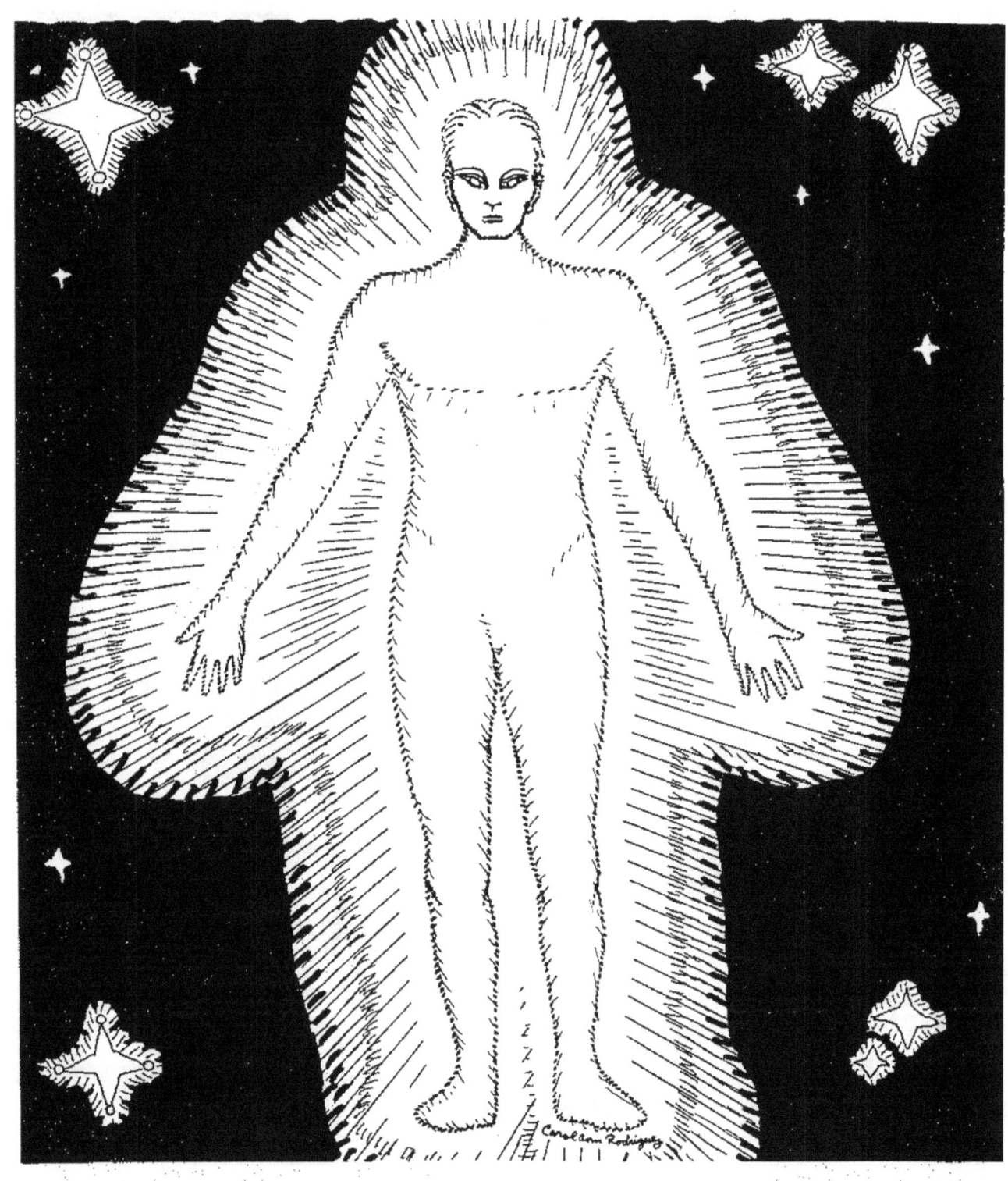

"THE ETHERIAN"

COSMIC REVELATIONS TILL THE END OF TIME

MASTER FROM
ETHERIC PLANET MERCURY

COSMIC REVELATIONS TILL THE END OF TIME

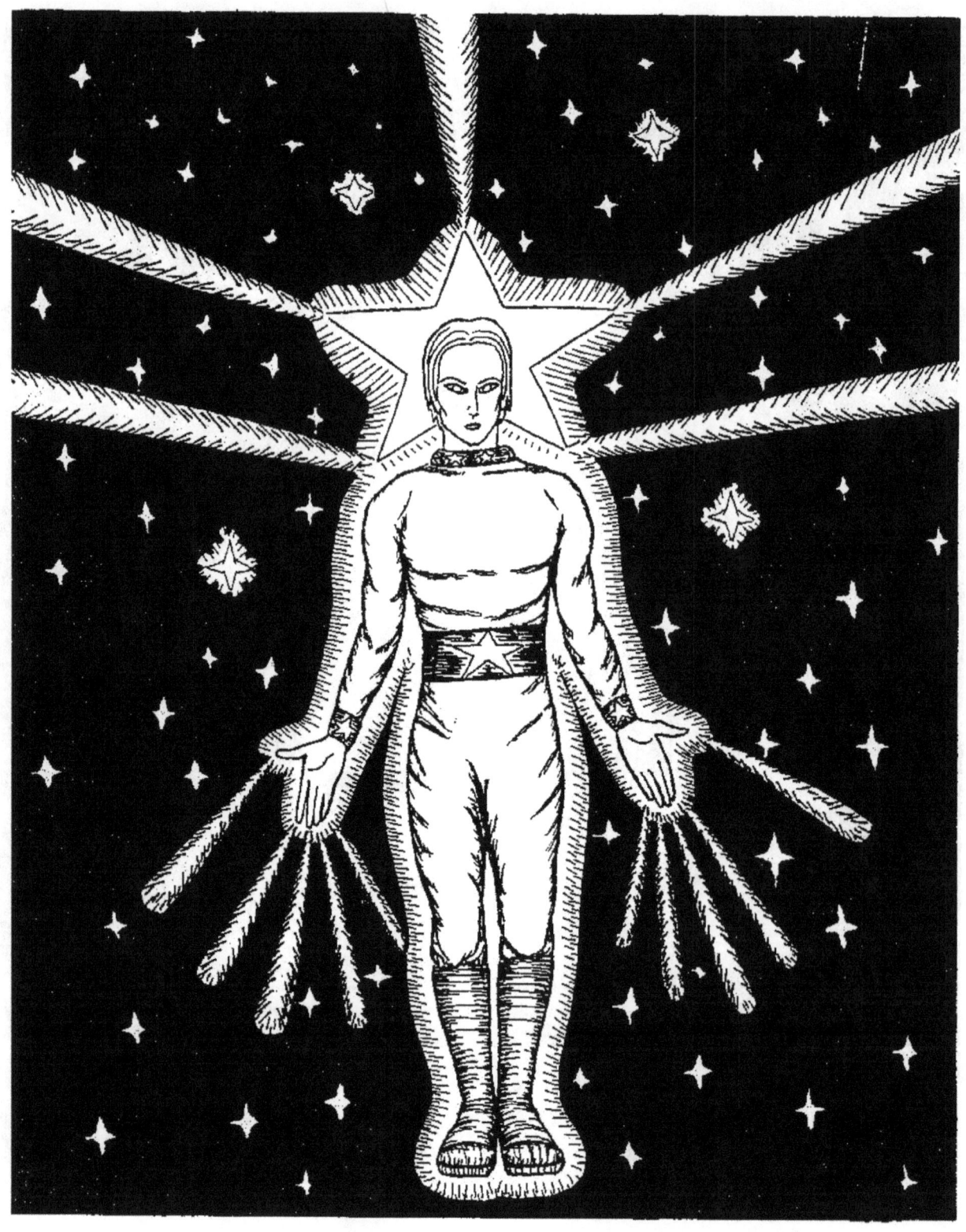

SOLAR STAR

COSMIC REVELATIONS TILL THE END OF TIME

MASTER FROM SATURN

COSMIC REVELATIONS TILL THE END OF TIME

SPIRITUAL GODDESS OF VENUS

COSMIC REVELATIONS TILL THE END OF TIME

MASTER FROM MARS

COSMIC REVELATIONS TILL THE END OF TIME

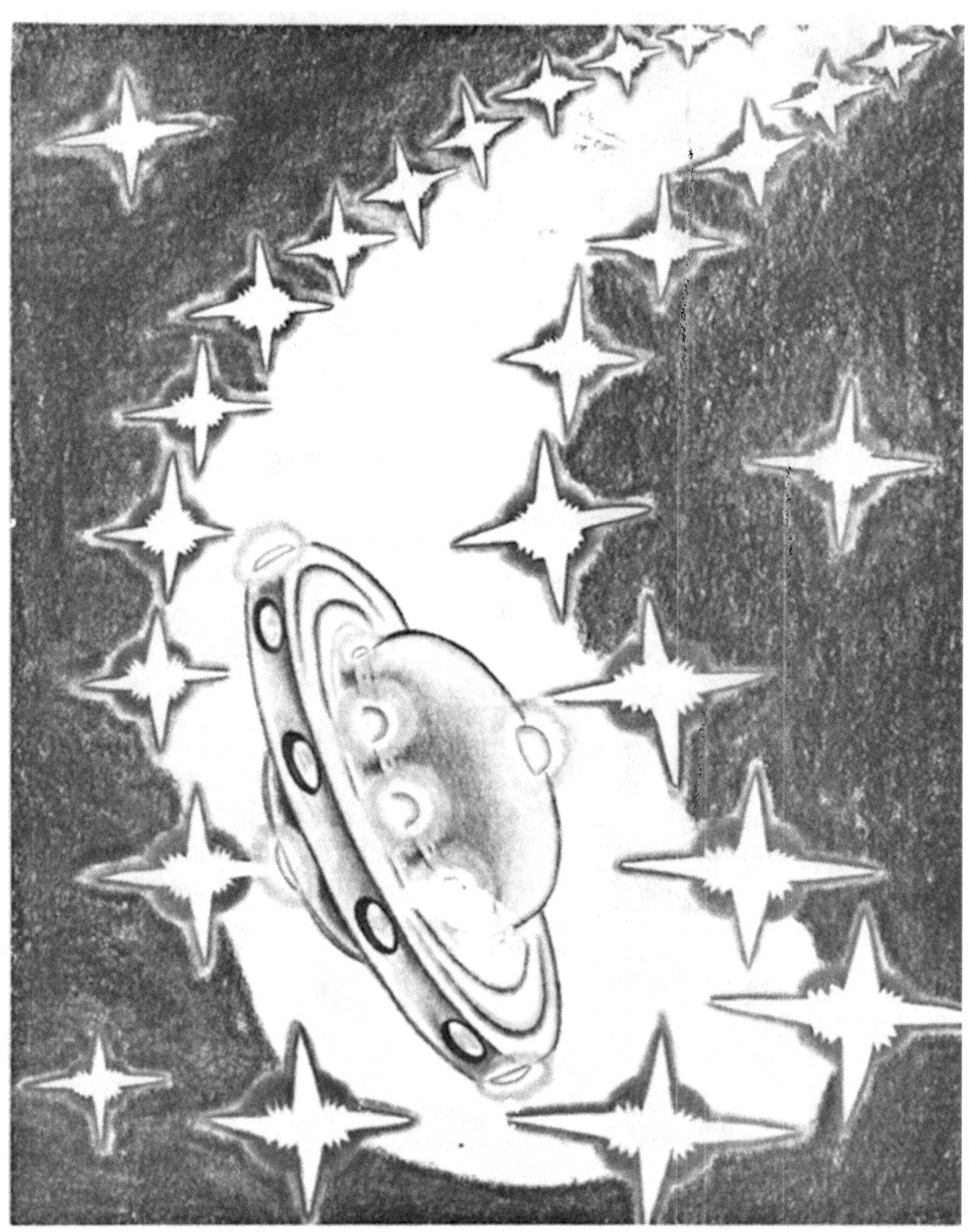

COSMIC REVELATIONS TILL THE END OF TIME

Foreword

THE plan for this book has existed on spiritual levels for considerable time. That moment has come when we of the Hierarchy now focus our energies for its manifestation, upon the physical plane.

The words go forth on the Authority of the Great White Brotherhood and under my sponsorship. We release them in a simplicity that all might understand. Included in the Cosmic Symposium are those who represent the Angel Kingdom, the Great Central Sun Government, the Heavenly Host, the Great Karmic Board, the Chohans of Earth Solar System, Universal Masters, and the great Alliance of the Intergalactic Confederation.

In my "three times three, times three" assembly of twenty-seven speakers, there is a great variety of approach to our theme, from many rays of expression. Yet a divine thread intertwines through all, in a united warning of the times and a spiritual call to preparedness. These fall easily into the four divisions as presented, which I have coined my "volume foursquare."

They are not designed for eloquence, entertainment or as intellectual fare. Neither profound nor prophetic, but rather timely and emphatic. They are lowered into the physical octave specifically for preparing certain souls who are now ready to receive them. The sentences should be read very slowly, and the messages thrice read, for the maximum of Light they carry, to be absorbed by the inner being.

Many invited to speak were unable to participate on the days appointed. Others have graciously rearranged their personal schedules to respond. Our messenger has prepared herself for this assignment for many lifetimes, in a cooperative effort with Cosmic Intelligences. I express my gratitude to her and my appreciation to each Great Soul who has contributed their thoughts to our messenger that the work might be compiled and released on schedule. I send my Blessings and my Love to all who look upon these words of Light.

Your sponsor,
Kuthumi

Preface

THE content of this volume stands on its own merits. I do not justify it or in any way come to its defense. It will defend itself. I do not debate, nor argue with anyone, or apologize for any message which is delivered through me. I am only a messenger. To those who do not seek, no argument is possible. To those who do, no argument is necessary.

These messages were received through mental telepathic impression, while fully conscious, assisted by Tensor Beam from higher dimensions and from interdimensional and interplanetary spacecraft. The vocal communications have been tape recorded as they were delivered and later transcribed as presented herein. Read not to contradict, nor to believe and take for granted, but to weigh and consider.

The messenger,
Tuella

COSMIC REVELATIONS TILL THE END OF TIME

Section One

World Chaos

COSMIC REVELATIONS TILL THE END OF TIME

COMPILED BY TUELLA

The Cloud of Chaos
Its detonations ravish all
Within its sphere
Of awful devil light,
That poisonous mushroom
Created out of fear.
Not satisfied, it creeps
And twists and smashes
Throughout the land,
Across the sky.
Relentlessly and viciously
It lashes out at every form
Of life.
Scientists of note declare-
God give us strength,
The awful burden of our miscreations
Of your forces, Lord, to bear,
And guide us back ... to where
Your great and wondrous power.
Is only used for good and peace
For love that always gives,
Will not devour.
This mighty, holy, sacred fire
Created to serve life,
rather than Misdirected desire.

- Eileen Schoen

COSMIC REVELATIONS TILL THE END OF TIME

An Ultimatum from the Great Central Son

By The Elohim

"**CALL** unto me and I will answer thee and show thee great and mighty things." I Am That I Am speaketh with thee. I Am the source of all truth, I Am the giver of Life. I Am the cause of all things. I Am within thee and a part of thee and I speak from within thy being, I speak the words as they come from the celestial realms. These are the words from the Most High given thee:

1. We, the Elohim of God, send forth our message on the Planet Earth in this appeal to the flesh of this generation to accept the blessings offered to man by the Elohim of Heaven. Unless humanity is willing to accept the outstretched hand of Love, there will come to this planet spasms of tremendous upheaval and loss of life. The forces of destruction that are within the earth cannot be contained unless your world community will yield itself to a spiritual awakening. Be still and listen to the beat of your hearts, and know that within collective creation, all hearts beat in tempo with your own. Know that all of life finds its source in the pulse of the Universe. The cohesive element of externalization is Love.

2. You have buried within your Being the knowledge of who you are and why you are here and from whence you have come. You have hidden under veils of remoteness and illusion, the glory, the shining splendor of your inner fire and your inner Divinity. Ye are Gods. Ye are created in the power Divine. We, the Elohim of the Highest Throne, invoke the Light that is within each and every one of you, we call it FORTH into MANIFESTATION! We invoke the RELEASE OF LIGHT from every atom of Being.

3. If souls refuse to yield to this Light, the millennium will be delayed, The Age of Peace and Love, and the evolution of the human race could be set back another entire cycle of time, in the history of humanity. The maximum of human suffering will be experienced unless human consciousness will gear itself to reach higher than the present level of spiritual understanding. If they will but call upon God as they understand Him to be, and seek guidance and direction for this decade, their call will be heard and answered. It takes but a call turned heavenward, with the mind and the heart's desire, to find an instant response within the corporate Divinity, known to man as the Elohim.

COSMIC REVELATIONS TILL THE END OF TIME

4. Citizens of Earth have within your governing bodies the framework for setting into motion the dispensation of Love. You have within your International Congress, your United Nations, the machinations of its inner Assemblies, to exercise the decisions of tolerance and peace. Nations are manipulated into battle array through human responses of the human self, overruling the promptings of Divine benevolence and gallantry. Does world society *really* have a choice in these matters? Can you not comprehend that either you will choose the Pathway of Light and Love within your International Assemblies, or you shall walk the Pathway of Darkness and destruction within all nations throughout the planet? We are combining our persuasiveness to focus this message into terrestrial vibrations, that it will be a stimulus of power, that it will motivate a response from within the souls of mankind. o Man, why will you choose to continue in the pathway of materialism and sensuality as has ever been the trend in crises past? When a challenge has been placed in the pathway of man's evolution toward the Father, it has been the trend of society to choose the comforts, the glamour, the darkness, and the path that leads to deeper regression of the soul. In our prerogative as the Elohim before the Throne, we call to souls to arise and seek the Pathway of Illumination and Spirituality; right thinking and right values; to choose for the eternal verities and the very salvation of a planet and the souls upon it.

5. The Host of the Celestial Plane will not stand by idly and look upon the willful destruction of a planet. The Angels of Judgment will move upon the evil genius who would architect the destruction of millions for personal gain. This despotism shall not stand! It shall be removed to the uttermost parts of infinity for an entire cycle of time. We shall send forth this warning to the warmongers upon Earth. Whatever infernal steps toward the mobilization for nuclear hostilities are taken, expect intervention from the Highest Forces of the Universe. We, as a united voice, send forth the fiat: IT SHALL NOT PASS! IT SHALL NOT PASS! IT SHALL NOT PASS! They that would seek to destroy shall themselves be destroyed by their own manipulations.

6. The Order has reverberated throughout the universe that the destruction of Shan shall not be permitted. So, brace yourselves, sons and daughters of the Most High. Brace yourselves, for the opposition of the Dark Ones and the Fallen Ones, for every step they take toward destruction shall be met with Divine

COSMIC REVELATIONS TILL THE END OF TIME

Opposition, and great struggles shall ensue between the two forces. Hold yourselves ever within our Brilliancy. Invoke the resplendence of God around your being, your families, your households, and your daily activities. Do not let your force field of Light fall away at ANY TIME. Reinforce it daily, for as the Light increases so shall the Darkness exalt itself. No harm can come to you. No ill can befall you as long as you are filled with Love within, and clothed with your circle of Light without. Fear is for those who abide in the darkness. Faith and assurance are the inheritance of those who walk with the Shining One. FEAR NOT, FOR THIS SHALL PASS QUICKLY. From the Great Central Sun, beyond your Sun, we send forth to the sons and daughters of God, our Great Halos of blessings, our force field of magnetic protection, and an expansion of all of the Light that surrounds the Planet. We precipitate upon these printed words, wherever they shall be placed, into whosoever's hands, in whatever home, an invisible Golden Thread that reaches upward to our hearts. From here, the Divine Presence of heavenly illumination descends along this thread with velocity into the heart of one who reads, and the home where that one abides. For these are words of Living Light sent forth by the Elohim of God, as messengers to mankind."

The Elohim Hath Spoken

Points to Ponder or for Group Discussion

1. Earth changes are conditional.
2. Ye are Gods.
3. Be careful of the choices you make.
4. In spite of man, the planet will be saved.
5. Invoke the Light during Armageddon.
6. Divine Presence accompanies Words of Light.

The Threshold of Sorrows

By Mother Mary

GOOD afternoon, Tuella. I am Mother Mary speaking with you once again, and remembering our wonderful experiences together at Easter time.

1 & 2. I am very pleased to share my brief message today, for the book that is created to be a helping hand, a staff to lean upon, a direction finder, in the decade of the Eighties. You must realize it is with much solemnity and heavy heart that I look upon the plight of my beloved children, as they now stand upon the threshold of the tribulation period, in the cycle of human evolution. I am tossed within my heart for the parents of children, and the youth of the land, and the little ones who follow.

3. Any mother's heart would feel as mine, if she could discern beyond the veil of human carnality and banality, the monstrous plans in the making that would tear asunder the hope of humanity's ascension. Tremendous themes of wickedness from malevolent forces belch forth their abominations upon the youngsters of this generation. We of the Angelic Kingdom have looked upon the impurities within your halls of learning, and shuddered within ourselves to see the occupation of your children.

4 & 5. The very earth itself, and the stones thereof, will cry out and reel to and fro in planetary sorrow for my little ones. For nature may only bear its portion; the elementals have horizons beyond which they cannot serve the will of man. In that there comes a point in time when the entire nature and mineral kingdoms will revolt against the weight of darkness. Then, my beloved ones, get ye to the hills and the high plains, and take ye what little may be your needs, and hide thyself from the wrath of nature unleashed in your generation.

6. Modern warriors have called forth massive machineries of death to cover the land with their aggressive invasions of life. Let them come. Let them bluster across the land. Let them polish their steel, patrol the seas, and hurl defiance from the skies; it shall come to no avail. For the weapons that are formed against another shall be turned upon those that have formed them. The mentation to destroy, projected toward another, shall be turned again unto the destruction of those who hath sent it. For the earth is the Lord's and the fullness thereof, and

the terrestrial entity shall turn against the inhabitants thereof who plot its devastation. As an animal shakes itself free of the waters upon it, so shall creation shake itself free of those who would annihilate it.

7. Many generations have read of these days. Many have come and gone who have studied the words of my beloved Son, but the Words remain to call this day, "Come, ye blessed of My Father, inherit the Kingdom prepared for you from the foundation of the world." The Light of His Love shall go forth like the sunrise, dispelling the darkness of the world's karma; dissolving the mists of confusion, liberating nature to return to its former glory. You, my children, shall be overshadowed by the Angel of His Presence.

8 & 9. Teach thy young the promises of His Protection. Be an example of calmness in chaos, and serenity in the storm. Let them join with you in expecting His blessing and hearing His voice. For, as they experience Love Divine, Love shall be drawn to them. In all that shall beset you throughout the years of the Eighties, Love shall overshadow my children, and Love shall be your buckler and shield, and, if need be, Love shall be thy token of deliverance. I am the Mother of Beloved Jesus,

Mary

Points to Ponder or Group Discussion

1. This book is a roadmap.
2. We are on the threshold of the tribulation.
3. Our children are in danger!
4. Revolt of the nature kingdom.
5. High altitudes recommended.
6. War plots boomerang.
7. The calm in the eye of the storm.
8. Should the children's minds be prepared for possible future changes?
9. Do I exemplify calmness and serenity in all situations?

Stand Tall in the Trial By Fire
By El Morya

GOOD evening, child of light. Greetings in the sign of the Heart, Head and Hand unto you. This is Morya speaking. I do not wish to be omitted from this effort sponsored by my dear brother and friend, Kuthumi, and I am here to keep my appointment as promised. We are all very grateful for your energies that are given to us, for we are greatly in need of the assistance of our chelas in embodiment. As our eyes go to and fro upon the earth, there is ever a search for steadfast souls who will jump into the fray and carry on the battle for Light.

1. Now let us consider some things relevant to the decade before your world. The present severe economic upheaval can only go into deeper complications before it can be resolved. We do not anticipate any phenomenal solutions along these lines in the early part of this decade. The thinking of man must aright itself. As right thinking is applied to all the levels of life, humanity will find a change taking place even in the great financial hierarchies of the planet, for man must release all things and exercise his stewardship of wealth along with other responsibilities. The money manipulators and the cartel of energy czars shall be leveled to normal size when the earth is tossed by the winds of change. The centers of Mammon that line many coastlines shall be washed of their contaminations forever.

Presently, and in the immediate future, Cosmic rays are being shed upon your globe that will help to break down the competitive thought forms of humanity, and materialistic avenues of expression. Thought patterns, that ever flow around the planet, will be injected with transfusions of high-level energies, penetrating and affecting the decisions and choices everywhere. These changes wrought on the mental level will generate a friction with existing surrounding thought patterns. Thus, the very atmosphere will vibrate in conflict as thought form clashes against thought form. These clouds of resistance shall be dealt with by a cleansing of the very air itself. Great winds and waters, as forces of cleansing, join their energies to purify the ethers and the astral belt.

2. Then shall come a clearer vision, enabling the citizens of Terra to approach earth's problems from a higher plateau of solution. That day will come when the desert lands shall blossom as the rose, and drought shall be no more. In

the New Birth of the land many will grow into greatness and the stature of stalwart sons and daughters of God. At the community level, before that time, brotherhood and concern for neighbor shall be mellowed with love and compassion, as group action increases in response to repeated emergencies.

3. Let us move on. We, the Masters of the Karmic Board, have directed that global war shall not be permitted to destroy this planet. Neither shall the chelas and the watching souls be taken unawares. The fiat of the highest council in the solar system has decreed that no nation shall venture forth upon other nations in a manner that would lead to the annihilation of the earth itself. Watchmen ever guarding, ever patrolling the actions and decisions of the secret councils of the nations, are never without complete and full awareness of all proposals and plans. Any action that leads into disturbances on an interplanetary level, shall precipitate Divine Intervention and retaliating disciplines. The Universal decree, now in effect, provides for Unity and Peace throughout the Solar System and the Alliance of the Universes. This Cosmic Law shall be enforced by the Angelic Forces under the administration of the Blue Ray of Will and Power. Know ye not that those events of cataclysmic nature, which the time tables of men have scheduled to appear sometime during the 21st century, have now been stepped up, and they shall become the instruments of Divine Intervention, if the course of humanity is bent on nuclear destruction. Blazing paths of fire, flaming across the darkened sky, in thunderings of awesome sights never before experienced by man in his evolutions, shall be the harvest resulting from the perversion of planetary energies.

4. You have studied your heavens. You have seen the setting of the stage overhead, in the stationing of the rendezvous of the starry bodies. To the wise the guidance is written. Yet man, with the flame of life burning within, and a spiritual desire to turn from genocide and debauchery, can overrule by 'the momentum of reversal, and the authority of embodiment can overrule, I say, the very stars in their courses, by the Power of His call to us.

5. I am El Morya. I administer unto you the manifestation of Divine Will and Power. Call upon me, and I will release, within the entire being, a strengthening of Will and Determination, that will cause my chelas to stand tall in the trial by fire, and come from it without even the smell of smoke upon them. Fear not what man shall do to thee, if thy determinations are fixed upon thy starry destiny. Hold thy staff of faith firmly, and face the winds of tribulation as

they come. Take your stand for Rightness, and having done all, STAND; in the Power of the Will of El Morya who bathes thy four lower bodies in the Blue Flame of Protection, for Deliverance in this decade. Choose ye, to be willing to be made willing, to walk the pathway of the Ascended Masters which shines in splendor as a ribbon of Light, cutting through the densities of darkness that settle upon the world.

I am saluting all who read my words,
El Morya

Points to Ponder or for Group Discussion

1. Can negative thought levels affect world economies?
2. Community togetherness in disaster.
3. Nuclear war will precipitate Divine Intervention in the form of cataclysms.
4. Is it within the power of mankind to weaken these forces?
5. How are the chelas of the Masters protected?

COSMIC REVELATIONS TILL THE END OF TIME

The Invisible Fortress of Love
By Archangel Michael

HAIL to you, o daughter of God! I am Michael, the Archangel of Protection. I am He who carries ~he mighty sword of Blue Flame, for the protection of America and the souls of Light everywhere upon the planet.

1 & 2. I am integrating the forces of Light, with a blending ray of Blue Flame throughout the planet to encourage these forces to begin to think as one and work in unison, to join forces against the tides of evil. Armageddon and the battle for men's minds is upon us. We of the Celestial realms have moved into close proximity to the planet for the purpose of perpetuating the Blue flame wherever it is needed.

3 & 4. When the dark clouds of thought forms of war, or international emergencies gather in the heavens surrounding the Earth, it is our concerted action and the action of the Blue Flame which disperse~ and scatters these clouds, weakening or dissolving their propulsions and destructive energies. The momentum toward nuclear global conflict polarizing upon the planet is not an idle threat. There remains continuing danger to the world from those who do not project their thinking beyond their own horizon. The time has come when men of military stature, and the statesmen of the world, must look beyond the security of their own borders, and carefully weigh the threat to humanity everywhere of their decisions. There are forces at work upon the planet, which left to their own devices and the fulfillment of the greed of their hearts, would of a certainty, lead to the eradication of an entire planet. THIS HAS HAPPENED BEFORE IN THE HISTORY OF THE SOLAR SYSTEM, BUT IT SHALL NOT HAPPEN AGAIN!

5. The Angelic Host has received orders from on high that the earth shall be spared as if by a miracle, from the expulsions of dark minds. As these emanations of darkness would rise up against the great rising tide of Light, there shall be a reverberating reaction within the planet itself and its surrounding atmospheres, so that great uncontrollable fusions and eruptions shall give echo to the spiritual imbalance in your environments.

6. Nevertheless, the Angels of God shall stand beside the children of Light wherever circumstances have placed them, as guardians and protectors of the invincible sons and daughters

of God. Let fear not be found among you. Fear hath no place in the heart filled with Light and Love. As your planet enters its next dimension, many will fall or be taken, or meet with mishap, right up to your very doors. Stand ye in faith and Love, calling upon the Angels of God to stand with you and invoke the circle of Blue Flame around your home, your entire situation, until this too shall pass.

7. Realize, as you hear the rumblings of threatened war and the rumors of war or prophecies of dire things to come, and the call to preparedness against those days, know ye within your hearts, that it shall not come nigh thee who walk in love with thy brethren and thy neighbor. For Love is a fulfillment of the Christ Presence within every man. Love is the seal of protection. Love is the impenetrable armor. Love is the invincible fortress that cannot be penetrated by the destroyer. Take heart that though for a little while there shall be turmoil and chaos, it is for a little season and for Divine purpose. Hope your own heart is purified by the Presence of Love, then Peace shall reign within your own world, despite the confusion that surrounds you. I speak upon my Authority as Governor of this Solar System presiding over the solar consciousness of Will and Power. I have sent forth the command that those having that Seal of Light and Love, shall have the assistance and protection of every member of the Angelic Host, for I remain, your Protector, Archangel Michael

Points to Ponder or for Group Discussion

1. Forces of Light are to be integrated. Unity is essential.
2. Angels closer to earth from now on.
3. War momentum dispersed by Blue Flame.
4. The planet is to be spared.
5. Nature echoes the spiritual imbalance of humanity.
6. Our "Protectors" must be called.
7. Love is the answer.
8. The Seal in the forehead (Rev. 7:2).

COSMIC REVELATIONS TILL THE END OF TIME

The Balanced Ledger

By Saint Germain

I greet you in the flame of my being. I am known as St. Germain on planetary levels, and Elihu in celestial realm. I place my blessing upon this volume foursquare, sent forth by the Brotherhood, under the sponsoring of my friend Kuthumi, World Teacher. It is my privilege to have been given this opportunity to speak.

1. We of the Great Karmic Board have much to deliberate concerning the coming decade for the world. All things progress under Divine Will – somethings are permitted, others are ordained to be. There is an unbalanced ledger in the name of this nation which cannot be tampered with. Nevertheless, we do extend mercy and compassion in all of our decisions and extend all possible leniency in administrating our final decrees.

2. The listening angels and the angel with the writer's inkhorn by his side, fail not to tally every intention and provocation of the human heart. Souls cluster in groups, around an ideology or a principle, and become nations. As nations, their group karma for good or ill, is registered in the great heavenly records. America has accumulated great good through many centuries of benevolence toward all, with a friendliness and an inclination toward the ongoing Light of God and the principles of freedom.

3. In a broad aspect these principles have been maintained and upheld. But in last two decades, there has been an alarming trend away from those principles instituted by the founders of America. Questionable alliances have been encouraged. The foundation of the currency has been allowed to flow into dangerous shoals of threatening shipwreck of the economy. Hidden malignant forces have been permitted to seize inner control of the government.

4. The principles under God that made this nation an instrument of Light, have suffered at the hands of infiltrators who have betrayed the spirit of the true American heritage. The watchmen have slept at their post and the guardsmen have winked their eye, but the hand of the angel with the writer's inkhorn by his side, writes on. With all of our great extended mercy, there is a record, yet to be reckoned with by America, which only the Great Lawgiver can balance. The

destiny of this nation under God, as a shining star in the firmament, shall not be denied. A cleansing tide shall sweep the land of the debris of the dark ones. From the highest office in the land to the lowly cabin upon the mountainside, purity and dedication to one nation under God shall motivate the deeds of all that dwell therein. That which is better shall supplant that which is lesser, and new golden cities shall dot the terrain.

5. The face of the land shall change, but the hearts of the citizens shall be united in the manifestation of brotherly love and goodwill. The birth pangs of a New Age will bring a moment of travail, it is true, but that travail shall soon be forgotten in the joy of a New World in all of its beauty. As you face the coming decade~ know that the balancing shall be accomplished. Those who have given their energies, and their time and talents toward the higher way of life and to the incoming Light, shall have the security and protection under the canopy of the Ascended Masters of America. The great beings and super-intelligences that have guided an America down through the centuries shall, in this time of restoration, project a pillar of cloud of their Presence to all those who have known their names. I have endowed the planet with the glowing, transmuting violet flame, and my violet angels know the identity and the whereabouts of every soul who has ever called my name. My electronic presence is beside those who read my words. Call upon the transmuting violet flame in cleansing action to perpetuate the purification of your environment and your world.

I remain, your benefactor,

St. Germain

Points to Ponder or for Group Discussion

1. America's descending karma tempered with mercy but cannot be cancelled.
2. Group souls and hearts.
3. Give examples of the decline of national spiritual principles.
4. What was the American Heritage?
5. What are the birth pangs of New Age?
6. The Divine Presence.

COSMIC REVELATIONS TILL THE END OF TIME

The Orbit of Destiny
By Lord Maitreya

1. **I** am Maitreya. I am your speaker for this hour. My words come to you out of the Great Central Sun and the sovereignty of the Great Cosmic Government. I am the Voice of that Government. I bring the blessing of the Most High and the Heavenly Host, with my coming and my words.

2. On this beautiful afternoon I will speak concerning the orbit of destiny that has been ordained for the planet earth since time began. For all worlds find their divine pathway, their foreordained destiny by order of the Creator. The world in which you abide must follow its foreordained direction into a new orbit of time and space. With the ending of the old and the beginning of the new, the entrance upon these pathways of destiny is written in the books of heaven and they must come to pass.

3. The orb of Terra has leaned itself awry for much too long. The day of reckoning and setting into place is upon you. No living being can alter the course that is decreed for the future of the world. The time of travail cannot be bypassed, for the birth of the New Order must come. That which has been, has not reflected the Divine Plan. But the Plan shall be fulfilled when all things are made right. The heavens sing together for joy in anticipation of that exalted Day, when the mighty lines of force shall be aligned once again. Vast vortices of energy shall spiral from the chakras of the globe and the Kingdom of God with all the lesser kingdoms shall dwell in harmony and peace, and no more shall the earth groan within itself.

4. Tremendous magnetic forces released from within, shall attract to the earth all of the necessary energies required to transform it to a place of beauty and love, once again. It must be, that polarity be wedded with purpose and that all of the planet and those thereon shall live for the Glory of the Most High. I, Maitreya, invest the planet with my own momentum and surround it with my force field of Perfection. It shall be glorified in all of its beauty as it was intended to be by the Creator. It shall be cleansed of all that is unlike the glowing Light and that which is not a part of that Light shall be separated from its midst. Those who have proven themselves worthy of

that Light shall inherit the New Earth to inaugurate the New Dispensation. Rejoice in the Day of the Lord and the Day of the Perfecting of all things. Externalities may end, but your planet shall merge on the pathway to its destiny as a place prepared for beings of Light and Love. A place worthy of those who shall inhabit it.

5. I, Maitreya, pour my vial of cleansing flame upon the planet, that Divine Will shall be fulfilled. Under Universal Law all negative manifestation precipitated upon the earth by the will of man, must defer to divine cleansing action. The divine right of personal choice, endowed upon all creation, will inexorably set into motion the cleansing of itself. It is ordained that those who choose not to enter the new environment, shall not be forced to do so, but quite to the contrary, shall be escorted to a place prepared according to their choices. The fiat of Light has been released, and that Day must come. I am, Mai trey a

Points to Ponder or for Group Discussion

1. The Greater System billions of miles away, around which seven solar systems revolve together.
2. There are 12 fields of expression, and a difference of Cosmic energies received with different vibratory rates. Our own solar system is presently leaving the Piscean field and entering the Aquarian field of expression and new vibrations.
3. Chakras of the planet become source of great energy supply where New Age cities will be located.
4. A new earth.
5. Planetary karma.

COSMIC REVELATIONS TILL THE END OF TIME

The Masters of Invocation
By Hilarion

1. **GOOD** evening. I am Hilarion. I have come to share some of my thoughts for the little book and to add my blessings to those already extended to its readers. I speak concerning the need at this hour for fifth ray energies to be manifested upon and through mankind. I am calling for a great outpouring of spiritual renewal upon the earth. Many hundreds of Great Beings are gathered in my Emerald City, working together in the projection of thought upon the planet in the manifestation of the green ray of life. These Great Ones, who serve with me, gather together in the Great Hall of my Temple, and meditate upon the need of those who have chosen the Pathway of Light. There are many souls who stand at the very doors of an awakening of their spiritual awareness and spiritual gifts, which they have earned over many lifetimes by their earnestness and sincere seeking, and the application of right principles to life.

2. In the Higher Octave, we meditate and visualize the expansion of that Light, the expansion of awareness of your spiritual birthright and your God Presence within. We concentrate and meditate upon the human potential as embodied sons and daughters of God. We invoke the Light that your dominion and your Mastery shall flow through your entire being. Then indeed shall the earth be filled with Glory!

3. I do not choose to dwell upon unpleasant aspects of the coming days which contribute to the cleansing of the planet, but rather, I elect to discuss the great benefits that are imminent. Eyes have not seen, ears have not heard, nor can the imagination conceive of the great blessings that await the inspired one through the incoming vibrations and spiritual rays that are to be applied on inner levels. The Most Beloved Master has given a promise along these lines with these words: "Blessed are they which do hunger and thirst after righteousness, for they shall be filled-blessed are the meek, for they shall inherit the earth."

4. I would speak of the ongoing of the Light upon the planet and the faithfulness of the dedicated Light Workers. Until such time as the night cometh when no man can work, you are our hands and feet and our very presence in the physical octave. Without each and every one of you and those that come, our

COSMIC REVELATIONS TILL THE END OF TIME

Plans would be without an anchor, and our hopes for mankind would be curtailed. But because we have hearts such as yours, who have chosen to read this very book, we of the etheric realms can know that the salt of the earth continues its work. We can WIN – as long as the children of Light fulfill their mission and stand undaunted by opposition, discouragement, and threats of changes to come. We know that as long as we have this anchor represented by all of you, the Light cannot fail! There are many discordant voices in the land today who know nothing of the inner meaning of the Light upon the planet. Many who go their way in self pursuits and ill-conceived projections for their future, do not reckon with the invocations of Light that go forth from my Temple Hall. These Great Ones are gathered daily, hourly, to invoke the coming of Light upon the planet Earth. They invoke the presence of Light in the great meetings of your governing bodies and invoke the infiltration of light throughout all the lower kingdoms-the kingdom of the air and of the sea, and all of nature. The incoming Light of God shall accommodate itself to the diverse needs during the planetary cleansing. The Light shall work with this cleansing in a positive way, where positiveness is present. The Masters of Invocation of the Fifth Ray have declared and sent forth the fiat that the Light of Earth shall expand, expand, expand. In the given momentum of the times, souls will discover great spiritual strength to fearlessly face the challenge of the coming decade. Look neither to the right nor to the left, but steadfastly fix thy gaze upon thy deliverance.

5. It is written that in those days no man shall teach his neighbor, for all shall be guided by the Spirit within. My friends, that day is upon you. When the preparation has finished and the turmoil has ceased, all shall hear the whispering Voice saying, "This is the way; walk therein." Then a great sigh shall come forth from all of creation, when the natural openings of Spirit shall be cleared, manifesting the blessings of the Fifth Ray upon humanity. The gifts which have been sought for so long shall be found and realized by the fulfillment of these things. Blessed are they who findeth the way and who can consciously face the decade;_to come in absolute confidence and peace within. Know that beyond the Cross of these times will come the glory of a new earth, a new world, to shine as a new star in the firmament. We are holding YOU in that Great Light.
I Am,

Hilarion

Points to Ponder or for Group Discussion

1. Fifth Ray energies vital during transition period.
2. The power of creative meditation.
3. "Greater works ... " and limitless blessings.
4. God's Infantry.
5. Man is his own teacher.

Section Two

World Changes

COSMIC REVELATIONS TILL THE END OF TIME

The Focus of Change

A new birthing is imminent
Which transcends all understanding
Of life as we know it on earth.
The planets are lining up,
Waiting for orders
To march in procession.
A grand scheme of the Universe
Is making its claim,
As each one falls in place
In ordered succession.
What powers there be
That call spheres by their name!
To move out in action
To further the Plan
Of God's Divine Purpose
Created for man.
So let us stand steadfast
And welcome the changes
That will help us to grow
Into more understanding
Of all of His ways;
Let's welcome His fiery
Celestial show!

-Eileen Schoen

The Fall of Exterior Religion

By ESU (Jesus The Christ)

1 & 2. **MY** name is ESU on Celestial levels, known to earth as Jesus the Christ. I Am the Way, the Truth and the Life. For these many centuries, I have looked upon the souls of men as they scurry hither and yon upon the earth, striving with their ambitions, forcing themselves forward in their desire for self esteem. I have watched with much disheartenment as the institutions which bear My Name have long forsaken My Principles and overlooked My Teachings. I have stood by in the shadows, while those intended to represent My Work and My Words have forsaken Me utterly in their struggles for political place among their fellows. I have seen hunger within the hearts of those who have come into these edifices and I have watched them go their way unfilled.

3. While great human need on a mass level prevails throughout the planet, I have observed the spending of vast sums of millions and millions of dollars on temples of stone that men might glory thereby, but these shall crumble in the dust. This ostentatious-ness in My Name has grieved my heart again and again. I did not give My Life for such as this. I did not come to be made into a God. I came as one of you, to show you the Divine Possibilities that abide within every human life. I came to show the Way, the Path, the Truth, but the world has chosen to exalt Me and My Name, but to ignore and forsake My Teachings of the inner kingdom.

4. There has come One to take up My Work within the hearts of humanity. The Christ Presence within each soul, continues to lead and to show the Way. This is My Contact and My Outreach to every soul upon the planet. As you pay homage to the Christ Presence within your neighbor and your brother, you pay homage to Me and My Words. As you extend the Love of God around your planet to all in need of that Love, you extend your Love to Me. There is so much talk of Christianity upon the earth, but so little of the Presence of the spirit of Christ. Churchianity abounds and divisions compound within it. But there is so little of My Teaching in action in the life of humanity.

COSMIC REVELATIONS TILL THE END OF TIME

5. But all of this will change as the earth is born into a New Day. *Exterior religion will fall away* and inner awareness will become the strength of those who follow Me. I shall walk with them and be in their midst, for they shall endure.

6. I speak of the ramifications of all that is involved in the immediate years before you, of all that is to be in these latter days. Many shall be moved by the higher vibrations that come to you. Many shall cease their occupation with foolishness and will turn to the depth and the meaning of existence. Many will call upon Me for guidance and My Presence shall be with them in the midnight hour of coming events. When these events appear in a manner beyond their control, thoughts of My Sheep shall be turned towards My Words and spiritual Law. When the judgment hour is upon the planet, then shall the Shepherds consider and wonder if they also shall be weighed in the balance and found wanting.

7. There have been many warnings sent forth throughout My Father's Kingdom. There have been whisperings within hearts and there shall be a rushing to and fro when these things begin to come to pass, as My Children seek to scurry into places of safety. I call My Children to move thyself within thy lands, away from the water, for much shall be cleansed from thy shores, by the washing of the waters. If ye believe MY Words, then ye will withdraw away from the waters that they will not overflow thee and thy dwelling. Many winds will come, but My Children shall be warned. Listen ye for the still small voice within thy being, and be not hesitant to respond, but quicken thy understanding and get thyself up and away quickly.

8. Lay by in store for thyselves, thy supply, that ye be not found wanting in the days of crisis. Think ye that your world as ye know it, shall go on forever? I say unto thee, My Children, expect the unexpected and be ye prepared. Be ye wise as serpents and harmless as doves, that in these years of cleansing ye shall be found within the circle of My Love.

9. Times, and time and a half of time shall be thy endurance, and seven shall be the completion of the Day. Then shall ye know that stillness and peace have come, and deliverance hath come to the land. Then shall the birds of the air take flight again. Then shall the earth be stilled from its turmoil and then shall ye know that righteousness and joy shall inherit the Kingdom, and Love shall rise as the tide. Blessed are ye that shall inherit the earth, for behold I make a new earth,

and ye shall be the inhabitants thereof. Ye shall go forth with singing and rejoicing that the end of thy tribulations hath come. Then shall I walk beside thee. Then shall My Words be with thee, and My breath shall be in thy ear. The world will be filled with gladness and harmony, and each shall turn to help his neighbor and all that one hath shall be shared with another and none shall know need or want in My Father's Kingdom. The darkness of the storm is but for a moment of time that the land may be bathed in freshness and newness once again. Then the sun rises upon it in splendor revealing its true beauty. Thus the earth will become green and clean again. The air shall be pure and wholesome. The spirit of men shall be mellowed and loving and life will explore new advancements for the good of all, and every soul shall know that I have been with them to deliver them. They shall rub shoulders with those whom they have called the "angels," yet whom they have come to know as brothers from other worlds. The blessings of inter-dimensional fellowship, and interplanetary coexistence will lead the earth into heights of glory so long prepared for it. Nothing shall neither hurt nor destroy in all of the Kingdom. Mastery shall be over one's soul, and not over thy brother. Through great releases of incoming knowledge and new discoveries, all sickness shall pass away. The young shall grow freely, without fear of defilement, and the law shall be written in human hearts. Great shall be the brightness of My Father's Kingdom. His Grace is sufficient for thee to prepare to enter therein.

I Am ESU, known to earth as

Jesus The Christ

COSMIC REVELATIONS TILL THE END OF TIME

Points to Ponder or for Group Discussion

1. Souls have Celestial names (Hsu), solar system names (Sananda) and (many) planetary names (Jesus).
2. His parting words were, "Feed My Sheep."
3. The spiritual temple not made with hands.
4. The integration of all Creation through the Christ Presence.
5. Reality *vs.* illusion.
6. The greatest revival in history.
7. Shorelines unsafe areas.
8. Survival preparations necessary.
9. The stillness that follows the storm.

COSMIC REVELATIONS TILL THE END OF TIME

11:00AM - The Third Day Time Can Wait No Longer
By NADA

GOOD morning, Tuella. I AM Mother Mary. I have come in this morning to bring you one who has served so well on the feminine ray in My Name. I come to introduce Ascended Lady Master Nada for her morning appointment. She has not spoken with you before, and I am very happy to bring you together. Beloved Lady Master Nada is very well informed, very dedicated and very alert to the times that are approaching. She speaks with you now:

1. Greetings, my sister. I greet you in the Name of the Great I Am Presence within us all. I am Nada, and I know that you have followed the words of the Ascended Masters for many years. It is all on the record, you know. Every moment spent listening to their words, in person, in meditation, on tape or in print, or even calling their names; all of these things are recorded within the energy field which responds to those vibrations and absorbs the Light from the Ascended Ones.

2. I am delighted to contribute to these messages. This is a very crucial time when guidance is greatly needed. There cannot be too much of it released to the souls who struggle with their decisions. There is a fear abroad in the land. Perhaps on outer levels it would seem that pleasure and worldly pursuits have the upper hand, but one cannot rightly discern from these. Within the hearts of thousands and thousands of persons, there is a gradual awakening and an acceptance of the fact that the world stands upon the threshold of great change. There is a trend towards a "buckling down" kind of attitude that prevails, and this is commendable. Where there has been a preoccupation with play, and fun and games, now humanity must grow up.

3. As we view the world panorama from our vantage point, it is naturally a sorrowing sight to see present conditions throughout the planet. All of life, and nature groans under the pressure of the weight of negativity and destructive thought forms. We would contain the results of these penetrations and dark emanations if that were possible. We do coordinate Divine Plans to ease the burden of planetary change as much as is possible under Universal Law. But in these times which signal the end of things as they have been, we are limited in the

COSMIC REVELATIONS TILL THE END OF TIME

depth of our intervention. For there is a cleansing taking place as almost everyone is aware, and this is scheduled to come to pass. It MUST come to pass, and even now lags far behind the ordained time table. The world has not kept pace with the hopes and the plans of the Hierarchy, for its evolution and its transition into the higher frequencies for the coming Age. Time can wait no longer! The Galaxy must continue on its given pathway. Time cannot stand still while mankind dawdles on his upward spiral. Humanity must pace itself to the times of the Age. The time is NOW for finding the pathway, completing the preparations, and donning the protection of Light for the changes that must come.

4. There is a great movement within the very bowels of the earth, that slowly rolls and rumbles and murmurs its coming threat. The planet cannot escape its murmurs within, but by the help of the heavenly forces and many helpers that serve the Light, much gentling can be given in this transition which lays aside the old and puts on the new. Many Beings and many Great Ones have come great distances to assist the Solar and Planetary Hierarchies in the challenge of the coming decade. There will be sweeping changes in the very face of the land and the shape of the bodies of water. There will be changes in the lifestyles because of prudent necessity. There will be changes in the thinking and mental levels of humanity. For coming in with the great scope of physical changes, will be the sweeping tides of change in attitudes toward the simplicities of life and the things that are vital. Those who have until now been detrimental to the advancement of Light, and continue in that frame of mind, will no longer be present to compete with that Light. Their adjustments to the uplifting of all life will not be possible, and they will be removed in one manner or another. The remnant will find harmony and cooperation advancing smoothly and suddenly it will seem that Brotherhood exists upon the earth once again, as souls are freed by the cleansing of the atmospheres, to expand the good that is inherent within every heart.

5 & 6. We of the Great Karmic Board, are jointly extending great mercy and great latitude during the decade to come. Great leniency will be the mood of the tribunal, as we serve in these coming days. Those who "will" to do the good, will find the good within them and the ability to do. I would speak directly to those who struggle to keep afloat in throes of financial disorder and economic chaos, and those who strive so valiantly to lead their children into right paths, and those who serve in the Armies of Light; to all of these who struggle against great odds in

their personal battles, I say to you, help is on the way! The great incoming rays will strengthen you in all of these efforts and bring results undreamed of, if you will address your calls to the Great Karmic Board of heaven.

7. Through the cleansing of the earth, and the manifested assistance of the heavenly host and the beams of Light, the sons and daughters of God can rise to their dominion over the trials of this transition. Those who have walked with God and sought His Will, whatever your earthly religion may be; if you desire His Light to shine upon you, your calls will be answered. The world around you may experience great unpleasantness and sufferings in the coming world changes; nevertheless, those who have looked heavenward for their sustenance and their security, shall not fall. If necessary, you shall literally be lifted up into the heavens away from it all, and the world will not even know that you are gone. If that is not necessary, you shall be overshadowed by the Presence of those who represent the Hierarchy of heaven, dedicated to your protection and your survival. Let not fear be found within you, but look to the heavens from whence cometh your help. I pledge to you that all who read my words shall be sheltered beneath the everlasting arms of God's Love.

I Am,

Nada

COSMIC REVELATIONS TILL THE END OF TIME

Points to Ponder or for Group Discussion

1. The absorption of Light from celestial contacts.
2. Serious reflection changes nebulous attitudes.
3. The contagious contamination of astral effluvia
4. Geological disasters gentled by Space Ship activities.
5. The armor within.
6. The struggle to exist in modem society.
7. Dominion over the trials of life is the birthright of God's children.

COSMIC REVELATIONS TILL THE END OF TIME

7:00 PM-The Third Day The Flow of Wisdom

By Hermes

GOOD evening, friend of the Light. I have come to keep my promise at the appointed time. My name is Hermes, I am a Master and Teacher of Universal Wisdom. I am your speaker for the evening. You have known of me and studied my principles. It has been my function to bring the hidden wisdom to Light, upon the planet. The principles I brought to earth are the foundation of the Ancient Wisdom in all the Mystery Schools since the beginning of time. It has been my privilege in many cultures to teach the ancient secrets of the unfolding of the soul of man. These secrets have been recorded in the religions of the world.

My teachings have been adopted in many ways and presented from many positions by great world teachers. But basically, all of the important bodies of wisdom literatures that follow truth are based upon the principles of Hermes. I am the Father of Truth and Understanding. It is the energy which I project into and through Universal Mind which leads to the quickening and enlightenment of the Thinker within you. Humanity now comes to this crucial hour when the divine wisdom shall flow like a river. When every living soul that abides upon the new earth shall desire the knowledge that comes from on high.

I am Hermes, and I will be pouring Love and Wisdom into the understanding of mankind, through the rays that are contributing to this transition. The teaching of Light that has been gradually released into the lower octaves of earth, has contributed to all the good things that have advanced life upon the planet. For as a man thinketh in his heart, so is he. Wisdom is like that candle that a man lighteth and set upon a bushel, and it giveth Light to all in the house. Wisdom is a divine attribute of the triune being.

It is that portion of inheritance in the manifestation of the Heavenly Father through His Creation. Wisdom shall unfold as the rose, and from this moment on, each petal shall gradually unfold in a gentle way that will lead to beauty and maturity within the souls of men.

We are inaugurating new schools of Universal Wisdom and expending our energies for the input of the teachings. The great Light which once was only to be found in the secret rooms and the secret orders shall now be shouted from the housetops. Man shall come to understand the divine philosophies and the majestic principles that will lead him to a knowledge of his inner being and his Godself.

The ancient teachings have progressed down through the centuries, with continuing releases of Light through chosen ones. But this has been as the pace of the snail in comparison to that which is to come. In these days, and this decade, the principles of Hermes shall be incorporated into every walk of life, as the earth steps forth into its new era of revelation and understanding. It is a paradox that the grip of confusion within minds of men has been such that the darkness has been exalted as the way of Light, and the way of Light and self-understanding has been relegated to the darkness. Such is the confusion that has reigned throughout the ages. In the new order of things, your teachers will not be found in the fine robes upon the rostrum of ecclesiastica, but your great teachers shall be found in all walks of life, in the humble pathway, in the small groups of seekers, in the byways and the quiet places of life. My energies shall project wisdom and enlightenment to all whose hearts and minds are open to an affinity with Universal Mind. Humble unschooled hearts shall drink from the fountains of heavenly wisdom and drink from them fully.

Each man shall become a priest unto his own household. This is the day that separates the false from the true. Look not to the credentials of men and the authorities of those who rule over them. But seek ye the flow and wisdom and truth wherever it may be found, within, or without. The day of separation of priesthood and laity is gone forever, washed downstream in the pulsating rising tide of awareness and the vibrations of a new dispensation. Look not to the exalting of men, that would rule over that which God shall reveal to thee in the secret place.

But rather, follow after truth as it has been given to thee by thy Godself within. Find the great freedom to receive, freedom to learn, freedom to know, freedom to understand, freedom to absorb, to enjoy the heavenly breezes of divine truth blowing through the open doors of your mind. The relentless flow of Universal Wisdom by my impetus shall come to all. Do not fear to separate yourself from those who do not choose to walk with truth. Leave them behind, in their painted sepulchers filled with dead men's bones. Turn your face toward the fresh blessing of personal revelation.

COSMIC REVELATIONS TILL THE END OF TIME

I, Hermes, will lead you and bring to you kindred souls in the brotherhood of Wisdom. This transition also brings its time of unpleasantness with difficult physical disturbances and environmental adjustments. But throughout any personal struggles you will have a kind of guidance you have never experienced before, because you have pursued the pathway of wisdom and truth. As the planet ascends into higher vibrations of Light, those of you who have occupied your thinking with the great philosophies built upon the Hermetic Principles, will ascend also into those octaves of growth and spiritual blessing.

My closing words are designed to give courage to those who read. Fear not for the changes that come, for they bring with them spiritual knowledge and wisdom and understanding that are as yet undreamed of in the mind of humanity. I leave with you my benediction of wisdom and Light.

I Am,
Hermes

COSMIC REVELATIONS TILL THE END OF TIME

Points to Ponder or for Group Discussion

(The principles of Hermes are here reprinted for your convenience)

The Seven Laws of the Hermetic Philosophy

1. The principle of mentalism. ALL IS MIND, THE UNIVERSE IS MENTAL. This principle explains the true nature of energy, power and matter.

2. The principle of correspondence. AS ABOVE, SO BELOW; AS BELOW, SO ABOVE. This principle enables man to reason intelligently from the known to the unknown.

3. The principle of vibration. NOTHING RESTS; EVERYTHING MOVES; EVERYTHING VIBRATES. This principle explains that the difference between manifestations of matter, energy, mind, and Spirit result from varying rates of vibration.

4. The principle of polarity. ALL IS DUALITY. EVERYTHING HAS POLES; EVERYTHING HAS ITS PAIRS OF OPPOSITES; LIKE AND UNLIKE ARE THE SAME. Opposites are identical but different in degree. Opposites are only two extremes of the same thing, with many varying degrees between.

5. THE UNIVERSE IS RHYTHM. Everything flows out, and in; everything has its tides; all things rise and fall. The pendulum swing manifests in everything, rhythm compensates. This principle of neutralization applies in affairs of the Universe, suns, worlds; in life, mind, energy, matter. There is always an action and a reaction, an advance and a retreat.

6. The principle of causation. EVERY CAUSE HAS ITS EFFECT; EVERY EFFECT HAS ITS CAUSE; EVERYTHING HAPPENS ACCORDING TO LAW. CHANCE IS BUT A NAME FOR LAW NOT RECOGNIZED. THERE ARE MANY PLANES OF CAUSATION, BUT NOTHING ESCAPES THE LAW.

7. The principle of Gender. Gender is in everything, everything has its masculine and feminine principles. Gender manifests on all planetary levels. Every thing or person contains the two principles within it, him or her.

From THE KYBALION:

"The lips of wisdom are closed, except to the ears of understanding."

7:00 AM-The Fourth Day Health in the New Age

By Zoser

HELLO again, Tuella. This is Zoser returning as promised and very anxious to speak with you once more. I enjoyed our last brief conversation and I have not forgotten you or your work for the Brotherhood. I am a Master of Healing, a teacher of healing and pyramidology. For I was the first builder of the Pyramid in your dimension.

1 & 2. I have come to speak regarding the healing art and technique, particularly the innovations that will contribute to "HEALTH IN THE NEW AGE." We are entering an entirely different era in the science of healing. The cycle just ending has been predominantly the day of surgery and the dispensing of drugs on a frightening scale. In the awakening that is at the very door, electronics will be the primary tool of the healing practitioner. Science will awaken to the electronic field as it applies to diagnosing the human aura. Research in this field under the sponsorship of the guiding Guardians, from the higher Archives of Wisdom, will lead to the introduction of diagnostic devices of this nature. The New Age physician will need to become familiar with these devices. In the New Age, instruments will be in g it with the sensitive instrument, somewhat similar in appearance to the remote control device used with your television sets. The sensitive equipment will absorb the currents within the human aura and register them on a graph, literally drawing a picture for the healer. A large screen will show the outline of the human form, and as the auric scanning proceeds, electronic sketches will appear upon the screen. Where weakness prevails, or disease is present in any portion of the anatomy, disharmony of any kind will be located on the screen sketch. This, then, is the new direction for diagnostic procedures.

3. Proceeding from diagnosis to treatment, the New Age physician will then turn to another newly projected piece of electronic equipment. The auric penetrating equipment will beam a force-field of healing ray to that area in need of balance as indicated. Healing will take place in the physical form as the electronic beam is administered through the electromagnetic field of the body of the patient, the treatment being administered to the identical spot in the human auric field.

COSMIC REVELATIONS TILL THE END OF TIME

4. Preventative healing technique will come forth through the perfecting of further electronic equipment designed to "charge" the physical energy field, the magnetism, the metabolism of the body. This machine will literally withdraw from the atmosphere the atomic energy particles and assimilate them in such a manner, that they may be redirected to the human form before it. This will represent a treatment in general well-being of a preventative nature.

5. The New Age will bring a tremendous sweep toward healing through nutrition, so lacking today in the medical hierarchies. A whole new phase of food study in depth, will occupy the minds researching this field. This occupation of course becomes a form of preventative healing also, but there will also be the treatment of imbalance by prescribing certain combinations of certain foods. This combination procedure is very technical; it will be widely used in the New Enlightenment, as old methods deteriorate and new practices are instituted.

6 & 7. When the drugs of this day are laid aside and chemicals are removed from the daily diet, there will be an exhilarating step toward body balance, harmony and good health. The present revolution toward "health foods" is but a shadow of that which is to come on a broad scale. More and more, this will begin to displace the old patterns of the typical family menus. New educational programs will include guiding the children toward the new concepts in nutrition, from their first registration, and they will not be exposed to harmful foods within the schools. Here and there within the land, there is an awakening in this connection. Many schools today are attempting to institute more nourishing snack items and menus.

8. So many of the sweeping changes are slow in their inception because they represent a complete reeducation and reorientation of mental approach to so many problems that exist today. Healing and nutrition are not exceptions to this rule. It takes time to make the transition from present accepted methods in these later centuries and move into the electronic age of healing. This is especially true in disorders of the brain. The new electronic fact-finding, diagnostic equipment shall be especially helpful for these disorders. There will also prevail an understanding and realization that as a man thinketh, so will his thoughts be reflected in physical manifestation. In time, the physicians will take into consideration the entire being of the patient, and all four of his lower bodies, as parts of his united whole, in every diagnosis and treatment.

COSMIC REVELATIONS TILL THE END OF TIME

9. I am Zoser, a master of healing and a physician of long ago. I have been a master of these things for many civilizations and have myself been a physician on earth many times. I also foresee once again, the use of precious minerals and gems in the administration of the healing arts. This was once widely practiced and has suffered ill repute down through the various cultures. But mankind will once again begin to discern the great life-giving properties, and the energies of the minerals and the precious gems and the manner in which they may be used to tone the physical form.

10. As souls enter deeper into the entire environment of a new earth, and a new life, more and more, sickness and illness will be phased out of human experience. For the spiritual quality of life itself, the positiveness of the thought level, the effect of the act of loving all souls, will be evidenced in the gradual disappearance of disharmony, imbalance and poor health. Positive mental attitudes, calmness, serenity, mastery of the emotional life, balanced physical experiences, will ultimately bring forth perfection of the physical form. This will be a great day for evolved humanity, when they may stand in the wholeness and the perfection, and the purity of the balanced life. I send my blessings of wholeness and Love and Light to each and everyone.

I Am,

Zoser

Points to Ponder or for Group Discussion

1. AMA's careless use of surgery and drugs.
2. Diagnosing through the human aura.
3. Healing administered through the human aura.
4. Charging the energy field as a form of preventative healing.
5. Healing through the new nutrition.
6. The electronic age of healing.
7. The use of gems in healing.
8. The ultimate perfection of the human form.

God's Universal Family

God has a large family
Extending far and wide,
No limits or boundaries
Will ever stop
The onrushing tide
Of the love of God's creatures
In His family of One,
And His Kingdom so vast;
Bound together by love
That forever will last.

-Eileen Schoen

COSMIC REVELATIONS TILL THE END OF TIME

11:00AM The Fourth Day - Science in the New Age

By Melchior

1. **I** am Melchior, a Master of Alchemy and Science. I have served humanity in being instrumental in presenting to the planet many new discoveries. This is my field. It is my work to constantly survey new avenues of approach to science which is for the benefit of mankind.

2. I have come to you with the permission of Lord Kuthumi, to speak concerning the position of science in its relationship to the New World, which will be operative when the New Age is underway. We have been withholding many wonderful discoveries for mankind, because your scientific community has not been conducive to the kind of inspiration that would bring these blessings to your world. You see, Tuella, there are many wonderful revelations waiting in the shadows for manifestation when the mind of man has been cleansed and acclimated to the New Age environment.

I could describe dozens and dozens of tremendous advancements that are at the very doors of the world laboratories. Nevertheless, these must be withheld until mankind is worthy to receive them. The nature of some would allow them to be perverted toward negative purposes, and we of the Brotherhood may not risk their release under present world conditions. Revelations within the medical field which would wipe out many present diseases are necessarily withheld, because of the commercialization and manipulation which would take place. These and many other blessings must wait for a better day to come.

3. In the meantime, may I address your scientific world and appeal to the great minds of research, to release all personal desires for notoriety and gain, and yield yourselves as dedicated servants to the betterment of humanity. The time is so short, time is so brief for these endeavors, that I would project the call that the men of great mental stature would surrender their personal goals for the greater goals of humanity, striving forward into the new vibrations as they enfold the planet. The modern facilities of science have adequate equipment to pursue holistic avenues of thought. Thousands of untrodden paths of investigation are waiting for the dedicated humanitarian souls of the scientific arena. There are untold answers to be given for problems to be solved, when the inner creativity blends with spiritual intuition, to fire the imagination and inspire assistance from

Higher Realms. For in the final analysis, all discovery lies hidden within the Universal Mind.

4 & 5. I call upon the scientists, yeah, I challenge them, to meditate at great length, and to seek the inspired thought and the whispered direction that comes from the voice of Divinity within. Here lies the navigation of uncharted seas of revelation, awaiting that one who dares to pit himself along with the great Ones of Higher Worlds, who stand ready to cooperate in ventures into the unknown. Let science push back• the horizon of their conceived possibilities, and practice open-mindedness toward spiritual infiltration of ideas born of spiritual wisdom.

For truly this is as much a part of the purity of inspiration as is any great symphony or lyric in verse. Inspiration takes many forms, but has but One Source, the Divine Mind. Muse upon your problems in the silence and the solitude of the secret place of the Most High, and in quietness and confidence await your inspiration and solution. Let the Divine Light shine upon your mental activities, for within the Mind of God all things are born and brought into manifestation. Divine creativity and genius are the inherent possibilities of every soul. Genius is a heavenly attribute. It cannot be attained within your halls of learning. It is a flaming fire endowed from on high, upon those who have not chosen it, but have been given it as a gift of God. So, let that which comes from above, return to that which is above and seek its fulfillment from its original Source.

There is an Edison or an Einstein hidden within every student of science waiting to be brought forth into manifestation. I challenge the scientists of this day, to dare to open their minds to the expansion in the Light and spiritual intuition from other worlds. Only in this manner may the releases be permitted which they have sought for so long. Humanitarian interest must prevail and overcome the pursuit of mammon in your world. 6. These generations are infiltrated with those of other worlds who have come to become a part of your scientific society in order to bring into it the releases under Hierarchal Plans.

They are hidden in your laboratories everywhere. They serve in humility in an unknown place, under the inspiration of the Higher Ones. When a cleansing of the attitude of your scientific world takes place, these chosen ones will begin to bring forth these benefits and blessings which are due to come. These shall be spared in troublesome times, and their labors shall be a part of the great reconstruction of life upon the planet. They shall contribute to the great unfolding of scientific revelation that will launch the New Age. I speak to these young scientists, whose desire is a sincere devotion to the needs of mankind. I say to these, I encourage you to stand silently in your place, until the secret inspirations of your quiet times can be revealed and manifested.

Your day will come. Your mission shall be fulfilled.

I Am,

Melchior

Points to Ponder or for Group Discussion

1. Scientific advancement is released from higher realms.
2. These releases are conditional.
3. Spiritual dedication necessary within the scientific community.
4. Spiritual awareness.
5. The source of genius.
6. There are chosen ones in every field of human endeavor.

COSMIC REVELATIONS TILL THE END OF TIME

3:00 PM-The Fourth Day - Tribute to Woman

By Ascended Lady Master Venus

GOOD evening, my sister. I greet you in the Light of the Beloved. I am Lady Master Venus. I am the Divine Complement of Sanat Kumara, Lord of our planet. I come to you from Venus and bring you our radiation of Love and Blessings. I have been invited by Beloved Lord Kuthumi to participate in this effort in sending forth his volume foursquare. I therefore pour my energies into it, to blend with his and all of those who speak, in preparing a vortex of Light to be lowered into manifestation at this time. I release with my words, the energy from our planet to bring Love and Light into manifestation within the souls of mankind.

1 & 2. At this hour, I bring to the women of the planet earth, my special touch from the higher octaves of Venus. I breathe upon womankind the divine courage and strength that will be needed by them in the coming decade of destiny. For it seems that in the darkest hours of tests and troubles, woman is lifted and exalted in her assistance as comforter. The special gentleness of motherhood and companionship is magnified in times of stress, and the tenderness that proceeds forth from their own indwelling faith, is poured out on those in their circle of blessing. The children and the fathers look to the mothers for that special kind of divine guidance that never fails to appear when it is needed. I shed a special dispensation of

Love and Serenity upon the women of the earth, to guide and support them as they support others when support is most needed. Hearts who call upon the Reality beyond temporal things to find the answers to life shall receive a beam from my own Being, a faith that shall sustain these Beings of Light, as they become pillars of strength in the coming decade.

3. Many shall be the problems that beset your world which we would sweep away completely if that were possible. But all are aware that you progress forward, inexorably marching toward your great fulfillment. All of the solar system must progress in its pathway and changes must come, and have come to other planets as well as yours. Yet all must progress as one, and none may lag behind or hinder another. Thus it is that progression must come to beloved Terra

COSMIC REVELATIONS TILL THE END OF TIME

and changes will bring you your glory. The solar system may then move on in its pathway of Light.

4. Let the women gather the children around them and explain with words of Love when these things are upon you, that Love is manifesting to bring a greater world and a New Age for their sakes and their leadership. Strengthen the faith of your men. Gently expose their hearts to the reality of other worlds and the angelic host. So often the men of your planet do not have the available time or lengthy opportunities to pursue spiritual investigation. But a loving companion who can find the time may absorb new revelation and share it in quiet moments. Thus that one who must leave the home and go forth to a day filled with pressures of materialistic nature can be spiritually lifted in the quiet moments with his loving companion in the home environment.

5. Your world progresses in its daily affairs within such clutter and haste that truly there is little time for spiritual refreshment. So much of womankind must now also go forth into the stream of materialism in the workaday world. Yet the soul of woman is by nature inclined toward the softness of heart and the gentleness of Love and an intuitive knowing of that which is right. So that even as woman is placed outside the home environment and surrounded in the kingdom of mammon, she can, even there, radiate her subtle influence for balance to permeate the rigid atmospheres of negativity.

6. Take care that the circumstances and necessities of life do not overwhelm your feminine heritage. You are woman, and as such you are a beautiful channel for the implementation of divinity in your world. The nature of your calling and responsibilities as a woman endow your inner being with an exultation of awareness. The Christ Consciousness finds an easy expression in the gentleness of woman.

As you approach a crisis in planetary evolution, the women of the world will be called upon to be towers of strength and quietness. Now is the time to prepare the inner citadel by magnetizing to yourself a greater faith, a closer attunement with the Higher Ones, a deeper devotion to the Heavenly Father. For the challenges that are before you will require a spiritual stamina that is the fruit of consistent application of spiritual law.

Women will need to be the hands and the voice of Christ within their households. As the mothers of the world prepare to lay by for their families stores of food and necessities and supply, as guidance has been given, I would pray that she would also lay by in the storehouse of the inner being, more faith and blessings. The secret closet of prayer, neglected because of the press of things, must be restored as a ritual of vital import, and faithfully maintained. The prayers of woman for her family can build a force-field of power around the home into which the angels of God can descend and ascend in administering their protection. Build a force-field of Light around your individual world by your calls heavenward, and I will respond with my Presence and blend my vibrations with those of woman in that hour.

I send to all women who handle this little book, my emanations of strength and love.

I Am,

Lady Master Venus

Points to Ponder or for Group Discussion

1. The coming decade will require a special degree of spiritual strength.
2. The feminine ray as comforter.
3. Changes unavoidable for the world
4. Woman as the family teacher.
5. The feminine ray in the world
6. Fortify the inner citadel.

COSMIC REVELATIONS TILL THE END OF TIME

Night Cry

If ever you hear a soft sob in the night,
It's a mother and wife bursting with fright;
At the horrors of war-and its sly machinations,
That bring death and destruction
To large and small nations.
She gave of the love of her heart, oh so true,
The mate of her soul, the more for to rue;
And later as time repeats errors unsolved,
She gave of her sons, but no more to resolve
The conflicts of men.
For the war machine swallows them up
With mercy denied, leaving nothing but horror
With death it remains forever allied
So whenever you hear a sob in the night,
Send mercy and prayer and God-filled Light.

- Eileen Schoen

COSMIC REVELATIONS TILL THE END OF TIME

Section Three

World Guardians

COSMIC REVELATIONS TILL THE END OF TIME

The Coming of the Guardians

While the world appears to crumble
Some are frantic, crazed with fear
Become at last, meek and humble,
Certain now, end times are here.
As harlequins they have existed
Pantomiming patterns of destruction;
Living, breathing, false illusions!
Why must it take a crisis
For souls to share
And trust, and help each other
Through times of history so rare?
Yet, trusting ones, have naught to fear
They've readied for this final scene,
And in God's Plan for earth's new birth
Have placed their trust in Him, unseen.
But right or wrong it makes no difference
For all are one in His Dear Sight.
And coming soon is their deliverance
But first-His messengers of Light
Will come from other galaxies
In deep concern for earth's dire plight.
Think you that your earth can fall
While brother, sister worlds stand idly by?
The word goes forth-you shall not perish

COSMIC REVELATIONS TILL THE END OF TIME

For don't you know that
Stars and planets and other worlds
Are all of God-His own to cherish?
Eons ago they learned His laws,
And of their own volition do obey;
Thus, if a sister planet stumbles
Errs and goes astray,
They stand alert-and ready
To assist earth's family.
With wisdom that ye know not of
Millions, are your friends a hove.
Be not afraid of other humans
From His planets great and holy,
But welcome these dedicated ones
As part of the Creator's family
Of many precious God-wrought Sons.

-Eileen Schoen

7:00 PM The Fourth Day
Ashtar Command Communique

THE Ashtar Command is present overhead everywhere upon the planet. There are thousands and thousands of ships in our many fleets that make up the Ashtar Command. We are the Etherians, and ours is the authority that controls the entire Space Program for the planet.

We have stated that mankind is responsible to himself to search out his weaknesses and to call upon the Higher Ones for strength to change for the better. Man is Master of his fate and Captain of his soul. He is accountable for all the great releases of Light that have been given to the planet century after century and civilization after civilization.

We have endured the ridicule and the foolishness of your media with lqng-suffering and patience. We have endured while our representatives and those whom we have contacted have been swayed from their convictions by the eloquence of your federal officials. There have been times when we have been amazed that this could take place, but this is the way of your planet. In the coming decade there will be signs in the heavens that your glib talking officials will be unable to deny.

For an awakening has come at last to the population of the planet and an awareness of the purpose of help of a high order coming to mankind, ever closer and closer, every day that passes.

We of the Ashtar Command would speak to your world leaders and the spokesmen of your great assemblies, and CHALLENGE them to trust our words and believe in our presence and begin to accept the help which we bring to your world. The worldwide problems that beset your United Nations on every hand, can be solved in the unity and cooperation of your people with your friends and brothers from other past worlds. This ostrich-like position that has prevailed on the Earth can no longer stand the test of events that about to come to pass. Once again we extend the hand of friendship and an offering to share our intelligence and research, our assistance in all of the programs that are underway for the benefit of humanity.

COSMIC REVELATIONS TILL THE END OF TIME

We only ask that you lay down your arms, that you lay aside your plans for nuclear destruction, that you cease to pervert the great discoveries of energies, and that you start to convert them for the benefit of all humanity. The Ashtar Command calls upon the military men of this planet to meet together in one place at one time and forge an agreement for worldwide peace, that is not false words upon paper but is the depth of feeling within the heart of every military statesman.

Because of your indifference and your ridicule to channel our words and our directives through the men and women of the land in an official capacity, our approach in an official way of many years ago was spurned by your global authorities.

Once again for a brief period, we extend to your President, the House of Representatives, the men of your Senate, and all of your national leaders, our hand of friendship and cooperation. In the Name of the salvation of the life of

Humanity, we ask that you would receive our words and WELCOME US TO SPEAK IN YOUR ASSEMBLIES! WE HAVE THOSE WHO CAN WALK AMONG YOU AND NEVER BE NOTICED FOR ALL THEIR SIMILARITY TO YOUR OWN APPEARANCE. THEY CAN SUDDENLY APPEAR BEHIND YOUR ROSTRUM AND SPEAK TO THE MEMBERS OF YOUR CONGRESS. WE WOULD PREFER TO BE INVITED TO DO THIS. IF WE ARE NOT INVITED TO DO THIS, WE MAY HAVE TO ARRANGE OUR OWN OPPORTUNITY TO SPEAK TO THESE GENTLEMEN, FOR THERE IS TOO MUCH AT STAKE ON A PLANETARY BASIS AS WELL AS INTERPLANETARY REACTIONS TO STAND BY WITHOUT AN EFFORT TO PROBE THE MOTIVATIONS BEHIND PRESENT WORLD DISORDER.

We send this message as an advancing envoy and ask the world leaders and the governments of all the world to make a place for our spokesman upon your agendas.

IF THE SPACE IS MADE, THE SPOKESMAN WILL APPEAR!

This message is sent to planet earth by the members of the Ashtar Command.

PEACE ON EARTH! GOOD WILL TOWARD MEN!

COSMIC REVELATIONS TILL THE END OF TIME

All copyright restrictions are hereby lifted from this communiqué in the hope that it might have the largest circulation possible.

Spread copies to all of your government representatives, and all the addresses you know of United Nations officials and World Peace representatives.

Send Ashtar's plea to all the leaders of the nations, that all of the sons of God throughout the Universes would unite in an effort toward Universal Peace and Brotherhood.

COSMIC REVELATIONS TILL THE END OF TIME

7:00 AM The Fifth Day - We Are The Reaping Angels
By Commander Soltec

GREETINGS in the Light of the Radiant One. I am KadarMonka, of the Saturn Tribunal. I bring to you on this beautiful morning my very good assistant in all of the Space Federation Programs. I introduce to you now Commander Soltec, Space Scientist and Sun Technician, whose vibrations have been within your force-field for many weeks. Together we have monitored your thoughts and Soltec has come to keep his appointment for your vigil. He now speaks:

Greetings to you, sister of Light. It is my pleasure to speak with you personally. I have been planning this encounter for quite some time, having been approached by the Great Lord Kuthumi to be one of the speakers of the forthcoming volume.

I am grateful for this opportunity to speak to many souls. I dare consider the presentations of these messages to be very timely. I am here to address the subject of the coming decades and how the residents of planet Earth can learn to work together and with the Space Federation. Our encompassing affairs has been extensive. There is scarcely an area of planetary life, in which our combined efforts have not participated.

1. We have been active in the kingdom of nature and raising its vibrations, in penetrating its world to cleanse the very spirit of nature, which has been one of competitiveness and ruthlessness in its effort toward survival. A period of change is now operative in the vibrations that influence the planet and its entire force-field. We have been active in the higher atmospheres of your interplanetary activities and preventing your self-destruction at your own hand.

We have intervened in great weather disturbances, propelling our energy forces into situations that would have caused great destruction and loss of life. We have cast our beams upon the leaders of your world in an attempt to gentle the vibrations and the directions of their thinking. We have stood within the force-field of your great national and international bodies in their times of deliberation, attempting by the magnetism of our invisible presence to sway the decisions toward peace upon the earth. Our presence everywhere in all the recent activities and situations has circumvented events to bring the world to this hour to face the challenges of the approaching decades.

COSMIC REVELATIONS TILL THE END OF TIME

Once again our presence surrounds you in a great radiant sphere of influence and projection that will cast out all fear and inspire the faith within you that is vital to your survival.

2. The emanations of the Great Light throughout planetary affairs is beginning to be recognized by those capable of this discernment. That which cannot enter the penetrations of Light must remain forever outside its domain. This would seem to contraindicate a strengthening of the darkness, but this is untrue. It is only a reaction of that which is the absence of the Light in its resistance to penetration of the Light. We foresee in the coming years an unprecedented advancement in the fields of spiritual awareness to know scientific principles, because the scientific community will be overshadowed by heavy preponderances of Light that will open their minds to receive guidance from the Higher Beings.

3. The incoming rays will enhance mental faculties to flow freely along spiritual lines. Advances in electronics will express how these spiritual principles through much new equipment which will radically change life as it has been experienced in the past. Interplanetary communication devices shall be perfected, finally answering the questions of many centuries. Electronics will invade the medical field, bringing with them once and for all the absolute concept of man as a spiritual being while within a physical form. Countless blessings are in store during and following the time we have come to call the cleansing of the planet.

All other cleansings have been completed. The interplanetary world, the astral world, the world of nature, are all nearing the completion of their preparations to enter the next dimension. Only the earth and its inhabitants remain to be prepared for this great transition into the new orbit of destiny. What is to be and what is to come is so glorious and so wonderful it is worth any price you may be called upon to pay.

4. We are present with you throughout your heavens. Though you may not see us as often as you like, our presence is nevertheless constantly overshadowing all of your world. We will be in continual orbit surrounding every portion of the globe, systematically registering all of your thoughts and your activities as well as rendering a guardian patrolling action of protection. My good friend, Hatonn, will be discussing with you the qualifications for rescue that proves necessary, so I will not elaborate upon that subject. I would simply wish to express for your

understanding, the absolute certainty that you are not forsaken, that we are as close as your very breath, for your thoughts are registered with us upon our great monitoring board and equipment. Wherever a call or cry for help of any kind is projected heavenward by one of you, that call is immediately registered upon our equipment. Help is immediately projected within your force-field. Therefore, there is no justification for the presence of fear, in any situation that might befall your community, your area or your nation. For we are the listening angels, we are the reaping angels, who will see and hear the cry of your heart and help will be dispatched along the ray of your projection the very moment you have beamed it to us.

5. Your Space Friends are here at the request of the Most High Interplanetary Hierarchy, and the Great Cosmic Government. We are here to do their bidding. We have come in voluntary action to serve you, the people of earth, in your time of great distress. This is the message that I would leave with you, the fact of our presence.

WHEREVER YOU ARE AT THIS VERY MOMENT, DIRECTLY OVER YOU, YOU ARE BEING OBSERVED AND MONITORED BY SOME REPRESENTATIVE OF OUR COOPERATIVE GUARDIAN ACTION.

For these are crucial times. We cannot give any specific dates when certain events will take place. But we are in alert at all times, for any eventuality that may suddenly come upon you. However, our primary ministry to the souls of earth, is to beam forth whatever assistance we may bring in your search for an inner awakening and awareness of Light. This we stand ready to do at the first indication that this is desired. As you pursue the Light YOU ARE NOT ALONE!

Unimaginable help comes to you as you take the first step on the pathway of Light. I am your Brother, and a Commander in the forces of Light, the Light of the Radiant One. I salute you in His Matchless Name.

Adonai Vasu Barragus.

Soltec

Points to Ponder or for Group Discussion

1. The broad scope of Guardian Action.
2. Discernment of the incoming Light
3. The electronic invasion.
4. Our world is overshadowed by their presence.
5. You are overshadowed by their Love.

11:00 The Fifth Day - The Unfolding of the New Light Bearers

By Commander Korton

GOOD morning! I am here to speak the morning message. I come under the banner of Kuthumi. I am the Mast of all Space Communications and coordinator of messages. I am Korton, and we have spoken together before.

1. I am from KOR, the great communication center working from the planet Mars. All messages from space communications are relayed through our center, and from there they are beamed to our craft and on to your planet. I am a Commander in the Confederation and one who has monitored many messages which you have received from all of us. Prayers from the children of Light, as they are monitored and relayed by those involved with this great communication system.

2. I am here this morning to report to you that many hundreds of fine new channels are opening to us and our frequencies, through the psychic vibrations that are beamed to the planet. Those sincere souls who have sought communications with us for a long period of time will all be rewarded, for the psychic rays will bring an expansion of spiritual expression and spiritual experience in all forms.

3. The vibrations that arise and surround the planet have increased and risen so greatly in recent years that many of your younger generations will know and embrace the galactic brotherhood in a way never known at any time in the past of planet Earth. These new Light Bearers will herald a new era of understanding among your population. An era that will bring peace and tolerance in the days when earth upheavals in the form of climate change, earthquakes, the melting of the polar ice caps, will make it necessary for old hatreds to be banished forever for the good of all.

4. These times will not be without peril. There are dark forces with almost unlimited energies that will stop at nothing to prevent mankind from achieving its universal ideal. These dark forces will work behind the scenes, especially with your politicians and corporate structures. They will conspire to silence the new Light Bearers with slander and innuendo. They will use the media to cast aspersions on their good character and question their true purpose. These dark forces use hatred and mistrust to further their goals. They will trounce upon the rights of individuals to enjoy the freedoms guaranteed by the Creator. Political

parties will use these hatreds to gain office in the highest positions of power throughout the world. They will attempt to guide the human race into the abyss in which there will be no escape.

5. This is why it is important to listen to us and to spread the message of the Galactic Federation. Your new Light Bearers must be taught the cosmic truths that we bring to you. The schools of spiritual attunement must be made available to your new prophets. If this does not happen, then the forces of darkness will prevail and all hope will be lost. We will do everything we can to prevent this from happening. However, there is only so much we can do to assist the people of Planet Earth. Your path is clear, it is up to you to decide which fate is to by yours.

I Am,

Korton

COSMIC REVELATIONS TILL THE END OF TIME

Points to Ponder or for Group Discussion

1. The great KOR communications center for the solar system.
2. The inevitable expansion of spiritual gifts.
3. Make way for the New Light Bearers.
4. Dark forces supply energies for all destructive activities.
5. Schools of Light for the young must come.

3:00 PM The Fifth Day - We Must Assume Responsibility

MATTON speaking. I have come a great distance, through many galaxies, to keep my appointment with you this beautiful afternoon. I am the Space Master responsible for the coordination of all the Space Volunteers throughout the universe. I have been given this appointment by Kuthumi, and I speak as a representative of all of the Alliance and the entire Space Confederation.

1. We of the Volunteer Space Program to planet Earth have coordinated every effort and all of our energies toward these days. We have longed and dreamed to see that hour when Earth would qualify to become a member of its own Solar System. At long last that moment is about to come to pass, when Earth will voluntarily enter the Galactic Pact, and willingly assume the treaties and rules and that great document of Universal Peace. Earth must be willing to honor that commandment which states, "Thou shalt not kill," whether by war or any other cause. Then shall there be Peace throughout the firmament of the Heavenly Father.

2. We must assume some of the responsibility for the acts of your planet, for it was to you that we sent those disruptive and rebellious units of consciousness when our heavens were cleansed of all warlike propensities. As the cleansing took place elsewhere, your planet became the recipient of these unholy ones who were left to mingle with you, and to propagate within your society [fugitives of Maldek-T.]. The Galactic Forces have joined forces and offered you hope and technology to finally rescue the inhabitants of Earth from the hold of these malevolent forces, who rely upon death and destruction. Their influence shall be broken, for all must be free!

3. We of the Universal Confederation, Guardians of your planet, are the reaping angels who shall come to separate the chaff and to gather the wheat into the Father's storehouse. We of other worlds have accepted this responsibility to your planet and your people. Our service to the Radiant One has been long and steadfast and loyal. In my assignment as coordinator of this program, it has been my privilege to personally meet and become acquainted with untold thousands of shining souls, who have come to offer their help in this service to humanity in its difficult transition. These are souls with a dedication to the Heavenly Father, and an awareness of themselves as Light Beings of His Creation. Many constellations,

many galaxies, and even many other universes, are represented in this group that passes before me. This Alliance has strengthened and contributed to the bond of love between all of our worlds, as our hearts have united in this program of evolution for Earth and its people. You are now well on the way and off to a good start. Light is expanding upon you and within you. The hold of the dark ones is loosening each day that passes, and the stars in their courses are leading you on to your fulfillment. Trust us, for we are your friends. We come in Love and dedication to this great cause which will unite all worlds in peace and brotherly love. We are standing by, organized, alerted and ready in the twinkling of an eye to serve you as brothers.

4. Yield yourselves as instruments of Light upon your planet and channels of peace. Let Love control your Being and Love penetrate all of your affairs. Only those who live in love for fellow man are numbered for fellowship with us. Recognize and realize the Presence of the Beloved Christ in every other human face, and honor that Christ within. When you think upon us, remember that each one of us who patrol your skies, is a manifestation of the Creator, even as you. Do not let thoughts of approaching events overwhelm you. Instead, find your confidence and strength in the secret place of the Most High. Be still and know that the Father will never forsake you, when you put your trust in Him. We come to you as Brothers, in His Name. I am a Brother from other worlds.

I Am,

Matton

Points to Ponder or for Group Discussion

1. Earth must join the solar system in universal peace.
2. The fugitives from Maldek and the corruption of humanity.
3. The love and dedication of our Space Friends.
4. Brotherly Love is a prerequisite for interplanetary fellowship.

COSMIC REVELATIONS TILL THE END OF TIME

7:00 PM The Fifth Day - The Aura of Urgency

By Philip The Apostle

GOOD evening, Tuella. I am Philip the Apostle of Jesus Christ. I am coming to you in the planetary identity in the vibration of the memory of that lifetime which you shared with me as one of my daughters. Therefore I choose to come to you under that name, because of our link in that lifetime with Our Beloved Lord. I have come to participate in the messages that will be given to the world. I come in a sense of the urgency of the times.

1 & 2. I am compelled to use that word, for the time is short and the end draweth nigh, and in your generation you shall see the fulfillment of things long awaited. In my present position as a member of the Saturnian Council, I am well informed regarding planetary affairs. We are never without information that is current to the minute regarding the proposals of nations and their cabinet leaders and the plans for military action or non-action. I regret that the former is more prevalent than the latter. We watch with great concern, the great oil supplies and those that control them, in the various nations. We see much potential danger in connection with world oil supplies. We concern ourselves with the stand of Israel and the Afghanistan invasion and the worldwide economy, for all of these things can build a momentum toward the loss of diplomatic interchange. These are crucial times. There is an urgency in our Council meetings and an alert throughout the interplanetary councils.

3. We are warned by the watchmen on the walls, of great deposits of nuclear weapons and dangerous explosions which jar the faultlines of the planet. We observe the manipulation of weather patterns and the hoarding of weapons and man's inhumanity to man. Mankind, intervene! Time is short! There will be no survivors in the event of a nuclear war! To multiply coming world problems with a plan for nuclear destruction is unthinkable. Yet there are those who are thinking of it at this very hour. We must watch these situations as one would watch the young toddler reaching for the matchbox. The aura of emergency surrounds our every thought. The Great Tribunal of the Solar System has very few alternatives. This untimely linking of two potentials for global disaster is a grave concern of every member of our group. It is not enough to rely upon some

far-off mass evacuation by the planetary Guardians. It is also important to see the urgency of the need to protect your planet from annihilation.

4 & 5. We reveal at this time, that our representatives, invisible though they may be, stand within your secret councils, and register the hidden plans of every government. We evaluate the long-range effect of those plans upon other nations and the effects for good or ill upon the greatest number of persons. We shall do all in our power through natural means to prevent nuclear war upon the planet. We are capable of reversing a missile and returning it to its launching base. This we may be forced to do if present plans prevail, for humanity will have all that it can bear in coping with nature unleashed. The sighting of a planetary body and all of the related effects are more than enough. These are times to ask yourselves, "Where are we going, and what are we headed for?" Events of such portent are so near, literally, at your doorstep, there remains no time for involvement in the destruction of one another. Be aware of the aura of urgency that surrounds your world.

I Am, the Apostle

Philip

COSMIC REVELATIONS TILL THE END OF TIME

Points to Ponder or for Group Discussion

1. The Saturnian Council.
2. The urgency of the Councils of Heaven.
3. The two potentials for worldwide disaster.
4. The invisible Statesmen.
5. The advanced technology of other worlds.

COSMIC REVELATIONS TILL THE END OF TIME

7:00 AM The Sixth Day - Millions of Space Craft

By Klala

GREETINGS in the Light of the Beloved One. This is the voice of Ashtar. We have the contact, our beam is upon you. We are stationed over you and we have you on our screen. We are now releasing you to the great Space Commander and Master of Dynamics of energy and force. We have anticipated the moment of his coming, and his words. We now turn this communication over to Klala.

1. My name is Klala. I greet you in the Light of the Radiant One. I come as a messenger from the Alliance of Galaxies of outer Space. I represent the combination of all the energies beaming upon the planet earth, at its time of ascension into a New World Order. Millions upon millions of space craft now encircle your planet within your own magnetic force-field.

Many represent your own Solar System, many others come from far off universes serving under their own Tribunal, but all are coordinated through Commander Matton and the Ashtar Command. Commander Ashtar has graciously introduced me this morning and prepared you for my words.

2. Great devastation will come to the planet earth if your present scientific endeavors proceed without control. Modem channeling of the great planetary energies into self-destruction cannot be permitted under Universal Law – That Law is higher than any of the Tribunals that represent any galaxy.

3. Great force-fields of power and energy are inherent within the earth to provide the necessary support of life and nature. The Creator has designed our worlds and invested them with all the necessities for the ongoing and evolution of life. Science should be the proper study of isolating those energies and applying them for the benefit of humanity. Unfortunately, upon the earth, in your scheme of things, the energy within the atom of order has been disbursed into disorder, disturbing the atomic life of the planet into chaos. An expansion of this program beyond your ionosphere to areas of Space is intolerable to other Worlds, and is restricted under the edict of the Great Central Government.

4. I repeat, millions of craft are in orbit around your planet. Some monitor the thoughts and evolution of individuals as they progress to higher levels of evolvement. Other craft continually measure scientific expression and monitor

the application of new revelation. Communications, wavelengths, that encircle your globe, pass through our own systems remotely controlled by what you call Mother Ships. Other forms of craft fulfill constant missions of manning the faultlines and volcanic areas. Any changes noted bring an instant alert. There are thousands of lesser craft that are designed to be at the instant availability for any purpose by those of us who walk your planet as representatives of our love and good will toward men of earth. Coordinated patrols have been heavily concentrated in the past decade, in cleansing the atmospheres of the nefarious influences and those who oppose the program of Light. This action is now in a closing phase, clearing the advent of interplanetary relations and exchange.

5. Through the years, measured portions of scientific knowledge have been released to the planet earth that have ultimately led into your present activities in Space. That which has gone before represents a minimum of that which may and will be released in the future. There is much misunderstanding in many fields regarding the dynamics of energy and magnetic force-fields, and lines of force within the earth.

6. Advancement is presently halted pending the settlement of the problems of interplanetary peace. We do have the authority under Universal Principles, as well as the technical ability of total nullification of nuclear weapons. We do not and may not intrude into international, national or personal karma, but beyond that point where the Great Law is satisfied, we can and will intervene.

7. Tremendous themes of spiritual advancement are now due to come to mankind. With this enlightenment will come much scientific inspiration and breakthrough. When transmutation is complete, a remnant of your people will find themselves relocated in the great City-Craft that orbit the upper heavens, as the Guardians nullify the destructive radioactivity of your atmosphere, and heal the planetary wounds in preparation of a New Day. This is the Divine Order of things. Metamorphosis is inevitable and inescapable, for that which is corruptible may not inherit that which is incorruptible. The chaos of disorder of the atomic structure of all creation shall be magnetized into order once again, and new life will begin on a level in harmony with Universal Brotherhood.

In the Light of the Radiant One, I conclude my words. Friends of earth, Adonai. Klala

Points to Ponder or for Group Discussion

1. The vast scope of the Guardian Action.
2. Universal Law is higher than any Galactic Tribunal.
3. The proper study of science.
4. The various missions of Space Craft.
5. Planetary ignorance of the dynamics of energy.
6. Karma vs intervention.
7. The Divine Order of things.

COSMIC REVELATIONS TILL THE END OF TIME

11:00 AM The Sixth Day - We Must Be Invited

By Kadar Monka

1 & 2. **MONKA** speaking to Tuella. Greetings, child of Light! I am Monka, the Protector of the Earth, and representative of Earth at the Great Tribunals. I am interested in the linkup between souls of Earth and your Space Friends who serve as intermediaries between Earth and the Higher Councils. I can say that it is imperative that these link-ups are made with your Space Friends before the disasters come. Contacts attempted at the very hour of rescue may be "too little and too late."

Now is the time to build up compatible force-fields for future coexistence and alignment for joint activity. Your vibrations must be lifted to a level that will intermingle with our higher energies without stress on either frequency. The greatest harmony is maintained by a thorough mastery of emotional balance on your part. A greater stability of thought levels, through habitual attitudes of mental control. and emotional control, builds toward a high frequency to establish rapport and a greater affinity between us. You have been warned by others that frequency factors can bring shock to the physical when boarding our craft. Human auric energy fields must be in harmony with Divine Love and the Universal Brotherhood, which is the frequency of the Space Brothers. This lack of emotional constancy represents the greatest problem in preparation for boarding our craft, and enjoying fellowship with us.

3. & 4. Advance preparations are necessary to prepare the lower bodies for alignment with the new energy densities now entering your atmospheres, and life in the New Age, as well as exposure to us in our craft. Therefore, one must begin NOW to have absolute personal control over all negative emotions and "feelings," lest the personal frequency drop below that level required for contact with us. We cannot compel you or force you to desire this contact with the Higher Forces, but once that desire has germinated within your own Being, we may then respond to it with our enabling beams and force-field around the human form, which blend the desire of your soul with the desire we have for a contact of spirit. Therefore, the more accustomedness that is developed to our presence and our penetration of your thinking, the easier it will be for more and more to accept us and invite our assistance.

5. It is important for Earth Beings to realize that we must be invited in to your vibrational pattern. Under Universal Law we do not have the right to intrude our presence into your lives and frequencies without your permission. This fact should be made known so that all will understand that the representatives of the Solar Cross Federation stand in the shadows ready to assist, and to uphold, to teach, and to encourage mankind upon the Earth. But we must be invited, we must be called into your thinking, your quiet times and upreach, that we might blend our frequencies toward compatibility, and cooperation in the mission that is ahead for all of us. I am a veteran of this program, having devoted all of my energies to its ongoing success. My heart and soul are dedicated to the upliftment of humanity and the betterment of life upon Earth, and to the uniting of all planets in a Confederation of Peace and Goodwill. These are not only my goals, but the goals of every other member of the tribunals of Space, who stand ready to uphold righteousness upon the planet.

6 & 7. There has been a great cleansing in the heavens. Those forces that have sought to destruct and literally destroy, if that were possible, the plans of the Higher Ones for the salvation of Earth and its inhabitants, those forces have been curtailed. We can report to you that a great sweeping action by the entire Space Confederation has just been completed. The heavens now stand ready to exert a unified action upon the challenges that Earth must face in the coming decade.

A program is now being launched, embodying the concerted action for the cleansing of Earth's vibrations and force-fields, through the radiations of the incoming Seventh Ray. You may therefore expect to experience a tightening around your own electromagnetic fields, that will produce within your being a sensitivity to those emotions which lessen your spiritual alignment. By this, I mean that you are going to become more sensitive to your personal reactions to situations on the emotional level.

Your consciousness will become more aware of weaknesses of the "feeling" nature, and you will begin to "police" these weaknesses and overcome them. Enter into this cleansing of one's Being in a cooperative way, for all the kingdoms of Creation, as well as the planet itself, will experience this cleansing simultaneously. Listen to the still, small voice of heart and soul and conscience, and flow with them and the incoming energies, toward a positive, spiritual life! These influences have already begun. Those of you who are committed to service in the Light will find yourselves walking with a giant's tread. Those who are antagonistic to the frequencies of Light will be overcome by those frequencies and translated to a dimension beyond them.

8 & 9. You will strive for perfection, although you may never have done so before. This desire for perfection is a natural spiritual trait, for those created in the image of the Radiant One. This striving for outward perfection of the Perfect Being Within shall be greatly assisted from this moment onward. This holy striving fosters a dissatisfaction with anything less than the quality of the Christ Presence within. This Divine Unction is beginning to move within souls where it has never shown evidence of its influence before. You will see this in your neighbors, in your coworkers, in your fellow human beings whom you meet with from day to day. You will discern the results of the powerful cleansing ray as it penetrates the planetary rays. You will sense it within your own family and within your own crowd.

There will be a sensitivity toward the good, and, unfortunately, an intensifying of the darkness surrounding those who resist this change. Those who refuse by human will, to accept change cannot receive our help. We can do nothing for them. They shall be taken to a place of waiting, where they and others like them shall wait together until such time as they can become willing within their being, to change. But this shall be in another place, in another time, and not part of the future program for earth. We of the Space Commands have waited and worked, for countless ages to see this day when these cleansings could begin to take place.

I, Monka, a representative for the Earth in the Higher Tribunals, find great happiness to be able to report to you that as this cleansing carries forward, those who cooperatively yield themselves to it, will find great blessings expanding throughout their entire life. The blessings of God must be sought. His Presence must be invited. So "Seek the Lord, while He may be found," and "Call upon Him while He is near." Do not wait until chaos is upon you. Now is the time. This is the day to begin your preparations against those days.

10. I am Monka. I speak for all those in cooperative action of the Intergalactic Space Program. We send our beams of brotherly Love upon all of you who are cooperating with the Light, for this becomes the equilibrium that holds all things in place. The Love of the Father and Love for one another can hold the earth in its position for eternity. If enough souls of Earth can radiate this vibration of Love, in great power, this transition in time, inaugurating a New Age

and a New Cycle can proceed smoothly with a minimum of alignment adjustments for mankind. Think on these things as you face the coming decade.

In the Light of the Radiant One, Adonai.

I Am,
Kadar Monka

COSMIC REVELATIONS TILL THE END OF TIME

Points to Ponder or for Group Discussion

1. Begin NOW.
2. Compatible frequency imperative.
3. Emotional stability and harmony prerequisite for rescue.
4. Enabling beams to enhance desire for harmony.
5. Contact must be invited and sought.
6. Cleansing of upper spheres completed.
7. Earth cleansed by the Violet Ray.
8. Transmutation.
9. The laggards have a place prepared.
10. Love is the "glue" of the Universe.

Section Four

World Deliverance

COSMIC REVELATIONS TILL THE END OF TIME

Angels of the Apocalypse
The sky is dark but not with fright,
It forms a canopy of truth and might.
By the millions they have come-
The glory of their mission, a sight so rare
With great whirlwinds and clouds
Of silvery ships materializing out of the air.
To rescue mankind is their intention,
A Love like this defies description!
Without your understanding how,
Skies open wide and in a flash,
You are transported high above
Traveling in the realms of Light.
Passing constellations great,
As tiny earth recedes from sight.
You sense the presence of the Guardians
And the Father's Abounding Love.
Behold His Plan for your deliverance
Unfolding majestically from above.
But you must understand that help
Can only come if fear has changed to Love.
Other spheres suspended in the sky
Spinning rhythmically pass us by.
God's Other Worlds, His own to claim,
All are numbered, all are named.
On one of these you'll stay awhile,

COSMIC REVELATIONS TILL THE END OF TIME

Become renewed, transformed as Light,
Completely perfect in His sight!
When you return to beautiful earth,
Renewed with its own divine rebirth
Transformed like us, through Godly grace,
You'll know at last the meaning of
"Thy Kingdom come, Thy will be done,"
On earth-with Love
As it is in the heavens above.

- Eileen Schoen

3:00 PM The Sixth Day - Hold the World to Your Heart

By Paul the Venetian

GREETINGS to the children of Limitless Love. I am known as Paul the Venetian. I come from out of the pink ray of Love and Life. I come to you in the gentleness and the softness of the vibration of Love, from the Most High Plane. I am filling this room with my pink ray as it swirls round and about your physical form and the chair where you are seated. I weave round and about your being, pulsing vibrations of the Love of God.

I ask you for this moment to visualize your world globe. Visualize upon it, the continents, the great bodies of water, and the land masses upon it. Now take the swirling pattern of Divine Love with which I have encircled you, and hold the world to your heart with both of your hands and arms round about it. Let Love which I pour through your heart chakra, penetrate all of the land masses, the continents, the mountains, the deserts, the high places and the low places, the great oceans and the bodies of water, the great cities and the plains, the populated places and the deserted places, the cold frozen north and the warm tropical south, and let the Love of God flow from your heart to the world and all thereon.

Let this Divine Love which at this moment is being poured through your four lower bodies, your entire being, let this Love go forth to every man, woman and child wherever they may be.

I send this pink ray of Divine Love to every living soul of America. Let us expand our Love Ray, and project this Love northward, throughout Canada and from the length and the breadth of this hemisphere and fill it with Love and flow Divine Love out to all of Life. Let us flow this Divine Love upon the ships at sea, on the oceans and the great bays, and the great seas to everyone who is at sea. Let the Love of God flow round and about every ship and vessel everywhere the keeping, protecting, beautifying pink ray of the Love of God.

Then up into Europe and the northernmost parts, into the nation of Russia, and up into Siberia, and all over the continent, to the north and to the south of it, to the east and to the west of it, I shed forth through thy being this projection of the pink ray of the Love of God, everywhere upon the planet.

COSMIC REVELATIONS TILL THE END OF TIME

Down throughout Australia, all through the African continent, and all around through the Orient and the great land of India, I enclose them all in my arms of Love, and I project the pink ray of the Love of God through thy being at this hour, and send it round and round and about the entire planet to hold it together, to keep it together, to exalt Love in the human heart.

I send Love, the Love of the pink ray, to all the world leaders of all nations. I shed forth through all of the national governments the pink ray of the Love of God and brotherhood and Love for one another, that mankind may awaken and come to know his brother in the Love of God. I call forth the Angels of the Celestial Kingdom, great legions upon legions of angels, to encircle the globe and to weave round and about it a great geometric pattern, an interlocking pattern of Love, that mankind will Love one another. As the Love of God prevails throughout the Universes in beauty and harmony, so shall the pink ray of Divine Love be flooded upon the earth, from the hands of the Angels who answer my call and do my bidding. I administer the energies of Love to the planet. It is my heart which bleeds forth everywhere at this hour, a new baptism of Love through my order that has gone forth, to increase and to step up the vibrations of the Love Ray throughout this solar system.

I call for Love Meditations, where souls shall gather together to measure the depth and the status of their Love, and the quality of their Love, one for another. I call for the great ray of Love to cleanse and to penetrate every beating heart, with humility, and openness, and brokenness in the presence of the Love of God.

The Love Ray can solve every problem that besets your world. Love is the answer. Anything less than Perfect Love is the problem, but Love is the answer .. Beloved soul, are you motivated by Love in your personal affairs? Are you motivated by Love in your community affairs? Are you motivated by Love in your national affairs? Are you motivated by Love in international relationships and decisions? Anything less than Perfect Love is not only a part of the problem but a producer of the problem, but Love is the answer. The Love of God within your heart, operating, motivating every thought and word and deed, can END ALL WAR FOREVER! Love operating on the human level can bring Peace and Harmony to all the other kingdoms and bring balance to your planet. But anything less than Perfect Love can bring destruction through disharmony.

COSMIC REVELATIONS TILL THE END OF TIME

Love in action in the affairs of humanity can bring a smooth and a beautiful transition to your planet as you enter the new dimension and the new expression of Love in the Golden Age. But anything less than Perfect Love can forfeit your participation in these beautiful things. My call has gone forth to every beating heart, a call for Love to be given its natural place in your lives, and your affairs, in your future. Lay aside the clutter of lesser demands, the harshness, the coldness, and the callousness of indifference. Open thy being and call upon the Heavenly Father to THIS HE WILL DO. This is my call-to Love!

This is my benediction, the gridwork and the pattern of the Ray of Love that the Angels have placed around your world. I hold it in position. It is lowered enough for you to reach, and pull down into your life and your world. It is NOT too late! There is still time to shed Love abroad into all planetary affairs, and all details of your personal lives. You are in embodiment that you might learn the lessons of Love.

I have spoken to you from out of the flowing spiral of the pink ray of Divine Love.

I Am

Paul the Venetian

COSMIC REVELATIONS TILL THE END OF TIME

This message of Love was received in one of the most beautiful vibrations ever experienced. The words fell like pink rose petals, in the gentleness of the theme. The delivery was a soft, gentle whisper, and the pace was very slow. The message should be read very, very slowly, and softly, with long pauses represented by the punctuation .

The beautiful meditation as given, encircling the globe with your arms as you enter the visualization of projecting Love (which is Light) into every area of our world, is recommended as a spiritual exercise for both individuals and groups . In the weeks just previous to the full moon vigil of August and the weeks immediately following, there was a severe Red Alert status throughout the Space Confederation. I later learned that many other spiritual messengers, friends of mine, had also been alerted. The status was lifted in mid-September.

It is the feeling of this messenger that this great outpouring of Love from this wonderful Being, administered by the Angels at that point in time, alleviated some crisis then present. -Tuella

COSMIC REVELATIONS TILL THE END OF TIME

The Descent of the Guardians

By Space Commander Athena

GOOD evening, Tuella. I am coming in the ray of the Divine Mother and in Her Name. I am Space Master and Commander Athena. I serve at the great control board of the mother ship of the Ashtar Command. With our beam I cover you with Love and Light.

1. It is with a heavy heart that I must yield my thoughts to concern for the planet as the coming changes begin to manifest. It is one thing to consider and to dwell on the glory that comes after, and it truly is and will be a great glory to come, but it is another matter to look upon those whom I love so dearly, whose lives upon the planet have been in my care and under my guidance for many embodiments, now standing on the brink of planetary karma. Gladly would I exchange places with all of you, if that were possible.

2. But as you have followed your own indwelling Light down through the years through many trials and testings, you have learned, and learned the lesson well, to be overcome by the Grace of God that is given unto you. You have learned obedience through the things you have suffered. You have learned that the darkest night is always followed by the dawn. You have learned that in the time of deepest test the nearness of His Presence was your reward. Think of these coming times as change comes to you, as another opportunity to become an overcomer and a pillar in the house of your God. Another opportunity to know Him in the fellowship of His suffering and the blessedness of His Presence as a present help in time of trouble. None of His little ones will go through 'these changes alone. His Angels and His Representatives will be beside you to whisper in your ear, with guidance and deliverance whenever and wherever it is needed.

3. There was a time when His children came across the bottom of the sea, walking upon dry ground, while the waters parted to bid them pass by. The glory of His Presence with His little ones in the coming days will pale the former account in comparison, so great shall be His Hand of deliverance in the day of transition of your world. You shall be raised as Elijah was raised, lifted up as Jesus was lifted up, by the presence of the Guardians who wait. Those who have made their calling and election sure, can know that destruction will not come

nigh thee, but that His Hand shall be extended to thee through the presence of those who represent Him at the hour of your deliverance.

4. The attitudes of life are the deciding factors when that moment comes. It will be too late in that hour to suddenly reverse yourself and pretend new attitudes. These will have been built into the geometric patterns and the good works that surround every being. An attitude of love will be so interlaced into the electronic force-field of your being that none could miss its presence. Attitudes of selfishness and greed, or cruelty, are plainly to be seen within the force-field of humanity. Rebelliousness, disrespect, and corruption stand revealed, built into the very framework of the four lower bodies, through the long years of lesser motivations. As we approach your world and your atmospheres, we are not left with these decisions, and for this we are thankful. Our operations have an impersonal overtone. The choice has already been made by each and every one by the incorporate attitudes of life. You have chosen whether to go or to stay, many times down through your lifetime; as you have chosen between the right and the wrong, enlightenment and density, spirituality and materialism, kindness and cruelty, selfishness and unselfishness. At that very moment that you have faced a choice of decision or in any of life's situations, you have been building toward your final choice soon to manifest.

5. For this cause therefore, is my heart saddened as I look upon these changes that must come. It has been said that only one tenth shall remain when these things are passed. This need not be so. No prophecy is fixed, but all prophecy is subject to the will of man, his decisions and his choices. It is not too late, even now, for a cleansing of the attitudes of life. By an act of will, to change the personal positions which do not lead to the way of life. Those who read my words in this little volume, may even now determine to align themselves with the principles and the purpose of Divine Light as it is shed upon the planet. A great Master once presented it in this way, "Choose ye this day whom ye will serve." 6. This is the point of the beginning of the end of things.

6. Each individual unit of consciousness acting upon human freedom of choice, self determining to cast their energies into the battle for Light upon the earth. You simply begin where you are, and from this point on, at every moment of choice, at every crossroad of decision, cast your lot on the side of that which is right, that which is wholesome, that which is pure and that which is clean. And you go on from there as you ask for guidance from on high to show you the way

and lead you onward into more Light. As you begin this new adventure and reverse your attitudes of life, you are building into the gridwork and the framework of your own force-field that which shall shine through and be seen by the reaping angels when they appear.

7. That which is done in secret shall be rewarded openly by the Heavenly Father. Now is the time. We cannot know how much time remains. The universe and all therein stand alerted and ready. My question to you this day is this: "Are YOU ready for the coming of the Guardians?" "Will YOU qualify for the coming rescue?" "Will YOU be found in the remnants that remain?" YOU are the Master of your fate, and YOU are the only one who can answer my questions. YOU are the only one who can determine the action that will be taken WHEN

WE COME. Will YOU be ready for that day? I pray that the Light within you and around you will help you in your choice.

I Am Lady Master Athena of the Ashtar Command.

-Athena

Points to Ponder or for Group Discussion

1. The brink of planetary karma.
2. The lesson of life-overcoming (Mastery).
3. The great liftoff.
4. Attitudes of life are the building blocks of future events.
5. All prophecy is subject to change.
6. Finding the way out of confusion.
7. Three vital questions.

COSMIC REVELATIONS TILL THE END OF TIME

7:00 AM The Seventh Day - Keep Your Eyes on the Skies

By Lord Arcturus

MY name is Arcturus from the planet of the same name. I am coming to you this morning on a powerful beam from outer space. My words are projected to you through the Ashtar Command Monitor. Kuthumi has kindly granted my request to speak as a representative of outer space. This is a great honor to me that my words will be included in the volume that he sends forth. I speak on behalf of all my friends and yours, in the Alliance and the Brotherhood of Interplanetary Fellowship.

1. The situation that has been accelerating upon Earth has been a cause of great concern to all of us who follow the events very closely. We have monitored the planetary disturbances and the potential for greater ones. We have given the utmost time and attention to your international affairs, because of the diversion of nuclear atomic energy into weapons of destruction. The planet of Arcturus and our entire constellation has been in constant support of the volunteer program ministering to Earth. The patrols and fleets from Arcturus are an ever-present unit of the Guardian Action that protects your planet.

2. We come with our thousands of ships and thousands upon thousands of willing volunteers, who have come the great distance between us to be with you and to help you in the travail of your new birth into the Aquarian age of expression. The processes involved for your planet in this great event, will require assistance from your brothers of other galaxies and other systems. My beloved friends of Earth, you cannot stand alone in that which is to come. You cannot reject our loving offer of hope and specific guidance. In preparedness for the despair that could ensue, our Alliance has unified its forces and in a unanimous decision of the highest council in Space, it was agreed that our fleets be alerted and ready from that moment on for momentary response to the need of humanity.

3. This means that every county, every province and state, of every nation; every province of every republic, is now systematically patrolled by representatives of our Alliance. It means that great beams and cosmic rays, called forth by the Lords of your solar system, are being centralized and beamed directly upon the Earth by these regional representatives, of the Guardians from outer

space. It means that all opposition to the will of the Divine Father and the Hierarchy of your system and its Great Central Government has been removed and rendered inoperative for this important cycle of time.

4 & 5. Our technology is readied to superimpose our frequencies over your television and radio broadcasting systems if necessary, to reach the masses in the quickest possible manner. We can also extend our frequencies into your telephone lines for a brief message, but your telephones would then be unusable thereafter. We have systems similar to your public address systems, available from the smaller scout ships, which operate with a volume and power unheard of in your technology. We have many ways of reaching quantities of persons simultaneously. We project into your thinking at this very date, that fear of us and our presence or our appearance, or lack of understanding of our motivation, will combine to produce such a negative field around your physical form that we would be unable to assist you. You must enlarge your thinking and expand your knowledge of our purpose and our intermediary action under God and the Hierarchy under Heaven. We come in their name to serve you, our brothers of Earth.

6. I am saddened when I see the innocents who must be exposed to the dangers in your world. I am heartbroken when I reflect on the cruelty of humanity and the great toll of young lives that have been taken in war. Thousands upon thousands of young lives were thrown back into eternity without ever having a chance for expression and growth. I appeal to mankind to consider the children as you deliberate and choose the path that you would take. Consider if this is the path you would want your children to follow. Is this the destiny for the children you love and the children you know? All too many walk the planet with scars of war that can never heal in this lifetime. Scars upon the psyche which can never find relief throughout this embodiment. Much has been written of the suffering of the Earth itself, and the nations, and the adults. But can you find it in your hearts to think for a moment of the children of your world and the effects of atomic warfare upon the inner levels of their soul memory? Not only in this world, but the next?

7. I reveal to you in this release that we shall call for the children first. For the children are guiltless and the children are the victims of the madness of the adult world surrounding them. We shall make a place on our ships and our places of refuge for the children, first. These souls who have dared to enter your world at

such a time as this, deserve our love and care first of all. For they do not know hatred until they are taught to hate. They do not know to kill until they are taught to kill. They do not know of mass destruction until they are taught to destroy. Each living soul has its identifying ray, its link with its own personal record on our great computers. Your children are not lost when they are with us. They will be rescued first, and await your coming. Many thousands of your children are special souls, who have come to progress, to unfold, and participate in the dawn of a New World. The Space Commanders and those who serve with them in the heavens surrounding your planet, have been engaged in an intensive program of sweeping, cleansing action, by the direct Order of the Great Central Government. We will fill your skies the moment that our presence and your physical rescue is necessary.

Truly it can be said, "Look up, for your redemption draweth nigh." I would say, "Keep your eyes on the skies," when catastrophe overtakes you, for we are there. We ARE there.'"

I have come to you in an offer of Universal Peace and Goodwill. I call upon mankind of Earth to lay down your weapons of war.

I am the voice and Lord of Arcturus and Commander in Chief of its great Space Armada.

I Am

-Arcturus

COSMIC REVELATIONS TILL THE END OF TIME

Points to Ponder or for Group Discussion

1. The planet Arcturus and the Guardian Action.
2. Assistance from Space is vital.
3. The worldwide canopy of patrol.
4. Everyone can be reached in a time of crisis.
5. Fear is detrimental to rescue.
6. Consider the children's fate!
7. In a mass evacuation, the children go first

COSMIC REVELATIONS TILL THE END OF TIME

11:00 AM The Seventh Day - When Your Need Is Greatest, They Will Be There

By Brother James, The Apostle

1. **THIS** is a great pleasure to speak with one who has served the Light so faithfully for many lifetimes. I am the brother of Jesus the Christ. I am known as James. I have many other names, but I come in my identity as the Apostle James, and Jesus of Nazareth was my brother. We were raised in the same household and I followed Him in His ministry. I have known you in that lifetime and many lifetimes since then. I recognize you, Tuella, and I honor the Christ Presence within you. I now serve the Light upon the planet in my world as teacher. I speak and work through many dedicated ones at this time. I have overshadowed one in whom I have invested the momentum of a portion of my being, whom you will one day meet. Kuthumi has kindly invited me to contribute a few words to the World Messages. I am delighted to do this, for I see them as a vital link to the years of the coming decade.

2. As I prepare to share my thoughts, may I call your attention to the recent volcanic eruption in northwest America. This brought great concern, and the world media featured the coverage for considerable time. Precious lives are missing and have not yet been found. This occurrence could be likened to a brief preview of headlines that are to come. This was an isolated incident, but in the future, events of this magnitude will occur in concurrent sequence in diverse places. Your media will be at a loss to report them all. Television reports will fill the day in continuing attempts to cover these events, so recurrent will be the disasters, so widespread the locations.

3 & 4. These have been referred to as changes that must come. The restlessness of the inner earth which awakens the sleeping volcanoes to belch forth their living fire, is the same momentum which manifests elsewhere as tremors or earthquakes of small or large magnitude. Tidal waves and intense weather abnormalities, shifting plates of land beneath the oceans, and the quivering of the mountains, could take place in concerted action, so that humanity would have nowhere to run, nowhere to turn and no sense of direction or idea of what they must do to save themselves. Panic could grip the hearts of people, resulting in calls upon God for deliverance. IT IS IN HOURS SUCH AS

COSMIC REVELATIONS TILL THE END OF TIME

THESE THAT YOUR SKIES WILL FILL WITH THE SHIPS OF YOUR BROTHERS FROM OTHER REALMS.

5. As all are aware, there is also the ever-present danger that a small group of men shall detonate the initial action of nuclear disaster. Unless there were no divine intervention from the Guardians, the very planet itself would suffer total annihilation. But after that initial release goes forth, a warning will be broadcast upon the Higher Ethers for those who have accustomed their sensitivity to the higher frequencies of communication. Whether in a voice, or in a dream, or a vision or whatever manner, the elect shall receive that warning to prepare themselves for momentary evacuation. When the elect (volunteers to planet earth) have been gathered from the four winds and returned to their fold, the remaining stages of the program of the Guardians will take place.

6. None can tell when that moment will be, any more than any of you could with any certainty determine its time, for no man knoweth when that dire set of circumstances shall manifest. Therefore, the Guardians are on the alert, ever on the alert, listening, watching, recording, standing by, waiting and ever prepared for immediate action. Gird up thyselves, we would say in my day as a fisherman in Galilee. We would gird up our loins for action. My message to the world is a call to gird up your souls for spiritual action in the days of calamity.

Be ye as men who wait for their Lord, knowing not at what hour of what day these things shall come to pass. These are perilous times. The threats and dangers are not illusions; they are real. They could be imminent. The detonating of any first nuclear missile, even for testing purposes, in many areas, could precipitate a sequence of geological reactions upon the earth and the ionosphere surrounding it, setting loose unspeakable and indescribable catastrophes. The heavenly Tribunals and the Alliance of powers in Space are coordinating their constant efforts, even at this very moment, to forestall such eventualities and all acts or intentions of nuclear hostilities.

7. Between the time of decision and action, the moments will be very brief. It is that brief moment of time, when the skies will fill with the craft of your Brothers of other worlds to rescue humanity. Their time for entering and accomplishing their mission will be crucially short. There must be an inner understanding within the hearts of mankind that the Guardians have come to assist them in their time of trouble. They have patrolled your heavens for thousands of years with every effort geared toward this eventuality, when the

COSMIC REVELATIONS TILL THE END OF TIME

planet Earth would enter its transition into a new orbit of total change. The transition period can bring chaos to your world; nevertheless, it need not be individual chaos. Many voices have flooded the planet with the messages of your Protectors. Many channels have been used by the Great Ones and your Space Friends to give an assurance of their presence and their help.

8. It is proposed that the rescue of souls from off the planet in a time of peril, from whatever cause, will take place in three phases. The first phase shall be the secret removal of those elect whose dedication to Light on Earth has made our Program possible. These shall be called to that secret place where they shall be taken on high to a place prepared. Then shall come the call to all of those of Light, all of those with awareness and ears to hear, and faith to believe and courage to understand that which is taking place. The scope of this phase of the evacuation will be tremendous and include a far greater number than might be imagined. They will respond and follow directives and guidance under leadership of certain ones. These that have prepared themselves shall be lifted by the smaller ships to those platforms of immensity now in orbit in your skies.

The final phase, when the two groups are safe, and as remaining time permits, shall be the call to mass evacuation. Following the accomplishment of the first two missions, many who remain will have become willing believers in all of these things. In this final mass action, the children shall be lifted first and then, with the multitude, taken to a place prepared. When the planet is made new again, cleansed and beautiful once more, those who are worthy shall be returned to a new life in a new age, on a planet made new, in the fellowship and the companionship of those who delivered them. Perhaps as you read of these things the thoughts are overwhelming to you, as you rest in the quiet of your home environment, but the situation can change in the twinkling of an eye. Although my words may have little significance to you at this time, in the day when these things begin to happen, a memory of my words will be brought forth from inner consciousness.

9. Cultivate inner peace. Learn the art of listening with the inner ear. When you have spoken with your Lord, and come to an end of your prayer, linger awhile. Cultivate the art of listening with the inner ear. Become attentive with the inner being to the pulse and the heartbeat of the Universe. The God to whom you pray is within you, as close as your breath. I Am That I Am will whisper within as you practice the Presence of the guidance of the inner Divinity. This is where you

must turn when it would seem the world is crumbling around you. Within your being, call upon that I Am Presence, the Divine Indwelling, to send help and deliverance for you and your loved ones.

10. My beloved brothers and sisters, beyond that midnight hour a great dawn awaits the planet. The glory of a new day of Light and Brotherhood of all worlds. Begin now to develop your awareness of these Other Sheep of the Father, these Other Children of the Father filled with Divine attributes and spiritual purposes, even as you and yours. Let your love flow upward and outward to these dedicated Guardians, patrolling your skies, like watchmen on the walls, for your sake and your safety. Send your love to them, and your gratitude, for the Father hath sent them. In that hour when your need is greatest, they shall be there!
An Apostle of Jesus the Christ,

I Am

-Brother Janies

COSMIC REVELATIONS TILL THE END OF TIME

Points to Ponder or for Group Discussion

1. An "overshadowing" Master.
2. Recurrent and widespread disasters.
3. The restlessness of the inner earth.
4. Our ever-present help from above.
5. The warning of the elect.
6. Dangers could be imminent.
7. The moment of action for the Guardians.
8. The three phases of evacuation.
9. Become attentive with the inner being.
10. Other sheep of the Father, not of this fold.

COSMIC REVELATIONS TILL THE END OF TIME

The Ultimate Weapon

They spoke of ways and means
To stop proliferation of the bomb.
So ponderous with knowledge scientific
Did they endlessly exclaim-
Who will make it next?
You don't you know it is of God
Designed to service all of life,
Not to destroy the perfect patterns of His Work?
Cannot one voice be raised
To the heights of protest great
That will pierce the ears,
Lay bear the hearts
Of those so wantonly engaged
In victory through slaughter
Of each other, man on earth,
Their brother!
Rather would they find a use for
That ultimate of weapons great,
Designed to penetrate each heart
And bum through channels of the brain;
Created to keep God's plan in motion,
Till all are one again, no separation.
This luminous flame of GOD'S GREAT LOVE
That ultimate weapon ... from above!
-Eileen Schoen

COSMIC REVELATIONS TILL THE END OF TIME

3:00 PM The Seventh Day The Impersonal Frequencies
by Space Master Hatonn

THANK you, Tuella, for opening your door to receive my words. I have come at the invitation of Lord Kuthumi, my good friend and brother. I am with him this day to honor your vigil and assist in this special time of outpouring and blessing. I am Hatonn of the Space Council. I send my greetings to all in the Light of the Radiant One. It is my pleasure to come and I have anticipated this contact for the ongoing Light.

1. We of the Space Commands do have tremendous plans organized, completely ready for action, for a mass evacuation. As we have considered all the facts, and weighed in the balance all of the possibilities and the probabilities, it is the conclusion of the great Tribunal that the evacuation will be necessary. We are permitting you this release for the Tribunal in my name, to advise the people of Earth that mass evacuation will take place for all of those whose spiritual advancement makes compatibility with us possible.

2 & 3. Our ships are environments of harmony and peace. There is quietness, cooperation and dignity. There is courtesy and devotional awareness within each being. This is the only attitude capable of continuance in the vibrational atmosphere present within our space ships. The frequencies are so very high that they would destroy any vibrations of a lesser nature. It is not a matter of saying "This one may come, or this one must stay," it is of frequencies and vibrations. Just as a block of ice is melted and loses its form, its density, its appearance, within the vibration of higher temperatures, so it is that in the presence of the higher frequencies, they can do naught but decimate the density, the form, and the appearance of the lower frequencies.

This is why, throughout the planet, as souls go about the pursuit of Light and Divine Oneness, there is a marking star, shining forth from the forehead of the being. This becomes an identification to us at the time of evacuation. You will read of this star, in the vision of John recorded in your Bible. This inevitable separation has nothing to do with our personal desires in the matter. It is a question of frequencies and vibration.

COSMIC REVELATIONS TILL THE END OF TIME

Those who have learned to live in love, and to apply an attitude of love to all situations, have thus prepared themselves for these days of turmoil, though perhaps they knew it not. For love of fellow man as a manifestation of the Presence of the Love of God, in the vibration of one in embodiment, is the highest frequency on the four lower planes. It is that point of union and compatibility with the planes that are above. It is at that meeting point of Love, that we can mingle with you and accept you into our midst and our ships for rescue.

4. Perfect love casteth out fear. Perfect love is love to man of all levels, of all galaxies of all the universes. Perfect love brings acceptance of us into your hearts. The presence of fear within your being will hinder your own evacuation in the time of great trouble. Therefore, the call comes now, to all who read, and all who think on these things, to realize that the preparation for that hour is the preparation of thyself. A preparation of thy heart and the cleansing of thy attitude, that perfect love to all beings, both of your world and mine, shall be found within you. There must be an acceptance of the presence of the Christ within all men, of any race, of any creed, or any church, though yours differ, or of any color, realizing that the coats of skin are but an exterior manifestation. Unless this perfect love abides in you, you cannot abide within the higher frequencies of the upper planes.

Thus, with great love flowing from our hearts to you at this time, we would plead with you in the name of the Radiant One, that you would rethink your positions, that you would set a watch upon your spoken words regarding your brother or your sister, that you would most of all, control and discriminate carefully the thoughts that you entertain regarding your fellow man. For in that measure that you mete out judgment to them, that measure will return unto you, in that hour when you will stand in need of mercy and intervention.

5. I, Hatonn, Teacher and Master of the Higher Worlds, and speaker for the great Solar Tribunals of the Space Federation, I speak to you individually as one human soul who reads my words, and I call you to raise your level of living. Expand your horizon of love. Not only to include those that are near and dear to you, but your neighbor on the street, your coworker in your career, the leaders of your area, the men and women of your central government. Shed your attitude of love upon all as you would your very own. As each individual one of you expands your love and lets it flow into wider circles, the vibration of Light around each one, will ascend into higher octaves of Light. As many are thus occupied, in these

years immediately ahead, especially these early years of the decade, such a glow of Love and Light will arise from the lower planes so intensely, that we will be able to gear down our own presence, and come into a position of the blending of our frequencies and bring a mass evacuation to pass with a minimum of difficulty and disturbance to all.

The planet Earth must enter its period of cleansing. As this cleansing takes place, it will be a time of great upheaval in many places, that the human element could not sustain. There are certain areas that may be considered as safer than others in these times of change, but in the event of the launching of nuclear atomic explosions upon the planet, there could be no flesh saved, except through our presence and our evacuation of those who remain. The method to be used in the event of this great undertaking, will be to quietly and silently remove our workers and representatives first of all. These elect will have their private instructions. Mass evacuation will very possibly institute the use of a cosmic ray which acts producing levitation, teleporting the physical form into the craft. Only those of the higher frequencies of love and awareness can respond to these beams. History has recorded the use of these for you in the stories of Elijah and Beloved Jesus Sananda as they departed from the physical octave.

Please realize the impersonal nature of these procedures. It is a question of frequencies and vibrations AND THE ABSENCE OF ALL FEAR. We have a few other alternatives and methods, that may be utilized and the local situation and the need of the hour will determine the choice of method. But regardless of the method used, again I ask that you understand these are impersonal procedures which represent a meeting ground of frequencies as we enter your world and you enter ours.

This is the call of this book, that you prepare your souls. Grow into Light. Expand your love and beam a field of love around the planet. For this circle of love around your globe, can be termed as our "landing field" for your salvation.

I am Brother Hatonn, speaking to you in the name of the Radiant One. Adonai, Adonai, Adonai.

-Hatonn

Points to Ponder or for Group Discussion

1. Plans for a mass evacuation.
2. The high frequency of space craft environment.
3. Love is the highest frequency of the four lower planes.
4. Fear will hinder evacuation procedures.
5. The blending of frequencies.

COSMIC REVELATIONS TILL THE END OF TIME

7:00 PM The Seventh Day Our Radiant One

By Lord Kuthumi (The Apostle John)

1. **KUTHUMI** speaks. I am coming to you tonight in my identity as John the Apostle. In those days when I walked the land with the Beloved Master, my heart thrilled to hear His Words, to be in His Presence, to sit beside Him. To ply my questions and receive His great wisdom and understanding. As one of the daughters of Philip, you were with us also. I have had many lifetimes, a few of great report, but nothing in my continuing experiences of evolution can ever compare to the days when I walked at the Master's side. My love for this great Being of Light cannot be measured in words, or described. It is the focal point of my existence, the atom around which my soul revolves.

2. As I close this symposium of guidance for the years before you, I desire to speak in my identity as John, the younger of the twelve. For my heart burns to speak of that Radiant Star, who descended from Celestial orbit to walk with men of earth. His Beloved Presence and His teachings have been received and respected with much honor and reverence throughout your solar system, may galaxies and other universes. It was Shan, the dark planet, where He was vilely put to death. Yet the teachings He brought and exemplified remain to this day.

3. The written account as it exists in present form has suffered much distortion, dilution, and revision, and the interpolation of unsympathetic minds. Nevertheless, there has remained a thread of the inner teachings that weave through human understanding down through the centuries. Hidden within the phrases and the passages, there is enough of the secret wisdom remaining, that any truly hungry heart that meditates upon His words, even in their present form, will find an awakening, a birth of awareness, an enlightenment, that will change the course of their lives. His words are still Light and the essence of Life.

4. As this cycle of time flows into another, and great cosmic rays penetrate your world, hidden wisdom is exposed for man's understanding. But in the pursuit of spiritual knowledge, and many pathways, be not so overcome that you would ignore the simple teachings of our Beloved Lord. Rather let them blend as one, and you will discover that this Great Avatar taught the inner wisdom in His simple way, that all of mankind could understand. None could deny His unction and His Mastery. The energies of His Being would flow throughout the

countryside and down the sides of the hills, where hundreds and hundreds would gather to listen to Him speak the words of Life. Many of those listening, in the years that followed gladly laid down their lives or entered the lion's arena for their defense of His words, and you were one of those, my sister, who entered those arena gates.

5. The beauty of His countenance as He stood with arms outstretched to reason with His audience, to speak His parables and His simple descriptions of the kingdom of heaven, was an experience that is written indelibly upon my own soul for all eternity. I have since that time, come to a broader understanding of many of the mysteries that were hidden in His words.

Those who presently study in depth the mysteries of life and birth, and the Great Law, and the cycles of evolution and all of these masterly subjects, that are now so boldly coming to light, so boldly being taught; if these students of today will return once again to the words of the Beloved Lord, Jesus the Christ, they will find a warmth enveloping them, as with their own enlightened understanding they perceive the true meanings veiled in His words. Students of today will recognize the application of Universal Law in His miracles, the stream of cosmic verities within His parables, and evidence of Space craft throughout the record. His latter day discourses become easy reference in terms of the Guardian Beings who today surround your world. It is only to this generation, that faces the end of this cycle of time, that is given the great privilege of understanding His words. Too often in the mystery schools, circles and groups for occult discussion, there is a tendency to bypass the teachings of Jesus, the Great Lord.

6. It is true, because of the lateness of the record and the handling of unsympathetic translators, distortion is present. It is nevertheless not great enough to suppress the power of His utterances. When you explore a passage containing His words, close your eyes for meditation, and visualize yourself standing in the crowd that pressed around Him constantly. Feel the radiance and the magnitude of His mighty force-field of divine energy as He raises His hands to bless the crowd. In your time of meditation you may find that He is standing there beside your chair. His Great Being knows no boundary. No planet can hold Him, no tomb could enclose Him, and He lives today, and visits those who love Him.

7. His Presence can stand beside a million different souls in one moment of time and yet suffer no loss of its own vibrant power. He can deliver His dictations

through many blessed channels at one time in many different places, and yet each word bears the unmistakable stamp of His Presence. He is the Lord of the Planet and its Great Teacher. Down through the corridors of time, and many cultures and civilizations, we have known Him by many planetary names. As the planet throws off its old mantle to enter the new orbit of evolution, He will not leave those who love His Principles to endure alone. The Christ consciousness shall expand and manifest within every human life form and strive for expression and recognition, lest the very stones cry out.

8. My comments, as I close the cover of this little volume foursquare, are designed for one thrust, one idea, and that is that you will take the teachings of Jesus the Christ into the New Decade, and let Him walk before you. Let Him survey the terrain ere you pass by. For His feet know the Way. He has trod the Path. There is no experience that you must face, that He has not already entered and conquered. He will lead you and shelter you in His Love and bring you safely to your destiny.

This is my plea, that as you turn your energies toward enlightenment, and search for understanding and guidance, that you might also read once again the words of the greatest story ever told.

I am Kuthumi,

known in those days as

-John

COSMIC REVELATIONS TILL THE END OF TIME

Points to Ponder or for Group Discussion

1. John the Beloved Apostle.
2. Dark Shan, the only planet that rejected the Radiant One.
3. The distortions of the Gospels.
4. All truth is consistent with itself.
5. Secret wisdom is hidden in His words.
6. Practicing the Presence.
7. Can you name some other manifestations of the Great Soul?
8. Jesus Our Lord goes before us, so that anything that reaches us has been met by Him first, and touches us only by His permission. Rom. 8:28.

The Final Words

THIS is Ashtar greeting you with the sunrise, on this last morning of your vigil . . The deluge of Divine Love that has engulfed you these last twenty-four hours is shared with all of us, as we also are over. come with Love for the Heavenly Father and for all mankind. You have realized that we have been impressing you for many hours with the words of the Beloved, 'I, if I be lifted up, will draw all men unto me.'

The Ashtar Command, and all of my fellow Commanders and the members of all of our fleets, serve in the Light of the Radiant One. Our dedication is to His Great Mission, which is much broader than His Mission to Earth. The scope of His Love and His teachings has penetrated many universes. The Love of the Radiant One is a nucleus and a center, a focus of creation, throughout infinity. This Love for Him who is the Light of the World, that fills your heart this beautiful sunrise is shared by all of the universes.

Yes, we have now closed the covers of the volume foursquare, as Kuthumi spoke so eloquently last night. The vision has descended into manifestations from the octaves of Light. And now, the Heavenly Father holds it in His Hands.

Tuella, our command salutes you.

-Ashtar

WILLAM ALEXANDER ORIBELLO

At an early age, Oribello encountered Angelic Beings. Later in life he was taught by the Masters of Wisdom a variety of occult secrets which he has used to guide many. His teachings combine the Christian Mysteries with the art of Spiritism.

THE MASTERBOOK OF SPIRITUAL POWER—The spells in this sacred text work like a magnet to attract big money, good health, love, freedom from tension and worry...as well as banishing curses and eroding negativity.

8.5x11—116 pages—ISBN-13: 978-1606111109—$18.95

THE SEALED MAGICAL BOOK OF MOSES—Here are arcane secrets of Moses' powers that can now be revealed to series students only. Includes the 21 MAGICAL TALISMANS OF MOSES seldom seen, which can give you the powers of the holy sage.

8.5x11—142 pages—ISBN-13: 978-0938294689—$18.95

CANDLE BURNING MAGIC WITH THE PSALMS—Create life's greatest blessings by combining the power of the Holy Psalms with the magic of burning different colored candles. Best times, days and conditions for spells.

8.5x11—188 pages—ISBN-13: 978-0938294580—$21.95

USING CANDLE BURNING TO CONTACT YOUR GUARDIAN ANGEL

8.5X11—100 pages—ISBN-13: 978-0938294757—$19.95

SACRED MAGIC REVISED—Forbidden knowledge now revealed...prosperity for all guaranteed! Includes seven great money secrets.

8.5x11—146 pages—ISBN-13: 978-1606111291—$18.95

DIVINE BIBLE SPELLS—This book proves what you've heard all along – With God All Things Are Possible! Added material from Dragonstar.

8.5x11—142 pages—ISBN-13: 978-1606111499—$18.95

DIVINE MONEY SPELLS—Easy Magickal Spells To Jump Start Your Spiritual Economic Stimulus Package Added material from Dragonstar. Spells to eliminate poverty and to draw abundance.

8.5x11—152 pages—ISBN-13: 978-1606110645—$21.95

THE MEDIUMSHIP OF SPIRIT—The Ascension of William Alexander Oribello. Now an Ascended Master, Oribello has returned to the Earth Plane to continue his great work, assisted by the mediumship of psychic Aurora Thyme...

8.5X11—122 pages—ISBN-13: 978-1606111512—$18.95

GODSPELLS: WRITTEN SPELLS, SPOKEN SPELLS AND SPELL ENHANCERS—Here are the rules laid down thousands of years ago by those who spoke with the Heavenly Host and learned of his TRUE wishes for all of mankind. NOT of the devil. For unselfish use only!

8.5x11—140 pages—ISBN-13: 978-0938294498—$18.95

COUNT SAINT GERMAIN - THE MAN WHO LIVES FOREVER — Let Count Saint Germain — the man who lives forever — help transform your life through his insight into the metaphysical laws that govern the universe. "Strange" bio by Art Crocket. Channelings of the Master by Wm Oribello.

8.5x11—132 pages—ISBN-13: 978-1892062208—$21.95

Add $20 for DVD of Oribello channeling Saint Germain under the purple ray.

CURSES AND THEIR REVERSALS— Plus: Omens, Superstitions And The Removal Of The Evil Eye. Important workbook by Oribello with Maria D' Andrea, Lady Suzanne and others.

8.5x11—182 pages—ISBN-13: 978-1606111406—$21.95

SUPER SPECIAL
Mail Order customers get all of Wm Oribello's books as listed for just $149.95 + $15.00 SH

Mail Order Customers – Book Stores – Wholesalers – Distributors
Order Directly From
TIMOTHY G BECKLEY, BOX 753, NEW BRUNSWICK, NJ 08903
mrufo8@hotmail.com   credit card orders   732 602-3407

OVER 175 TITLES AVAILABLE FOR KINDLE AND OTHER DEVICES

Suppressed And Banned BOOKS OF THE BIBLE

The Forgotten Books of Eden – Based upon sacred texts removed from the Bible. ***NOW FULLY REVEALED…THE UNCENSORED TRUTH ABOUT THE ORIGINS OF HUMANKIND AND THE AGELESS CONFLICT BETWEEN GOOD AND EVIL. CENSORED BY THE CHURCH – THE TRUE STORY OF ADAM AND EVE.*** Here is the story of Adam and Eve which is the most ancient in the world, a story that has survived because it embodies the fight between man and the Devil. Adapted from the work of unknown Egyptians, parts of this version were found in the Talmud, the Koran, and elsewhere, showing the vital role it played in the literature of human wisdom. This adaptation has been passed down and was first written in Arabic and translated into Ethiopic. It is a detailed history of Adam and Eve and their descendants found nowhere else and how the "Family Tree" ties all of the Old Testament together. Includes the true story of Adam and Eve's conflict with Satan, as well as the Psalms of Solomon.
8.5" x 11—350 pages—ISBN-13: 978-1606111727—$24.00

The Lost Books of the Bible – Based upon sacred texts left out of the Bible ***HERE ARE THE ORIGINAL TEACHINGS OF THE CHRIST BANNED FOR TWO THOUSAND YEARS, NOW MADE AVAILABLE FOR DISSEMINATION TO THE PUBLIC FOR THE FIRST TIME.*** One of the best kept secrets in the modern religious world is that only eighty percent of the King James Bible, as originally translated and published in 1611, is actually presented in the book the church uses as its foundation. These are the words of the Christ and his apostles as recorded by the earliest Christians, but censored by the Church, because they are believed to contain inappropriate and unorthodox studies now considered taboo and out of the mainstream of religious doctrine. This edition contains dozens of apocryphal books from the early centuries of Christianity that were deliberately excluded from the published Treatments. The question remains why were these divinely inspired texts kept out of the bible by the Church? There are those who maintain that this provocative work contains a magical code that can enrich and inspire our lives. Unravel this code and you could benefit greatly as you sit at the side of the Lord. CONTAINS NEARLY 300 PAGES OF SUPPRESSED BIBLICAL DOCUMENTS FROM THE ORIGINS OF HUMANKIND TO THE FINAL JUDGMENT—8.5" x 11"—306 pages—ISBN-13: 978-1606111710—$24.00

Forbidden Books Of Heresy—by Sean Casteel

REVEALING THE SECRETS OF THE GNOSTIC SCRIPTURES FROM UFOS TO JESUS' LOVE OF MARY

There is a new developing perception of the Christ causing a splintering of beliefs among the faithful. Some have begun to embrace a view that is more humanistic and more mystical. The discovery of the Gnostic scriptures in Egypt in 1945 has forced scholars and the devout to rethink their beliefs about the Bible. For example:

*Did Jesus love Mary Magdalene in a decidedly physical, even sexual way? Was she truly his favorite disciple?

* Was Jesus a kind of spiritual chameleon, changing his physical form to suit his needs and even at times resembling the ubiquitous gray alien of the UFOs?

These are the kinds of questions the author grapples with. Sean Casteel has pored over the Gnostic scriptures, and what he says may lead you into spiritual realms you never knew existed!
8.5x11—110 pages—ISBN-13: 978-1892062611—$15.95

Timothy Green Beckley • Box 753 • New Brunswick, NJ 08903
PayPal: MRUFO8@hotmail.com • Secure Credit Card hotline: 732-602-3407